MW00996901

THE MANAGEMENT TEAM HANDBOOK

THE MANAGEMENT TEAM HANDBOOK

Five Key Strategies for Maximizing Group Performance

Marie G. McIntyre, Ph.D.

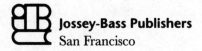
Jossey-Bass Publishers
San Francisco

Jossey-Bass books and products are available through most bookstores. To contact Jossey-Bass directly, call (888) 378-2537, fax to (800) 605-2665, or visit our website at www. josseybass. com.

Substantial discounts on bulk quantities of Jossey-Bass books are available to corporations, professional associations, and other organizations. For details and discount information, contact the special sales department at Jossey-Bass.

For sales outside the United States, please contact your local Simon & Schuster International Office.

 Manufactured in the United States of America on Lyons Falls Turin Book. This paper is acid-free and 100 percent totally chlorine-free.

Library of Congress Cataloging-in-Publication Data

McIntyre, Marie G., 1947–
    The management team handbook : five key strategies for maximizing group performance /
Marie G. McIntyre. — 1st ed.
      p. cm. — (Jossey-Bass business & management series)
    Includes bibliographical references and index.
    ISBN 0–7879–3973–0 (acid-free paper)
    1. Teams in the workplace. 2. Executives. I. Title. II. Series.
    HD66 .M3943 1998
    658.4'036—ddc21
                                                        98–8923

FIRST EDITION
HB Printing   10 9 8 7 6 5 4 3 2 1

THE JOSSEY-BASS

BUSINESS & MANAGEMENT SERIES

CONTENTS

**To my husband John
with love and appreciation**

PREFACE

Why do we need a book on management teams?

Management teams run the world. From large corporations to small family enterprises, from the military to the local library, from the Red Cross to the community food bank, all business, government, and not-for-profit organizations are guided by the decisions of management groups. Sometimes these managers do an outstanding job, and sometimes they preside over disaster. Most of the time, they produce acceptable results, but without living up to their full potential.

Long before the current trend toward team-based organizations, the groups of managers who ran companies, agencies, or departments were referred to as "management teams." They could have been called committees, boards, or councils, but using the word *team* seemed to reflect an underlying recognition that for an organization to succeed, managers would have to work together toward some common goals. Management groups have often failed to live up to the team label, however.

Many years ago, when I first became a manager, I joined a management team of bright, motivated, well-meaning, but highly independent people who knew little about the world beyond their own organizational walls and seldom collaborated or communicated outside of team meetings. And our meetings weren't exactly models of collaboration either!

Unfortunately, we represented a pretty typical management team. Today, when I am asked as a consultant to help an organization create a more team-oriented culture, my first question is, "Does your management group work as a team?" After a long pause, the response is usually, "Well . . . not really." Management groups frequently talk about teams these days but still have difficulty becoming one.

This paradox is created by several management team characteristics, which are described in the Introduction to this book. The root cause may be that the management role has not historically been defined in team-oriented terms. Good managers were *strong, independent,* and *authoritative.* They could *plan, organize, direct,* and *control.* Decision making was *tightly compartmentalized* and governed by *specific policies and procedures. Interdependence, collaboration, flexibility,* and *teamwork* were words seldom mentioned. Today, though, the environment in which organizations operate has become highly complex and unpredictable, requiring managers to process greater amounts of information, adapt quickly to change, and successfully coordinate the activities of interdependent functions. Rosabeth Moss Kanter (1989), one of the leading theorists on organizational change, has indicated that to survive in this difficult environment organizations must develop several critical attributes: agreement on a clear direction, regular exchange of information and ideas across organizational boundaries, reduction of conflict and isolation among departments, and consideration of multiple perspectives when making decisions. For an organization to function in this fashion, however, the management team directing the organization must itself first be able to exhibit these characteristics. Teamwork starts at the top.

Management groups also need to serve as a positive role model for other teams. But they have been given little guidance on how to do so. Despite the increasing focus on work teams in recent years, scant attention has been paid to the management team. Much information is available on teamwork, and much more can be found on management, but few resources exist to help managers put the two together. This knowledge gap creates a problem for any management group trying to succeed in today's challenging environment. They need an answer to one key question: "How can a group of managers become an effective team?" The search for a response to this question led to an extensive research project, which became the foundation for this book.

Who Will Find This Book Useful?

Leaders and members of traditional management teams—that is, groups of department heads who report to an upper-level executive—will certainly find that *The Management Team Handbook* describes the world they inhabit. They are the primary audience for the book. The information and strategies provided apply equally well to management teams in business, government, or not-for-profit organizations.

Other managing groups can also benefit from the advice offered here. Boards and councils, for example, have a rather different role than do internal management teams, but they face many of the same challenges. Relatives involved in running a family business may not think of themselves as a management team, but in fact they need to function as one. A group of entrepreneurs struggling to get a fledgling venture off the ground may not yet have any employees, but they are a management team nonetheless. Any member of a group leading an organization or department within an organization should find this handbook helpful in becoming more effective.

People who assist managers from a consulting capacity will also find practical information and advice in this book. Human resource managers, training and development specialists, and organizational development consultants are all in a position to help management teams implement effective strategies and become more productive.

Finally, the book can be of help to people who are preparing to fill a management role. Graduate and undergraduate students of management, as well as those who teach them, will find that the book provides real-world examples of strategies to adopt and pitfalls to avoid.

What Are the Goals of the Book?

The Management Team Handbook was written to provide a useful, practical guide for team members and leaders who wish to make their management teams more productive, responsive, and successful. This book fills a gap in the existing literature on teams by focusing on the specific factors that determine the effectiveness of *management* groups.

My hope is that managers do not simply read the book and then give it a comfortable niche on their bookshelves, but rather continue to use it as a reference as new circumstances or challenges arise. Although some people may read it from cover to cover, I expect that many more will seek out the specific situations that are of current concern to them and then return for additional information as conditions change.

Three themes run throughout this book. First, I wish to convey clearly a sense of the unique purpose, dynamics, and challenges of a management team. Second, I emphasize specific, practical suggestions that managers can use to improve the performance of their own teams. And finally, I use true stories and real-life experiences to provide both good and bad examples of management team performance. For this third aspect of the book, I am indebted to colleagues and clients, past and present. Because obtaining permission from all of them would have been difficult, I have tried to alter the description of their circumstances so that they cannot be easily recognized.

The overall purpose of the book is to help management teams operate more effectively, thereby increasing the success of the organizations they lead. Specifically, the book is designed to accomplish these objectives:

- Describe how management teams are different from other teams
- Identify the characteristics that tend to interfere with teamwork in a management group
- Define the five key success factors that determine the performance of a management team
- Provide tools to help readers assess the performance of their own teams on the five success factors
- Present specific strategies to help team leaders and members implement each of the five success factors
- Explore solutions to common problems that prevent management teams from reaching their full potential
- Offer suggestions for handling special situations, such as selecting new team members, managing team transitions, or fixing a sick team

A final goal is to help management teams become better role models for other teams in their organizations. When management team members are able to collaborate effectively, then the groups that report to them are also likely to do so, creating greater teamwork at all levels.

The Introduction to *The Management Team Handbook* defines what is meant by *management team,* describes several types of management teams, and differentiates them from other teams found in the workplace. Four attributes that create obstacles to teamwork in management groups are discussed.

Chapter One introduces the TEAM model, describes the Management Team Research Project, defines the five success factors, and discusses the special needs of different types of management teams.

The next five chapters each cover a success factor in detail. Each chapter includes these sections:

- A detailed description of the success factor covered in that chapter
- Strategies that can be used to implement the success factor
- Common management team problems and suggested solutions
- A team assessment survey to be completed by team members
- Questions to encourage discussion of the team's strengths and weaknesses

Chapter Two focuses on success factor one, strategic goals, with particular emphasis on the need for both executive and middle management teams to engage in strategic and operational planning. Some of the problems discussed include the challenges of a turbulent environment, executives with conflicting goals, and lack of direction from upper management.

Chapter Three covers success factor two, extensive networks. The importance of developing and maintaining contacts that can provide useful information for decision making is emphasized, with strategies suggested for both internal and external networking. Some of the problems addressed include territoriality, friction between line and staff functions, adversarial employee-management relations, and limited time or money for networking activities.

Chapter Four focuses on success factor three, collaborative relationships. Strategies for developing supportive working relationships among team members are discussed, including the need for trust, respect, and effective conflict management. Some of the relationship problems covered include personality conflicts, development of cliques, lack of opportunities for interaction, overlapping roles, competitive reward systems, and dysfunctional organization structure.

Chapter Five looks at success factor four, effective information processing. Meetings are highlighted in this chapter, because most management team decisions are made in that setting. Establishing clear objectives for a meeting, promoting thorough discussion, encouraging expression of different views and new ideas, and ending with specific action items are the primary strategies covered. Some of the problems addressed include interminable discussions; wandering from the agenda; making decisions too quickly; and managing team members who are too talkative, too quiet, or too critical.

Chapter Six is on success factor five, focused action. It discusses implementation strategies that can help the team move from talk to action, emphasizing the importance of defining specific results, developing action plans, establishing a time line, and involving all appropriate people. Suggestions are offered for encouraging behavior change in organizations. Some of the problems covered include difficulty in measuring results, dealing with team members who don't pull their weight, starting projects that never get finished, and fending off interference from upper management.

The remainder of the book helps managers keep their teams in good working order. Chapter Seven discusses the need for "routine maintenance" on a management team. Key strategies include providing opportunities for the group to work together, managing team performance effectively, and taking time to have fun.

Chapter Eight stresses the high cost of making poor management selections. I review common pitfalls in hiring and then describe an eight-step method for planning and conducting an effective selection process.

Chapter Nine deals with critical transition points for a team, including changes in membership, the arrival of a new leader, turnover in upper management, and redefinition of the team's function. For each transition point, the impact on the team is described and suggestions are offered to both team leaders and members for managing the change successfully.

Chapter Ten helps managers identify groups that are truly dysfunctional. Chronic team problems are covered: toxic team members, hostile cliques, intense rivalries between members, problems with upper management, high turnover, and ineffective team leadership. For each problem, I describe symptoms and suggest cures.

Finally, the Conclusion provides twelve guiding principles that managers can use to influence the performance of their management teams, whether the manager is the leader or a team member.

*

Companies may have become flatter and middle managers may be less prevalent, but management teams will exist for as long as there are organizations. If any complex activity is to be performed by large numbers of people, a group is needed to establish direction, coordinate efforts, facilitate communication, and make strategic decisions. Because the management team is the leading group in a complex system, its output provides input for every other group in the organization. Characteristics of the management team are therefore mirrored to some degree by all the departments and functions under their direction. Because management teams have such a critical and widespread impact, making them more effective can improve the performance of an organization and create a more enjoyable, productive environment for everyone who works there. I hope that this book is used to help achieve that goal.

ACKNOWLEDGMENTS

There are many "true stories" in this book. Here is the first one.

Once upon a time, a not-so-terribly-young woman with a responsible corporate position decided that it was time to look to the future. She could see two paths ahead. One was straight and clearly marked, leading directly up a corporate ladder. The other was a winding road, veiled in mystery and with an unclear destination. She was intrigued by the second path but knew that she could not travel it alone. Fortunately, she found a Wise Advisor to provide guidance, and a Helpful Friend to ease her passage. As she traveled the mysterious path, many other friends and colleagues, old and new, offered knowledge, assistance, and support. Much to her surprise and delight, she even found Prince Charming along the way. So far, she is living happily ever after.

I am the woman in the tale. Choosing the second path was the decision that ultimately led to the creation of this book. Traveling that road meant finding and finishing a doctoral program, leaving the security of the corporate world, starting a consulting business, conducting an extensive research project on management teams, and combining the research results with twenty years' experience to produce a book. Undertaking the journey would have been impossible without the friendship, help, and support of many people. One of the joys of writing a book, I find, is having the opportunity to thank them publicly.

My Wise Advisor was Stan Smits. Twenty years ago, he was directing the unique graduate program that first introduced me to the study of management. More recently, over a period of seven years, he devoted many hours to discussing the merits of different doctoral programs, exploring various research topics, considering alternative designs for the management team study, and sharing his extensive knowledge of research methods and management literature. Stan, you have profoundly affected my life, and I will be forever grateful.

Tom Gaines is the Helpful Friend. When I began my consulting business, Tom referred me to my first client. He continued to recommend my services to people throughout his wide network of contacts and is responsible, directly or indirectly, for many of the client relationships that I have today. Whenever I review the projects I am working on at the moment, I am amazed at how many of them can ultimately be traced back to Tom. In earlier years, he promoted me into my second management job, nominated me to participate in Stan Smits's graduate program, and recommended me for the job that brought me to Atlanta. He is someone who genuinely enjoys helping his friends. I feel very fortunate to be one of them.

Creating this book required research, experience, and support, for which I am indebted to many colleagues, friends, and family members. For assistance with the Management Team Research Project, I am grateful to the people who made it possible for me to survey management teams in their organizations: B. J. Bennett, John Brady, Rusty Durham, Don Howard, Jerry Jackson, Gail Lazenby, Jay Levergood, Paul Mullins, Jo Ann Pinder, Beth Pollard, Fred Schultz, Peter Van Der Gracht, and Linda Weigel. Without them, this research could not have been conducted. I also want to thank Ken Matheny for providing constant encouragement and support, Joanna White for enhancing my knowledge of group dynamics, and Bill Curlette for sharing his vast knowledge of research methods and statistical techniques.

My experience with management and management teams began many years ago, when I worked for a state government agency. Bill Anderson, who hired me, was my first good management role model. Page Truitt, who promoted me, was willing to take a risk and put a woman in a management job—something that had never been done in that organization. Then Cecilia Lewis and Bill Cobb also took their chances when they hired a government manager to work in a fast-paced technology company (an opportunity that would never have come my way without Claire Blehr's assistance). John Tekowitz promoted me into my first corporate management position and rapidly expanded my responsibilities. I am also grateful to Jay Levergood for always taking the time to answer questions and educate me about the business world.

As a consultant, I have appreciated the opportunity to learn from Daryl Connor, who many years ago taught a yearlong course on organizational change that was the foundation for my knowledge of organizational development; and for the wisdom of Peter Block, whose book was an early inspiration. Ginny Hall served as my "self-employment mentor," offering advice and encouragement during the transition from corporate life to consulting practice. Although they are not consultants, attorneys Jim Coil and Rick Boisseau have served as absolutely remarkable role models of outstanding client service. They would be amazed to know how often I have thought of their example when dealing with my clients.

Because independent consulting is a rather solitary occupation, I am fortunate to have some consultant colleagues I can call on for information or inspiration: Patti Hughes, a valuable friend and the finest internal consultant I have ever met; Jim Stephens, who for more than twenty-five years has been a role model and great source of philosophical conversations about management, organizations, consulting, life (and golf); Lynn Moore, who shares clients, resources, and the occasional frustrations of self-employment; and Hodge Golson, who is always willing to provide helpful information, including some extremely useful background material for the management team research. I also want to express deep appreciation to Rose Grant, who for many years—first as an employee and later as a friend—has proven that she can indeed find the solution to any problem; and to my assistant, Julie Dobrinska, who handles the details, helps keep clients happy, and preserves my sanity.

I wish I could list all the clients who have contributed to my understanding of management and organizations, but space prohibits me from doing so. If you are a client, please accept my thanks for the knowledge that I gained from the work we have done together. Clients probably learn something from consultants, but I believe that consultants learn much more from clients. Since many of the examples in this book come from client organizations, I have tried to alter descriptions and circumstances so that people and organizations cannot be identified (except possibly by those involved in the situation).

An idea cannot become a book without a publisher. Jossey-Bass was the only publisher to whom I sent a proposal, because, as a manager, I had always been impressed with the practical, user-friendly style of its business books. Now that we have worked together for a year, I am even more impressed with the people there. Cedric Crocker, Susan Williams, Julianna Gustafson, Paula Goldstein, Nathalie Mainland-Smith, Tanya Hanley, Judith Hibbard, and Tom Finnegan have all been accessible, helpful, informative, and just darned nice people to work with.

Management jobs, consulting projects, and books are all wonderful things, but the true meaning in my life comes from the members of my family. They have had little direct involvement with this book but have had everything to do with my ability to write it. My mother and late father, Katherine and Bill McIntyre, have always provided constant love and support, as well as a lifelong example of honesty, integrity, responsibility, achievement, and respect for all people. My brother, Michael, continues to be my delightful companion through all of life's stages, sharing his unique insights and observations. Gail Rogers—a sister in every respect but genetic—always listens, helps, and cares. Katherine Hoover, my daughter, was the light of my life as a child; as an adult, she has become a person I truly admire and one of my best friends. Her husband, Steve, has been a wonderful addition to our family (especially since he is the only one of us who can fix anything), as have Alice and Louise, our other "additions by marriage." Our two newest family members have brought a special dimension to life that I believe only grandparents can understand: Marie Allison, who has loved books almost from infancy, and Alexander, who for the moment is content just to eat them.

Finally, a word about Prince Charming. Shortly after setting out on the winding and murky path that led to this book, I met my husband, John Gambs, whose love, support, belief, advice, humor, and caring allowed me to travel the rest of the way. This book is dedicated to John, because he makes all things possible.

M. G. M.

THE AUTHOR

Marie G. McIntyre, Ph.D. has operated a management consulting business in Atlanta since 1990, with the primary goal of helping people work together more effectively. Her interest in management teams began in the mid-1970s, when she was promoted into a management position and had her first opportunity to observe managers operating as a group. She now assists managers with such activities as strategic planning, team building, implementing organizational change, leadership development, and conducting organizational research through the use of surveys and focus groups. She also teaches consulting skills to people who use their expertise to help others, including many managers in the staff departments of organizations.

McIntyre works with a diverse group of clients in business, government, and the not-for-profit sector. Business clients have included companies in telecommunications, health care, banking, insurance, aeronautics, electronic systems, retail, consulting, advertising, manufacturing, and distribution. She has worked with government agencies involved in transportation, human services, revenue collection, advocacy, higher education, rehabilitation, corrections, library services, public health, personnel, and administrative services. Not-for-profit clients have ranged from large membership organizations to small community groups.

Before starting her own consulting practice, McIntyre worked for nine years with Scientific-Atlanta, a Fortune 500 company, where she was a director of human resources. Prior to entering the business world, she held line and staff management positions in two government organizations. Still earlier in her career, she also spent two years in a not-for-profit agency. McIntyre received a B.A. degree in psychology (1969) and an M.Ed. in counseling (1974) from the University of North Carolina at Chapel Hill. She earned an M.A. in public administration (1978) and a Ph.D. in organizational development (1996) at Georgia State University. She has taught in the Georgia State M.B.A. program, is an adjunct faculty member at the University of Georgia's Institute of Government, and helped develop training for the Atlanta Olympic games. Her professional affiliations include the American Psychological Association, the Society for Human Resource Management, and the American Society for Training and Development. During her career, she has served on the board of several organizations and has been a frequent conference speaker.

THE MANAGEMENT TEAM HANDBOOK

INTRODUCTION

THE CHALLENGE OF DEVELOPING A MANAGEMENT TEAM

Some True Stories

The president of a technology company is meeting with his management team to discuss a potential new product. "Based on our projections," says the marketing manager, "we anticipate that sales will drop a bit after the first quarter but really take off by the end of the year." Without further discussion, the group agrees to invest in the new product—which proceeds to lose six million dollars. Several management team members later say they are not surprised. They expected the product to fail.

The director of a large government agency never holds staff meetings. Because division managers meet with her individually to discuss their concerns and make decisions, little communication occurs across division lines. An investigation reveals that the agency is unable to account for millions of dollars in government funds because their new information system receives incomplete data from the operating divisions. The director is forced to resign.

The vice president of human resources announces to his managers that the new CEO plans to reduce labor costs by laying off 20 percent of the production workers and replacing them with temporary employees. "Wait a minute," says one of the managers. "Doesn't he realize that we just barely won a union election here last year? If we bring in temps, those organizers will be back in a heartbeat! Being unionized would wipe out any savings from hiring temporaries." The layoffs take place, and the union organizers return.

In each of these situations, a poorly functioning management team contributes to a serious organizational problem. The technology company loses millions of dollars because of an ineffective decision-making process. The government agency becomes embroiled in a public scandal because division heads fail to communicate. The human resources function is unable to act in the best interests of the company because of conflicting goals from upper management. If these teams were more effective, such problems might be avoided.

Management teams affect the performance of all business and government organizations. The decisions they make impact every aspect of our lives, from the kind of car we drive to the way our taxes are collected. Every day, newspapers carry stories of organizations that prosper or fail as the result of decisions made by their management teams. In one national survey, 54 percent of equity investors rated effectiveness of the management team as the most critical factor for business success (Clark, 1993). Yet most of the time these teams operate with little guidance on how to do their job most effectively.

The ability of management teams to lead may be more important now than ever before, because of the overwhelming complexity of today's world. Senge (1990) has observed that we are now creating far more information than we can absorb; we are accelerating change much faster than our ability to adapt. In this dynamic environment, information processing and decision making—the two primary tasks of a management team—have become increasingly difficult. Decades ago, Herbert Simon (1947) suggested that organizations could overcome "irrationality" in decision making by developing detailed procedures and creating structured bureaucracies. This approach might have worked well in the past, but today's organizational climate requires managers to act rapidly, maintain flexibility, and work together cooperatively. Simply calling the management group a team is insufficient; managers must truly be able to demonstrate teamwork if they are to provide strong leadership.

Based on a study of more than seventy management teams, this book describes a five-step process that can turn your management group into a true leadership team. You will find suggestions for making a management team more effective, handling team transitions, and resolving problems that affect teamwork.

But first, let's consider exactly what is meant by the term *management team*.

What Is a Management Team?

In business and government organizations, "management team" specifically describes a group of managers at the same organizational level who are part of the organization's formal management structure. Although engaged in widely varying types of work, most management teams share a number of similarities:

- Membership on the team is a function of position rather than selection.
- Team members head different organizational units but report to the same higher-level manager, who is the formal leader of the team.
- All members of the team have individual goals for their departments, funds that they use to reach those goals, and people reporting to them who are charged with accomplishing the desired results.
- The managers meet regularly to share information and engage in joint decision making about activities within their area of responsibility.
- Between team meetings, members may work together to complete shared projects or resolve common problems.

There are exceptions, but this description applies to the vast majority of management teams.

A small enterprise may have only one management team, while larger organizations could have several teams at each level of their hierarchy. The typical management team—to the degree that such a thing exists—is a group of middle managers responsible for running a line department in a business or government organization. However, our definition of a management team also includes executive teams, staff management teams, and the teams that run not-for-profit organizations. Boards and councils, although not management teams in the traditional sense, are charged with many management responsibilities and therefore face a number of the same challenges. Each of these groups has certain distinguishing characteristics.

Executive Teams

An executive team is the top management group in a company or agency. If the leader of your team does not have a boss who works inside your organization, then you are probably on an executive team. In small organizations, the top team may be the only management team. In large corporations or government agencies, the managers who lead major, autonomous divisions may also be considered an executive group.

Line Management Teams

The line departments in a business or government organization are those producing, delivering, or selling the organization's product or service. They are responsible for the activities that directly determine the success or failure of the organization. Line management teams focus most of their time, energy, and attention on achieving the goals that have been set in these areas.

Staff Management Teams

Staff departments exist to support the line functions. Through application of special knowledge and abilities, they are able to help the organization accomplish particular goals in specific areas. Information systems, accounting, legal, human resources, and safety are examples of staff departments. Staff management teams concentrate primarily on offering expertise in their designated area of responsibility.

Not-for-Profit Management Teams

Not-for-profit organizations exist to provide a service to a particular group or community. They are usually funded through contributions, dues, or grants rather than from the sale of goods and services or direct appropriation of tax dollars. Because not-for-profits take many different forms—from large charitable organizations with a CEO and sizable staff to small community or professional groups that rely on elected officers and volunteers—their management teams vary widely in composition and structure.

Boards and Councils

Boards and councils are composed of people who come together periodically for joint decision making but have no other connection as a group. Boards generally exist to provide governance and oversight to an organization; councils usually comprise people with shared interests who wish to coordinate action in a particular area. These diverse groups range from the board of directors for a multinational corporation to a state government council on aging or the advisory board of a small community nonprofit group. Because boards and councils are engaged in management-related functions, many of the strategies for creating an effective management team also apply to them. This is particularly true for the executive committee of a board or council.

All of these management groups face similar challenges in creating a leadership team. Before exploring the challenges in more detail, though, it may be useful to differentiate management teams from other types of teams found in organizations.

How Management Teams Differ from Other Teams

The teams found in organizations come in various shapes and sizes, with each one having specific attributes that affect the way members work together. The most common team structures are project teams, work teams, and standing committees.

Project teams are formed to complete a specific task and are therefore focused on one common goal (although they sometimes lose this focus). A project team may be asked to develop a new product, reengineer a work process, coordinate the move to a new facility, select a new information system, or perform any of an almost infinite number of other activities. Because members of the team are chosen for their ability to contribute to the successful completion of the project, different departments and organizational levels are likely to be represented. A project team may have a number of managers among its members, but this does not make it a management team. Project teams are not part of the formal organizational structure and are usually disbanded when their job is done (McGrath, 1996).

Work teams, on the other hand, are a fundamental component of the organization's structure. A work team is made up of several employees in the same department whose combined efforts directly create the core products of their organization. They are given tools, technology, and other resources with which they are expected to produce specific results (Hackman, 1990). An automotive manufacturer, for example, may have work teams whose members combine their efforts to produce a completed automobile. A customer service work team may be charged with identifying and resolving customer problems. Work teams are required to operate within certain parameters and are therefore given guidelines and procedures to follow in completing their tasks.

Standing committees have continuing responsibility for a particular area of work that is not part of the members' primary job functions. Business and government organizations use standing committees to administer suggestion programs, identify training needs, organize social functions, and oversee charitable contributions, to cite just a few examples. Members of the group usually come from various departments and are expected to serve on the committee only for a specified period of time. Rotation of membership is needed to bring fresh perspectives to the task and keep members from being overburdened. In business and government organizations, standing committees are not considered part of the formal structure; but such groups may actually constitute the official structure of boards, councils, or certain types of not-for-profit groups. If standing committees make up an organization's structure, they are usually used to perform the tasks necessary for organizational survival, such as membership recruitment, financial management, board development, and so forth.

Management teams can be distinguished from other types by a combination of characteristics:

- The team is part of the formal leadership structure of the organization.
- Members all hold leadership positions in the organization.
- Members are on the same organizational level and report to the same person.

- Both membership and leadership on the team are functions of the individual's position in the organization.
- Members regularly come together to make group decisions that affect their entire organization or department.
- Members share information that helps them perform their individual jobs more effectively.
- Members often need to work together outside the team setting.

The work of a management team is critically important, for this group is, in effect, the central information processing unit in a complex system. Decisions made and actions taken by the management team reverberate throughout the organization, affecting the results of all other teams and all other people within their scope of responsibility. For this reason, management teams must learn to demonstrate leadership and provide a model of teamwork for others to follow. However, turning a group of managers into a leadership team can be a challenging assignment.

Barriers to Teamwork in Management Groups

"Management team" may sound like an oxymoron to people who have spent their lives trying to accomplish results in your average organization. In fact, some research indicates that management groups do have more difficulty than other teams in carrying out interdependent tasks and developing positive relationships (Hackman, 1990). Turning managers into a team can be challenging for several reasons:

- The primary function of a management team is to make critical decisions.
- Management teams are composed of the heads of different organizational units.
- Management work tends to attract personalities who focus more on individual accomplishment than teamwork.
- Management teams operate within a complex framework of organizational relationships.

Understanding these challenges is the first step in building a successful management team.

Management Team Decisions

Decision making has long been identified as the most critical aspect of a manager's work (Mintzberg, 1973; Simon, 1983). The primary function of a management team, therefore, is to make decisions that require input and information from different organizational units. Launching new products or services, changing the information system, coordinating a workforce reduction, or moving to a new location are all examples of decisions that cannot effectively be made by one person or department alone. On an ongoing basis, the management team is likely to make decisions about long-range and short-range goals, management of resources, establishment and enforcement of policies, development of critical success measures, evaluation of results, and assorted administrative issues. Management teams are therefore continually engaged in group decision making.

Anyone who has been part of a group decision-making process knows there can be many potential pitfalls on the way to a good collaborative decision. Goals conflict, information is lacking, lines of authority are unclear, or relationships become strained. To complicate matters further, many decisions made by management teams have a critical impact on one or more team members, on the function to which they belong, or on the entire organization. If the stakes are high, the decision-making process can easily become warped by self-interest, stubbornness, excessive caution, or unwise risk taking. When management teams in Hackman's study (1990) were found to be ineffective, a frequent cause was that their internal decision-making processes did not work well.

In short, decision making is a complex activity. The fact that management teams exist primarily to make decisions rather than to simply share information or meet well-defined expectations means that there are many opportunities for difficulties to occur.

Management Team Composition

A second challenge arises from the fact that management team members usually represent separate organizational units, which often have conflicting needs, interests, and concerns. As the head of a unit, each manager is likely to be responsible for a set of goals, a budget, various types of equipment, a group of employees (often including lower-level managers), and a physical space. Disagreements can arise concerning any of these.

In one manufacturing organization, for example, two units that shared a fax machine frequently bickered about who tied up the machine longer, who used up the supplies, who failed to replace the paper. In another company, the sales and production departments were constantly at war because salespeople promised customers delivery dates that the production manager viewed as unrealistic. The salespeople, of course, felt that production was too slow. In a social service agency, the unit responsible for casework felt that the intake unit did not provide enough information about new clients, while the intake unit thought that this information should be collected by the caseworkers.

Because managers of different units frequently face actual or potential conflicts with one another, relationships on a management team can be easily disrupted by outside events.

Management Personality Types

Another teamwork challenge is that management work tends to attract people whose personalities are somewhat incompatible with a team approach. Because generalizing can lead to dangerous stereotypes, it is important to acknowledge that managers vary widely in personality and work style. Nevertheless, people attracted to management jobs have often been found to share certain traits: they are likely to be analytical, biased toward quick action, and high on need for control.

Analytical people tend to focus on facts, figures, and objective information and are less likely to be attuned to the interpersonal aspects of a situation. They are more adept at logical analysis and critical thinking than at developing and building relationships. Since cooperative relationships are the cornerstone of teamwork, teams composed of highly analytical people often break down because of relationship difficulties. One study of management teams found that if the majority of individual team members excelled at critical analysis, the team was less likely to be successful (Belbin, 1981).

People with a bias for action want to see quick results. They tend to make fast decisions and prefer not to spend time discussing alternatives or debating pros and cons. They are often frustrated by the time it takes for effective team decision making, so they tend to cut the process short. Teams composed of action-oriented people run the risk of making hasty decisions without considering all relevant information.

A high need for control is usually consistent with a preference for independence and autonomy, and with a desire to direct the activities of others. Although these traits are valuable in many areas of management performance, they are obviously inconsistent with teamwork since being part of a group requires cooperation and interdependence. Teams whose members have high control needs may spend a great deal of time arguing and find that group decisions are not carried out as expected.

The fact that many management characteristics are not compatible with teamwork is one of the primary reasons why creating a leadership team is a challenging task. If individual team members are not naturally inclined toward collaboration, extra effort is required to develop a productive team environment.

Organizational Relationships

The final challenge in creating a leadership team lies in one of the realities of organizational life: all organizations consist of a complex network of relationships. Management teams are embedded in an organizational structure that greatly affects their ability to produce results. For this reason, they must be able to effectively manage upward, communicate outward, and focus downward.

"Managing upward" refers to the need to develop and nurture relationships with upper management—a critical task for teams below the executive level. To clearly understand goals and priorities, a management team must have a good communication link with the next level of management. Without this link, the team can find it difficult to be productive. In one company, for example, the head of human resources did not like the CEO and tried to minimize contact with him. As a result, the human resource management team had little knowledge of the CEO's goals, priorities, and preferences. After the team spent considerable time preparing to conduct an employee attitude survey, they suddenly found that the CEO did not like employee surveys. The project was scrapped.

"Communicating outward" means maintaining regular communication with other organizational units. To make informed decisions, a management team must have access to information about relevant activities in other parts of the organization. In one company, the information systems management team selected and installed a new program for tracking costs, but without consulting the operating divisions. When the new system was implemented, many of the assumptions about operating division costs proved to be incorrect. The team then had to throw the program out and start over.

"Focusing downward" involves coordinating the activities of employees who report to management team members. To produce results, team decisions must be translated into actions by those who actually do the work. Otherwise, the decisions have no effect. The management team of one government agency, for example, held several meetings to decide how to improve service to people who called in with problems or questions. The team gathered data, analyzed results, discussed issues, and outlined needs. The only problem was that in all that time, employees who answered the phones never received any training on how to handle calls, so the poor service continued.

Because management teams are embedded in a larger organization, they must successfully manage a complex network of relationships if they are to successfully achieve results.

Is It a Hopeless Task?

Of course not! Members of management teams have a challenging assignment, but a potentially rewarding one. A highly functioning leadership group challenges assumptions, pushes the limits, and insists on excellence. Team members combine their resources, explore their differences, and have fun while they work hard. And they can achieve amazing results. Being part of such a group makes you more effective as a manager and a leader.

So, how does a management group become a leadership team? The next chapter describes the results of a research project that discovered five key strategies for increasing management team effectiveness.

PART ONE

CREATING A LEADERSHIP TEAM

CHAPTER ONE

FIVE KEY STRATEGIES FOR MANAGEMENT TEAM SUCCESS

Management teams play a powerful role in the success or failure of organizations. But despite their prevalence, we know very little about how they operate. Much research has been done on managers and on teams, but little on managers working as a team. For that reason, the Management Team Research Project was designed to answer the question, "How can a group of managers become an effective team?"

To find the answer, more than five hundred members of management teams in business and government organizations were surveyed, using an instrument designed specifically to evaluate management team performance. The research sample consisted of seventy-two management teams having at least four members including the leader. These team members were asked to rate their group's functioning in a number of areas related to team performance in general and management team effectiveness in particular.

A management team was considered to be effective if it was able to accomplish three things:

1. Help team members work together more cooperatively outside the team setting
2. Help team members function more effectively in their jobs
3. Achieve organizational outcomes valued by senior management

The first two criteria were assessed by asking all team members to indicate the degree to which their management team experiences helped improve working relationships and job performance. These questions were included on the survey. To evaluate the third factor, senior executives (chief executive officer, president, commissioner, division manager, etc.) were asked to rank all management teams under their supervision according to the effectiveness of their output. Since the "output" of a management team is represented by the decisions made, these top managers were told to consider the quality, quantity, and timeliness of team decisions.

On each of the three criteria, teams rated in the top 25 percent were compared with those in the bottom 25 percent. Factor analysis was used to identify the characteristics that differentiated highly rated teams from the less effective ones. Based on these research results, we developed the TEAM model (Team Effectiveness Analysis for Management), which is shown in Figure 1.1. The model identifies five success factors critical to the development of a leadership team.

Success Factor One: Strategic Goals

To focus activity and effort, all teams must have a clear understanding of their overall purpose and the goals they intend to accomplish. For top executive groups,

FIGURE 1.1. THE TEAM MODEL.

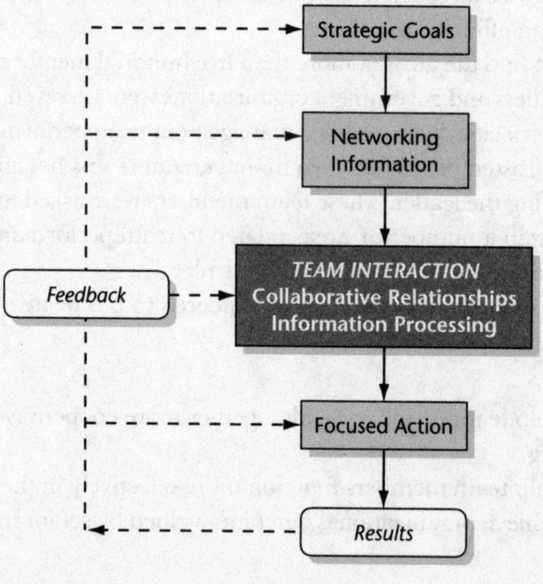

strategic goals develop through ongoing interpretation of the organization's changing environment and identification of appropriate directions to pursue. For middle management teams, an understanding of goals develops through clear and continuing communication with upper management. In fact, maintaining frequent, positive communication with the next level of management was one of two characteristics that led senior executives in our study to rate teams highly. There appeared to be a reciprocal relationship between perceptions at the two levels: middle management teams that felt positively about senior management were more likely to be rated as effective in senior management rankings.

Success Factor Two: Extensive Networks

To make good decisions, teams must have access to critical information from both inside and outside the organization. Sources of information may include contact with people from other departments, connections with other organizations, participation in professional associations, attending workshops, or reading trade publications. Having access to information was the second factor affecting senior management's ranking of teams in our study, possibly because teams with effective networks are better able to anticipate potential difficulties, make changes when necessary, and use more creative approaches in solving problems and making decisions. They may also be able to provide senior management with new and helpful information, thereby creating a positive impression of their abilities.

One interesting aspect of our findings was that relationships outside the team, with senior management and others, seemed to have the greatest positive impact on top management's perception of a team. The implication for middle management teams seems clear: if you want to be well thought of by upper management, develop effective communication networks outside your own department—and be sure to network with your boss!

Success Factor Three: Collaborative Relationships

To cooperate in achieving team goals, management team members must be able to develop positive, supportive relationships. Participants in a study of work teams had difficulty specifically defining this aspect of team effectiveness, but many of them simply described it as "working well together" (Larson and LaFasto, 1989). For the teams in our research, the most important factors in building collaborative relationships appeared to be trust, respect, and successful conflict management. Researchers have also found that previous successful experience in working together improves collaboration (Watson, Michaelsen, and Sharp, 1991). In our study, the quality of team relationships had a significant effect on team member perceptions of the group's effectiveness, but less impact on the opinions of senior management. Hostility among team members did negatively affect senior management perceptions, however.

Success Factor Four: Effective Information Processing

To make good decisions, a management team must effectively process the information received through networking. Decision making is a complex task, requiring clear objectives, expression of different viewpoints, encouragement of new ideas, and consideration of important information. One interesting finding from our research was the strong relationship between leadership and the decision-making process. If a team's leader was viewed as effective, team members also had positive perceptions of the group's ability to use information well. No similar relationship was found between leadership behavior and the other four success factors. This finding appears to indicate that the leader of a management team has more influence over this aspect of team effectiveness than any other.

Success Factor Five: Focused Action

To accomplish results, a management team must make the transition from discussion to action. Our research found that critical factors in this process include defining specific results, developing an action plan, moving forward in a timely manner, including all appropriate people in the planning process, and following up to ensure that plans are carried out. This success factor received the lowest score among participants in our research, implying a comparatively high level of frustration among management team members with the results of their decisions. Some dissatisfaction with outcomes may be related to Senge's observation (1990) that in today's turbulent environment, frequent change can make the result of an action difficult to anticipate. Low scores on this success factor may also reflect a tendency on the part of managers to focus more intently on negative outcomes than positive ones, possibly to prevent similar mistakes in the future. Additionally, managers may be highly aware of negative results because they are more likely to receive punishment for mistakes than rewards for successes.

The relationship among the five success factors is shown in Figure 1.1. Direction and information flow into the team from the external environment. (Although the team itself may set goals, they are nevertheless driven by factors external to the team.) During team interaction, collaborative relationships and effective information processing help the members translate goals and information into action. These actions produce results, which provide feedback about the team's effectiveness. This feedback loop is critical for the team's continued learning.

If these five success factors were present in a management team, the members worked as a productive, cohesive group. If they were not, the team had difficulty fulfilling a leadership role in the organization. In terms of overall team effectiveness, no one factor appeared to be more important than another, a result that is not surprising given that studies of work teams have often found factors affecting team performance to be highly interrelated (Larson and LaFasto, 1989; Katzenbach and Smith, 1993). Although five separate success factors were identified, each had an impact on the others. The reciprocal nature of the success factors seems to indicate the importance of attending to all of them, since a problem in one area is likely to "infect" other aspects of team performance.

Challenges for Different Types of Management Teams

Even though the five success factors are interrelated and apply to all management teams, some teams do have unique characteristics and special needs that increase the importance of particular activities. For this reason, certain groups need to give special attention to specific success factors:

- Executive teams
- Staff management teams
- Teams in government organizations
- Teams in not-for-profit organizations
- Boards and councils

Many management teams fall into more than one of these categories—for example, the board of a not-for-profit association or a staff team in a government agency. If your group is described by one or more of these categories, you may wish to pay special attention to the chapters mentioned in that section.

Executive Teams

Executive teams are responsible for guiding an entire organization and coordinating all major functions. Their decisions determine future success and affect many people both inside and outside their organization. Developing cooperation and teamwork in executive groups is often particularly challenging, since top teams—especially those in larger organizations—are usually populated by managers who are accustomed to exercising power and authority, who have bigger-than-average egos, and who like to be in charge. One researcher who studied many types of teams found that top management groups often had considerable difficulty operating as a team (Hackman, 1990).

Executive teams need to pay particular attention to the following success factors.

Strategic Goals. Clear goals are especially important for top management because they are responsible for providing leadership and vision to the rest of the organization. Unlike other management teams, the executive team does not report to a higher-level group. Executive teams in business do need to communicate and consult with the board of directors, and executive teams in government must be responsive to the appropriate political body; nevertheless they are expected to take the leadership role in establishing organizational direction. Managers and employees are always uneasy if the top group appears to lack clear goals, because they know that their future is at stake. (Success factor one, strategic goals, is discussed in Chapter Two.)

Extensive Networks. External networking is a critical responsibility for executive teams, because they need input from the environment in order to establish direction and make course corrections if necessary. Top teams cannot be effective decision makers unless they have access to reliable sources of outside information. If they remain too internally focused, the organization inevitably starts down the road to obsolescence. In business, outside connections may include major customers, public officials, the media, industry groups, and community organizations. Critical contacts for government officials may include politicians, taxpayers, service recipients, the media, and professional associations.

Internal networking is also important for executive groups because top teams must not lose touch with the workforce. This isolation can easily occur in large organizations because of the many layers between top managers and those who deliver the goods and services. Since top teams must depend on others to carry out decisions, they need to ensure that accurate information flows down from their level and up from below. Top managers also have a role as "head cheerleader" in their organizations, that is, their relationship with employees has a motivational function, even if communication can only occur through memos, e-mails, and occasional face-to-face interactions. Smart CEOs recognize the importance of this connection. As one of them said, "If you take out the people, all we have are empty buildings and idle machines." (Success factor two, extensive networking, is discussed in Chapter Three.)

Collaborative Relationships. Top managers are competitive and independent by nature. They like to be in charge and run their own show. Whenever people with these preferences are on a team, encouraging them to work cooperatively can be a challenge. To further complicate the situation, top team members are usually managing dissimilar functions with goals that may conflict. If they lack understanding of shared goals, their departments can easily develop tunnel vision and work at cross purposes. But rather than openly disagree, executives tend to avoid interaction and operate autonomously, allowing "walls" to develop between their functions. To achieve the best results, top management teams must constantly strive to foster cooperation and open communication among their members. Teamwork among top managers greatly enhances the accomplishment of goals throughout the organization, whereas poor relationships at the top often create confusion and hostility at lower levels. (Success factor three, collaborative relationships, is discussed in Chapter Four.)

Staff Management Teams

The most important task for staff management teams is to provide good service to their internal customers, the line managers. The problem, however, is that staff functions often have the dual role of helper and monitor: they provide assistance to line departments but must also see that certain standards are met—obviously an uncomfortable combination. As members of a professional group, staff employees frequently feel a dual allegiance: to the organization and to their profession. If organizational behaviors fail to conform to professional standards, they may experience conflicting loyalties.

Staff management teams need to pay particular attention to the following success factors.

Strategic Goals. Staff managers must clearly understand how they can best help the organization. In developing their goals, consultation and coordination with line managers is essential. At the same time, staff management teams need to provide leadership to the organization within their area of expertise and must therefore educate upper management about their function. Because of their professional allegiances, these groups run the risk of becoming too focused on their own special interests; they must be sure that their goals are always congruent with the needs of the organization and do not become self-serving. (Success factor one, strategic goals, is discussed in Chapter Two.)

Extensive Networks. External networking is vital to the success of a staff organization, since staff employees can only add value by keeping up with knowledge and trends in their specialty area. Joining associations and reading professional publications is especially important. Internal networking is also critical for maintaining communication with line managers and overcoming the built-in adversarial nature of this relationship. (Success factor two, extensive networking, is discussed in Chapter Three. Problems with line-staff relationships are included in the section in that chapter on overcoming barriers.)

Government Organizations

Government organization refers to any component of a local, state, or federal government that is largely supported by tax dollars. Government organizations differ from the private sector in several ways. First, success is harder to define. In business, profitability provides a clear measure of achievement; government agencies must balance competing interests and different interpretations of their role. As a result, researchers have found that goals in government are often unclear or conflicting (Osborne and Gaebler, 1992). Identifying customers is also more difficult. In business, customers are those who purchase products or services; government agencies have several groups of "customers": the people who receive services, the taxpayers who provide funding, and the elected officials who represent the taxpayers. Because agencies must function successfully within a political system, they need to be responsive to different constituencies, which may have conflicting needs, interests, and goals. Finally, whereas a business spends money earned through its own efforts, government managers are always spending other people's money in the form of tax dollars. This fact has many implications for the way that government managers operate. They must always be aware of their role as public officials as they make decisions or spend agency money—and this awareness must extend to the conduct of their personal lives as well.

Government management teams need to pay particular attention to the following success factors.

Strategic Goals. Managers in government need to be sure that their goals are clear and reflect the needs and concerns of service recipients and taxpayers. Remembering that their overriding objective is to serve the public interest (a fuzzy goal in itself), they must take care not to become self-serving. Government management teams need to clearly define their customer groups and determine where these groups have conflicting interests that need to be balanced. For these teams, another goal-setting challenge is that the top executive is often an elected or appointed political official. Politicians are sometimes reluctant to take strong positions for fear of alienating voters, so the agency may have difficulty getting upper management to commit to specific goals, particularly if they might generate any controversy. In our study, middle management teams in government were much less positive about their relationship with upper management than were middle managers in business. If a poor relationship exists with senior executives, middle management teams are likely to have more difficulty reaching agreement with them on goals. (Success factor one, strategic goals, is discussed in Chapter Two.)

Focused Action. Because success is harder to define in the public sector, a management team may have difficulty identifying desirable results. Even if goals are clearly defined, evaluating outcomes can be challenging, because government agencies often work in areas where results are hard to measure. The need to show positive outcomes is critical, however, because the agency must be able to compete for funding. Outcome measures must be developed in the context of public and political perceptions, since considering how results are viewed by various constituencies and interest groups is fundamental to survival in the public sector. For these reasons, government management teams must make an extra effort to define meaningful results and then clearly communicate them to the appropriate audiences.

Government agencies must also fight the tendency to obstruct effective action with red tape. Because mistakes often bring down the wrath of the political system, managers can get caught up in "CYA" activity, creating an abundance of policies, procedures, rules, and approval levels. These efforts to prevent errors, however, increase cost and reduce effectiveness, making results more difficult to accomplish. Because of this tendency, the public sector often tends to be rule-driven rather than mission-driven (Osborne and Gaebler, 1992), inhibiting the ability of managers to solve problems and accomplish meaningful results. Government management teams must always balance the need to prevent errors with the need for timely action. (Success factor five, focused action, is discussed in Chapter Six.)

Not-for-Profit Organizations

The majority of not-for-profit organizations are engaged in an ongoing struggle for funds, membership, staff, or other resources. Many of them must recruit and motivate volunteers to successfully accomplish the goals of their organization. Not-for-profit enterprises often use their board members as a source of resources, volunteer help, management expertise, and connection to other organizations. The board is usually populated by people who have a special interest in the work of the organization but may have differing perspectives on its purpose and direction.

Not-for-profit management teams need to pay particular attention to networking (as well as to the success factors listed below under boards and councils).

Extensive Networks. Because not-for-profit organizations are seldom rich in resources, they need to use their networking skills to secure funding, raise capital, recruit staff and volunteers, increase membership, and solicit help from larger organizations. Their management teams are most effective if they are active in community or professional organizations and adept at building a base of support. Smart leaders of not-for-profits know how to use their board as a networking tool and recruit members strategically to accomplish specific goals. (Success factor two, extensive networking, is discussed in Chapter Three.)

Boards and Councils

Boards and councils vary in the degree to which they actively participate in decision making for their organizations. Some simply sign off on the recommendations of an executive director or CEO, while others are more directly involved. Meetings of these groups are usually somewhat formal and structured, with long intervals in between; quarterly meetings tend to be the norm. Much of the work is performed between meetings by subgroups (executive boards, standing committees, or task forces) and brought to the full group for review, discussion, and approval. Unless they are engaged in committee activities, members of boards and councils usually have little interaction with one another outside of formal meetings. Boards and councils need to pay particular attention to the following success factors.

Collaborative Relationships. Because members of boards and councils often have no other connection with one another, they lack the foundation of positive relationships that helps promote communication and cooperation. People in these groups often know little about the background and expertise of other members and are therefore unable to put their opinions and comments into a meaningful context. This lack of familiarity may inhibit the expression of different opinions, but differences that do arise can quickly deteriorate into hostilities. Another danger in these groups is that members who do have relationships with one another may form cliques. If two or more members are acquainted through other activities or organizational affiliations, they naturally tend to band together. For long-term success, boards and councils must provide members with the opportunity to get acquainted and interact outside meetings. Special efforts should be made to orient new members to the group and help them develop relationships. To provide more interaction time, some boards and councils have their members eat meals together or meet in locations where everyone has to stay overnight. (Success factor three, collaborative relationships, is discussed in Chapter Four.)

Effective Information Processing. Because boards and councils meet infrequently, they do not have the shared history of joint decision making that most other management teams possess. This lack of shared experience, combined with undeveloped relationships, means that to make decisions effectively they usually need strong leadership. The leader must be sure that members understand the role of the board in relationship to other components of the organization (such as the staff, director, executive board, or committees). The objectives and agenda for each meeting should be clearly communicated. Some groups find that decisions are made more easily if they use a structured format, such as Robert's Rules of Order, during the business portion of their meeting. If a board or council lacks leadership, structure, or an understanding of roles, meetings can deteriorate into aimless discussions or hostile debates. (Success factor four, effective information processing, is discussed in Chapter Five.)

*

Even though different types of management teams have different challenges, focusing on the five success factors can help any management group improve its ability to lead effectively. The next five chapters explore each success factor in more detail and present:

- Reasons why the success factor is important for a management team
- Strategies to use in implementing the success factor
- Potential problems with the success factor and suggested solutions
- Surveys to assess your management team on the success factor
- Discussion questions for your team to explore the success factor

The goal of this book is to provide a resource to help you create a true leadership team. In the remainder of Part One, you can evaluate how well your group is currently functioning and identify strategies to maximize your team's effectiveness. Assessment surveys and discussion questions are provided at the end of each chapter to help you relate the material to your own management team. Part Two then provides suggestions to keep your management team operating effectively, including strategies for selecting team members, managing team transitions, and fixing a "sick" team. Since management teams are dynamic bodies, constantly reacting to shifts in organizational direction, this book also serves as an ongoing reference to use when conditions change. As a leader or member of a management team, you have an important and challenging assignment. The information provided here is intended to be a helpful guide to consult as you and your team continue the difficult but rewarding job of providing leadership to your organization.

CHAPTER TWO

STRATEGIC GOALS

How to Establish Direction for Your Organization

True Story: The Company with No Plan

Part One: The Problem

Five senior managers in a manufacturing company are meeting with a consultant. "We know that this company needs to begin thinking strategically," says the marketing vice president, "but we aren't sure how to go about it. Do you think you could help us?"

"I do that kind of work," replies the consultant. "And I might be able to help. One question, though. Why isn't the CEO in this meeting?"

The managers glance at one another. "Well," says the chief financial officer, "That's one of the issues. You see, the CEO has been here a long time and knows this company from the ground up. He can tell you the name of every machine in the plant. But he's not too keen on the idea of strategic planning—just doesn't see the point in it. We thought that maybe we could get something started ourselves."

"Hmm," murmurs the consultant. "You have no plan now?"

"Oh, we have a five-year plan," says the human resources director. "But I don't think it's very strategic. Bob Hughes puts it together every year, and the CEO signs off on it. Then we all get a copy. I think mine is somewhere in the files. Would you like to see it?"

"Maybe later," replies the consultant. "Tell me a little about how you use the plan."

"Well, we don't really use it," says the marketing vice president. "Actually, I really can't remember the last time I read one of Bob's plans."

In this manufacturing company, senior managers are frustrated by lack of direction from the top. The CEO is dedicated to the business but focuses his attention on operational details instead of overall goals. As a result, operating divisions in the company develop their own objectives, which sometimes come into conflict with one another, causing problems with both productivity and relationships.

The Importance of Goals

Shared goals form the foundation upon which all teams are built. Without them, any team finds it difficult to function. In studies of groups, shared goals have been found to promote consistency in members' behavior (Katz and Kahn, 1978), provide a framework for interpreting data (Pugh and Hickson, 1989), and help people screen information from the environment appropriately (Morgan, 1986). For a management team, goals help direct action, develop cooperation, and align organizational units both horizontally and vertically.

Action

A primary function of goals is to direct action productively (you are much more likely to score a touchdown if you know where the goalposts are located). Shared goals are especially important for management teams because these groups exist primarily to improve organizational decision making. The decisions made by team members, both collectively and individually, determine how employees prioritize activities and use resources. If these decisions are made without a framework of clearly defined organizational goals, resources may be wasted or misdirected. In one health care company, for instance, a great deal of time and money was spent putting all the managers through a management development program— shortly before most management positions were eliminated. The higher the team in the organization, the greater the impact of their decisions, so shared goals are particularly critical for executive teams.

Cooperation

Research on cooperation has found that group members naturally assume a competitive posture unless they clearly understand their shared goals and interests (Tjosvold, 1988). Destructive competition is more frequently found in Western cultures, which tend to place a high value on individual achievement. Competition can develop quite easily among management team members, since their departments frequently have conflicting objectives. Although competition has many positive functions, competition among team members is usually harmful, interfering with the achievement of common goals. In one manufacturing company, division managers failed to refer potential customers to one another because they were competing for bonuses based largely on increased revenues. None of them wanted to help the others get more business. As a result, the company as a whole lost potential sales opportunities.

If managers are to work cooperatively, they must agree on a set of shared goals that supersede the interests of their individual units. Otherwise, unhealthy competition develops, causing relationships to deteriorate. A member of one highly competitive management team told a consultant that having a root canal was more fun than attending team meetings, where managers were constantly engaged in arguments and power struggles.

Horizontal Alignment

When group goals are lacking, because they have not been developed or have not been accepted, members are less likely to coordinate their efforts and more likely to concentrate on activities that benefit them personally. Because the individual departments represented on a management team have very different functions, they can easily develop tunnel vision and begin to operate only in their own interest. This inward focus can be harmful to other units and to the organization as a whole. If the salesforce in a manufacturing company begins closing deals by promising unrealistic delivery dates, for example, the production department may start to suffer from overwork, missed deadlines, and possibly poor product quality. These production problems may in turn affect the company's reputation with customers. When management team members clearly understand overall goals—not just those affecting their own departments—these horizontal "goal gaps" are less likely to occur.

Vertical Alignment

The relationship between superiors and subordinates in an organization has been described as the "vertical dimension of group effectiveness" (Cota and others, 1994). Vertical alignment of goals is particularly important for management teams, especially in larger organizations where management groups occur in layers. Each member of a senior management team may have several managers as direct reports, thereby creating another management team. For decisions to be made effectively, each level must understand the goals of the levels above it. For instance, the accounts payable unit shown in Figure 2.1 must understand the goals of the accounting division, the finance department, and the company. Vertical alignment

FIGURE 2.1. VERTICAL ALIGNMENT.

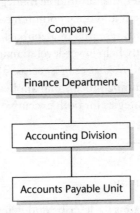

begins with a clear articulation of goals by the executive team and ends with employees taking the steps needed to accomplish those goals. Management team members should always remember that decisions only come to life through appropriate action by employees, which is more likely if goals are clear all down the line.

Strategic and Operational Planning

To establish clear goals, all management teams—whether they are responsible for a large organization or a single department—need to engage in both strategic and operational planning. Strategic planning establishes the overall purpose and direction for the organization, while operational planning determines the specific goals and objectives that turn the strategic plan into reality. Unfortunately, many management teams complete only half the process. Some groups attend retreats to develop a mission statement, articulate their values, and set broad goals (such as "improve communication with our customers") but fail to define the specific steps needed to put those goals into operation. Other management teams write detailed objectives every year, including time lines and completion dates, but never take time to consider whether those specific steps are heading in a direction that will create successful outcomes five or ten years down the road.

Although the steps in planning are similar for all management teams, executives have a somewhat different focus than middle managers do. Executive teams must provide direction for the entire organization, so the most critical element in their planning process is a thorough study of environmental trends affecting the organization's future. For teams below the top level, the most critical planning task is to clearly understand the goals and expectations of upper management. Results of our study indicated that for middle management teams goal clarity is only possible through frequent and open communication with the level above. This finding supports previous research (Katzenbach and Smith, 1993) showing that top managers can greatly help lower-level management teams by working with them to identify goals and measures of success. The following discussion provides an overview of the planning process that applies to all management teams, and then outlines specific strategies for both executive teams and those at lower levels.

The Planning Process

Phase One: Strategic Planning

Strategic planning aims to describe and determine the future of an organization by clarifying its purpose, identifying factors that may affect future success, and articulating critical priorities. Unless their environment is unusually stable or extremely turbulent, most organizations should undertake a strategic planning effort approximately every three years.

Strategic planning takes time. If your team has never undergone such a process before, be prepared to spend several months gathering, analyzing, and discussing information about your organization and the environment in which it operates. The result of your efforts will be a list of the strategic priorities that must be addressed in order to create a successful future for your organization. These are the priorities to which you will then dedicate resources—time, money, people, and energy—for the next few years.

Although the management team needs to be the driving force behind strategic planning, the best results are obtained when people representing a cross-section of the organization are involved in the process. One way to promote wider involvement is to consider the management team a steering committee and then create a larger planning group that includes representatives from throughout the organization. The steering committee makes major decisions about both the process and the final plan, but the entire planning group participates in the activities described below. Most planning group members are employees and lower-level managers, but some organizations include board members, customers, volunteers, or contract workers. Many teams find it helpful to hire a consultant to guide the planning process, but outside assistance is not necessarily required to produce a useful plan.

Each component of the strategic planning process is designed to answer a critical question. In answering these questions, the management team provides the information needed to identify actions required for future success. The results of strategic planning should be communicated to everyone, since all employees, from senior vice president to truck driver, need to know where their organization is headed. The steps in strategic planning are shown in Figure 2.2 and discussed below.

Mission. The mission of an organization describes the reason for its existence, answering these questions: "What is our purpose, and why should we continue to exist?" Many management groups get too involved in producing a mission *statement* and fail to spend enough time exploring alternative views of the mission itself. Having this discussion is quite important, however, because how you define your purpose determines how you invest your financial and human resources in the future. Suppose, for example, that you run a company that makes film for cameras and video recorders. You might define your mission in any of the following ways: to produce film, to provide photographic services, or to make imaging systems. The company's future could proceed in several directions, depending on which statement of purpose you adopt. If you intend to provide photographic services, you may decide to acquire a camera manufacturer or open a chain of photo developing stores; if you define yourself as a maker of imaging systems, you may begin to develop equipment for medical uses. If you simply see yourself as a film manufacturer, you may just keep on doing what you're doing.

The mission of an organization usually remains constant for a long period of time, but recognizing when your purpose needs to be redefined is critically important. A library system that viewed itself solely as a supplier of books or reading material might fail to provide videos, audiotapes, computer databases, or Internet access, resulting in a declining customer base as more people seek information in formats other than traditional text. If, however, library management defines the mission as providing customers with access to information (not just books), these additional services are more likely to be offered.

A mission is usually articulated in the form of a mission statement. Since team members should use their energy to define a useful purpose and not to argue about word usage, try to avoid getting trapped in a group writing-and-editing session. The team can reach agreement on what the mission must include and then assign one or two people the task of drafting a statement of purpose to be brought back to the group for discussion. Your mission statement should meet these criteria:

- Accurately reflect what you do or what you should be doing.
- Serve as a guide for making decisions about future activities.
- Include all major groups in your organization.
- Communicate concisely, using simple words and avoiding jargon.
- Clearly explain to someone *outside* the organization what you do.

FIGURE 2.2. COMPONENTS OF STRATEGIC PLANNING.

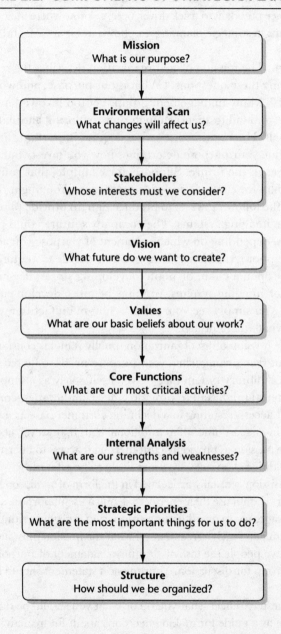

Mission
What is our purpose?

Environmental Scan
What changes will affect us?

Stakeholders
Whose interests must we consider?

Vision
What future do we want to create?

Values
What are our basic beliefs about our work?

Core Functions
What are our most critical activities?

Internal Analysis
What are our strengths and weaknesses?

Strategic Priorities
What are the most important things for us to do?

Structure
How should we be organized?

One library system that expanded its purpose beyond providing books but still wants to encourage children and adults to read describes its mission this way: "We intend to be the best source of free information for both educational and leisure purposes, encouraging the love of reading and the pursuit of knowledge in our changing and diverse community." This simple statement has several implications for the manner in which the organization plans to operate in the future:

- They will consider a variety of strategies for giving customers access to information.
- They will not charge fees for providing access to information.
- They will continue to encourage people to read.
- They will respond to changing community needs.
- They will serve the needs of diverse constituencies in their community.

Environmental Scan. An environmental scan identifies forces and trends in the larger environment within which the organization operates, to answer the question, "What changes have occurred that will affect our organization and what changes do we expect in the future?" For executive teams, this may be the most important stage in the strategic planning process, since ignoring major environmental trends can cause organizations to decline and die. Unfortunately, many management teams either ignore this phase or fail to do a thorough job. A cereal manufacturer, for example, experienced a steep decline in market share after failing to anticipate the popularity of lower-priced grocery store brands.

The first step in an environmental scan is to identify critical areas that should be studied. These often include, but are not limited to, customers, competitors, political trends, technology, legal developments, demographic changes, socioeconomic trends, and best practices. The next step is to create task forces to gather and evaluate data in each area. This information is then used to identify significant trends that should be considered in setting priorities for the future.

Stakeholders. People who have a vested interest in the success of an organization are considered stakeholders. Identifying stakeholders answers the question, "Whose interests must we consider as we develop plans for the future?" Stakeholder groups may include customers, employees, managers, shareholders, taxpayers, or anyone else affected by the organization's work. In fact, stakeholders don't necessarily have to be people: the board of a humane society quite logically listed "animals" as a stakeholder group.

Vision. Vision refers to a description of the ideal future, answering the question, "How would we like to be able to describe our organization and its impact five to ten years from now?" Once the organization's purpose has been defined and critical trends identified, a picture can be created of a future organization that is successfully meeting the needs of all stakeholders. Having team members literally draw what the ideal future will look like is often helpful in defining the vision, since the act of drawing calls on the more creative part of our brains. The themes represented in these pictures can then be included in a written summary of the vision.

One unorthodox vision statement was developed by a group of civic leaders in a city on the West Coast of the United States. Here is how they described a successful future for their community: "Everyone should be able to see the mountains, and all children should be able to walk to a park." Although on the surface this statement seems quite limited, these two goals actually have many implications for public policy, among them that

- Air pollution must be prevented
- Construction of high-rise buildings must be limited
- Crime must be controlled
- Space must be set aside for recreation
- Sidewalks must be built

Even though most descriptions of the future are more detailed than this one, all vision statements provide the foundation for developing the organization's priorities and goals. Creating a meaningful vision of the future is one of the most important steps in the planning process.

In addition to simply describing the ideal future, the management team also needs to determine how success will be defined. The group should address the question, "What results or outcomes will let us know that we have succeeded in moving our organization in the desired direction?" In the example of the West Coast city, measures of air pollution levels, crime, and recreational space could all be used to evaluate progress. (You will find a detailed discussion of defining results and establishing outcome measures in Chapter Six, Focused Action.)

Values. Values are the principles that guide decisions and actions in an organization. Value statements are developed in response to the question, "What are our beliefs about the way we should do our work?" One method for defining values is to list all stakeholder groups, plus any other factors critical for the organization's success—such as technology or work processes—and then ask, "What are the values that we must exhibit in each of these areas in order to achieve our ideal future?" One planning group expressed these values in relation to employees: teamwork, continuous learning, independent decision making, and commitment.

Once values are identified, two further steps should be taken. First, the values must be translated into behaviors by completing an "if . . . then" statement for each value; for example, "If we value continuous learning, then we will support employees with the resources and training needed to upgrade their skills." After all the values have been translated into statements of behavior, then the group should evaluate the degree to which the organization currently demonstrates the behaviors needed to promote each value. This may simply involve an immediate assessment by the group, or it may require more extensive data gathering (see the section on internal analysis below).

Core Functions. Core functions are the basic activities at which the organization needs to be proficient in order to create a successful future. The identification of core functions answers the question, "What are the fundamental activities that this organization must be able to carry out effectively?" In defining core functions, both current and future needs of the organization should be considered. Failing to identify these fundamental areas of expertise can lead to serious errors or omissions in organizational decision making. One nonprofit organization, for example, had never identified recruiting and motivating volunteers as a core function. When this oversight was discovered through the planning process, the members immediately realized why their organization had been struggling to survive; they were then able to take steps to remedy the situation.

The review of core functions may lead to a useful discussion of make-or-buy decisions, that is, what expertise should be developed internally and what should be purchased from others. A health care organization failed to consider this question thoroughly when it decided to internally develop a software program for updating medical records. The task was clearly beyond the capabilities of the company's information systems department—a fact that unfortunately did not become apparent until after the new system was in place. The make-or-buy issue was more successfully addressed by a struggling nonprofit group that had previously hired several consultants to help with fundraising, producing less-than-spectacular results. As a result of their planning process, the board decided that fundraising ability was needed in-house and hired someone with experience in this area.

Internal Analysis. An internal analysis evaluates the organization's current functioning and ability to meet anticipated future challenges, answering the question, "What are the strengths and weaknesses of this organization?" The assessment should determine how effectively core functions are being performed and how well value-based behaviors are being demonstrated. To conduct the internal analysis, task forces can be used to study various aspects of organizational functioning. These groups may need to compile and analyze existing data or gather additional information through surveys, interviews, and/or focus groups. The result of this process should be a comprehensive summary of the organization's ability to achieve current goals and meet future challenges.

Strategic Priorities. Strategic priorities represent the critical actions necessary for the organization to effectively carry out its mission in the future, answering the question, "What are the most important uses of our financial and human resources?" Strategic priorities are broad statements of direction that are translated into specific goals and objectives during the operational planning phase. Another library system identified strengthening connections between the library and the community as a strategic priority. In the operational plan, goals were established to move the organization in that direction: develop partnerships with other organizations, have staff members join community groups, increase public communication about library services, and recruit volunteers from diverse groups in the community.

If the preceding planning steps are completed properly, strategic priorities usually emerge rather clearly at the end of the process. In fact, this result at times seems almost magical, as managers who have been immersed in data, discussion, and analysis suddenly realize that they can easily see what needs to be done to create a successful future. These priorities represent what is often referred to as a "gap analysis": the actions needed to close the gap between where we are now and where we want to be. To focus resources appropriately, strategic priorities should be limited to an achievable number, usually from four to eight.

Structure. Once strategic priorities have been identified, the management team needs to consider whether the current organization structure is appropriate for future needs, by answering the question, "How do we need to be organized to address our strategic priorities?" This is an important consideration because structural problems often inhibit the accomplishment of critical goals. A technology company that for years had been organized along product lines determined through strategic planning that the same customers could use many of their products. This led them to decide that reorganizing into customer-focused business units would bring more success in the future. As another example, a not-for-profit management team determined through planning that they needed to pay more attention to public relations but realized that this core function was not represented anywhere in their organizational structure. They quickly decided to create a new board committee devoted to the activity and hire a staff member with public relations experience.

Two points must be kept in mind when considering changes in your organization chart. First, there is no perfect organizational structure. Each one has costs and benefits, which is one reason that reorganizations occur fairly regularly. When the problems with one structure become too troublesome, a new one is implemented to correct the situation. After a time, however, difficulties with the new structure become apparent, and another reorganization takes place. Your goal should be to find the structure that best supports your current strategic priorities. This may simply mean shifting managers' responsibilities with no change in titles and positions, or it may involve a wholesale reshuffling of departments and people.

Second, anticipating structural change often triggers intense territoriality among team members. Changes in structure usually mean shifts in the balance of power, and few managers willingly cede power to others. As a result of the strategic planning process, one large government agency decided to implement some of the quality practices used in business organizations. A primary goal of this initiative was to push a great deal of decision making down to lower levels. All the managers involved applauded the move to delegate responsibility downward— that is, until some of their own decision-making authority was taken away, at which point they all found reasons why no changes should be made.

Because people tend to act in their own self-interest, it is usually impossible to reach a consensus decision about structural change. When considering a reorganization, many leaders find it useful to get input from team members, sometimes even having the group draw several possible organization charts and debate the pros and cons of each; however, the final decision usually must be made by the person in charge.

Phase Two: Operational Planning

By identifying the most important priorities, the strategic planning process lays the groundwork for defining targeted actions through operational planning. To accomplish results, the transition from strategic to operational planning is critical. If this transition is not made, organizations may suffer from the bookshelf syndrome, in which a strategic plan is created and then placed on a shelf to gather dust while business goes on as usual.

A strategic plan only comes to life when the priorities identified through that process are translated into specific goals and objectives. As most managers know, goals are general statements of desired results, while objectives describe specific outcomes to be achieved. To be useful, an objective must include a description of measurable or observable outcomes, a designation of the person or group responsible for achieving them, and a date by which the results are to be accomplished. Goals generally aim at a one- to three-year time period, while objectives make up the annual plan.

For each strategic priority, the team should identify three to five goals that move the organization in the desired direction. Managers in the throes of a planning process are often tempted to develop a long list of goals, including every activity that might be helpful. Though this brainstorming may be quite useful for creating an initial summary of possibilities, narrowing goals down to a number that can actually be accomplished is critical for success. Once goals are agreed upon, the specific outcomes needed to achieve them must be identified and turned into objectives. (Detailed strategies for putting a plan into action are discussed in Chapter Six.)

Phase Three: Annual Review

Strategic and operational plans must be reviewed annually. If major changes have occurred or are anticipated, then the strategic plan may need to be revised. Under normal circumstances, however, a complete strategic planning process should only have to occur about every three years. Operational plans ought to be rewritten each year, with goals updated and new objectives established. At the time of the plan review, successes should be celebrated, and factors impeding goal accomplishment should be identified and addressed.

Additional Strategies for Executive Teams

Some material in this section may apply to any management group that has several management teams reporting to it.

Strategy One: Get Buy-in on Your Plan from Your Governing Body

Top managers, including CEOs and government department heads, need to get buy-in on their plan from the board or political official to whom they report. The degree to which these parties need to be involved in plan development varies among organizations, but in any event, the governing body needs to sign off on the final decisions before they are more widely communicated. Most governing bodies are only interested in strategic priorities or goals, although some may want to see specific objectives as well.

Strategy Two: Establish Direction for All Major Organizational Functions

The strategic and operational plans of top management should drive the plans of every other management team in the organization. If the executive team in a domestic manufacturing company decides to develop international markets, for example, then the strategic and operational plans of the production, sales, marketing, accounting, information systems, human resource, and legal departments should all reflect this shift. Clearly, then, members of the executive team must forge a strong communication link with managers at the next level, who should use the top team's plan as the basis for their own planning process. Hackman (1990) found that management teams whose parameters had been clearly established by senior management generally performed well, whereas teams subjected to chronic uncertainty tended to falter. If the top team fails to establish direction for the rest of the organization, then the organization's future is highly questionable.

Strategy Three: Ensure That All Management Teams Complete a Planning Process

Preparing and maintaining strategic and operational plans should be a performance objective for every manager who leads a management team. Executives need to require each of their direct reports to establish and follow a timetable for completing an annual plan for their departments. They must also ensure that this objective is built into the organization's performance appraisal system for managers. In coordinating plans throughout the organization, the top team must promote both horizontal and vertical alignment by linking the plans of lower-level teams appropriately to one another and to the overall organizational plan. Having team members share plans for their individual departments in management team meetings helps establish these connections.

Strategy Four: Be Accessible to Lower-Level Teams During Their Planning Process

Our research clearly indicated that middle management teams can only be effective if their goals are linked to those of upper management. For this reason, top managers must clarify expectations for each function reporting to them and should be available for consultation during their planning processes. This does not mean, however, that executives should become directly involved in managing the planning process of their direct reports. Their role is not to micromanage, but to clarify expectations, be available for consultation, and provide feedback on plans as they are developed.

Strategy Five: Maintain Ongoing Communication with Lower-Level Teams

The most effective midlevel teams in our research agreed upon performance expectations with senior management, received regular feedback about their performance, and were given advance information about anticipated changes. By maintaining regular communication links with the teams below them, executive teams help to ensure that those managers are able to update their plans in accordance with organizational needs.

Strategy Six: Demonstrate Commitment to Goals Through Your Actions

People in organizations learn more about goals from what managers do than from what they say. Because of their broad impact, the actions of executives are closely scrutinized by other managers and employees. When senior managers take action that is consistent with their stated goals, they send a clear message that these goals are important. If executive behavior is not congruent with stated objectives, however, people often grow confused about what is expected of them. The executive team of a large medical center stressed to employees that they must be friendly, helpful, and responsive to patients and their families; yet one senior vice president never spoke to employees she passed in the hall or responded when they spoke to her. Clearly, this executive was not modeling the behavior that the senior team was trying to promote. When lower-level managers are not sure what the true goals are, they may become resentful and begin to view top management as hypocritical. If executives sense this resentment, they may get defensive, creating a vicious cycle of declining communication.

Additional Strategies for Middle Management Teams

Strategy One: Consult Upper Management During Your Planning Process

Our research has found that middle management teams can only be effective if their plans are aligned with those of the managers above them. Teams that develop goals totally unrelated to those of their organizational superiors risk being viewed as incompetents or renegades. For that reason, managers below the top level need to clarify the goals and expectations of upper management before undertaking a planning process. As your department goes through strategic planning, the team should be sure to share information with the level above at appropriate points in the process; for example, upper management should be in agreement with your mission statement, be included in your environmental scan, and have input into your internal analysis. This does not mean, however, that the next level of management should take an active role in directing the planning process; they should simply be available for consultation.

Strategy Two: Establish a Regular Communication Link with Upper Management

Once the plan is completed, the management team needs ongoing discussion with upper management about organizational goals, department objectives, progress made, problems encountered, and anticipated changes. This communication link usually occurs through frequent communication between upper management and the team leader; the latter should view these meetings as an opportunity to learn more about the organization, the industry, and the activities of other departments, as well as a chance to develop a more positive relationship with the boss. Information from these meetings should be shared with the team and used to make any needed changes in the department's goals or objectives.

As discussed in Chapter One, our research found that senior management's perception of a team's effectiveness was largely determined by the quality of the relationship between the team and senior management. There appear to be two key components of this relationship: the amount of communication the team receives from upper management and the degree to which the team has a positive view of these executives and their actions. These two components may have a reciprocal effect. More communication with senior management may create positive impressions, while more positive impressions may foster increased communication. This reciprocity seemed to exist in reverse in Hackman's study (1990), which found that teams perceived by senior management as ineffective were not used in organizational decision making, thereby ensuring a further decline in their effectiveness.

Strategy Three: Solicit Feedback from Upper Management

Goals are meaningless without regular feedback about progress, so management teams need to routinely solicit upper management's perspective on achievements, problems, and priorities. Teams are more likely to seek out feedback if they anticipate praise, but negative perceptions may be even more important to hear. When poor impressions of performance are ignored or left uncorrected, they eventually cause problems for the leader or the entire team. If the team begins to sense that problems exist, the team leader may need to engage the boss in a conversation about what is expected and how to achieve it and then take action to remedy the situation. Even if no problems exist, regular feedback sessions give the team leader an opportunity to adjust the group's goals to organizational changes and to inform top management about group accomplishments that might otherwise go unrecognized.

Strategy Four: Invite Upper Management to Team Meetings

Having an opportunity to interact with upper management helps the team clarify goals, build relationships, and develop firsthand understanding of the executive's perspective on organizational issues. The meetings may include some or all of these activities:

- Update on organizational goals and issues by upper management
- Progress reports to upper management on major activities in the department
- Discussion of critical decisions the department is facing
- Open question-and-answer session between team members and upper management

During these meetings, the team leader needs to refrain from talking too much and give members the opportunity to interact with upper management. If team members have had little exposure to executives or tend to be reticent, the leader may want to have a prep session to discuss the agenda for the upcoming meeting, answer members' questions, and encourage them to speak up.

Overcoming Barriers to Establishing Goals

Executive teams define their own direction, so their problems with goal clarity usually result from failure of the top executive to focus on planning, conflict between two top executives, or a constantly changing environment. For middle management teams, barriers to developing clear goals usually arise in one of two ways: the goals of upper management are not well defined, or the communication link with upper management is broken. In this section, we consider some of the problems that prevent management teams from articulating useful goals:

1. Top management fails to plan.
2. Top executives have conflicting goals.
3. The organization's environment is highly turbulent.
4. There is little communication with upper management about goals.
5. The management team leader has a poor relationship with his or her boss.

At the end of the chapter, you will find a survey and a set of discussion questions to help determine whether your own team has any problems developing goals.

Problem One: Top Management Fails to Plan

For a variety of reasons, ranging from personality type to organizational crises, executives may fail to establish goals. This is the problem faced by the management team in the true story at the beginning of the chapter, where the CEO is not particularly interested in planning and prefers to occupy himself with details of the manufacturing process. He has been successful with this style in the past and sees no reason to change.

If a "goal vacuum" exists at the top, leaders and members of management teams usually become frustrated with the lack of direction and begin to define their own goals. One thing is certain: combining people and resources always produces action, but poorly directed action wastes resources and may eventually create serious problems for the organization.

To overcome lack of top management focus, a management team should make every effort to initiate upward planning (as described in the suggestions below). Frequently, managers grumble and complain about lack of direction from upper management without taking any steps to change the situation. Achieving ideal results may not be possible, but managers can usually increase goal clarity by initiating communication about the subject appropriately.

Suggestions for action:

1. In any discussion about goals, do not be critical or imply that the executive is not doing a good job.

2. Suggest to the executive that the management team might benefit from going through a planning process. Try to relate your request to some aspect of the business that the senior manager finds particularly interesting. If the executive feels that this undertaking is too lengthy or expensive, try to get agreement on taking one step toward planning, such as doing an environmental analysis or agreeing on a vision of the future. Indicate that the senior manager can then decide whether to take the next step.

3. If top management is not likely to approve a planning process, arrange a meeting to discuss your own department's goals. Indicate that you are trying to provide direction for your own management team and would like the executive's input. You can then use this opportunity to relate the work of your department to larger organizational goals.

4. If the executive tends to have trouble focusing on the future or does so only in vague terms, prepare a written summary of organizational goals as you understand them (even if they're not written anywhere). Relate goals for your department to these organizational goals. Use this document as the agenda for a discussion, asking the executive for agreement or suggestions.

5. If major changes or crises have rendered former goals obsolete, prepare a written summary of your observations about how the change appears to have affected both organizational goals and those of your department. Again, use this as the agenda for a discussion, asking for the executive's input.

6. In these discussions, try to reach a common understanding with the executive about organizational goals and agree on a specific set of goals for your department. Document your conversation by sending a written summary to the executive after the meeting.

7. If the executive tends to shift direction easily, you may need to have these discussions frequently. In that case, it helps to arrange regular progress reviews during which you can continue to validate your goals.

Problem Two: Top Executives Have Conflicting Goals

Sometimes "top management" is more than one person. If these people have conflicting goals, life can be quite confusing for a management team. For the top team, the problem occurs when the two top executives (say, the CEO and the chief operating officer) are at odds about the direction of the organization or how it should be run. For lower-level teams, a similar situation arises when their immediate boss (say, a senior vice president) has a strong disagreement with top management.

In one privately held company with both a CEO and a president, the CEO, who founded the company, was a visionary leader with a million ideas and hands-on management style. As the company grew, the CEO recognized the need for a more structured approach to management, so he hired a president with many years' experience in large corporations. The new president reorganized the company, developed policies and procedures, and stressed the importance of documentation. Periodically, however, the CEO would drop in on company managers and give orders contrary to the president's direction. Within one year, the entire top management team left for other jobs. They were exhausted from constantly heading off in one direction with the president and then being jerked in another direction by the CEO.

Managers in this situation usually feel they are walking a tightrope. They either try to please both people, which is quite stressful, or take sides, which can be both stressful and hazardous. Obviously, no management team can succeed for long in this kind of environment, and sometimes the only solution may be to leave for greener pastures.

Before giving up, however, you may want to make an effort to resolve the problem.

Suggestions for action:

1. First, assess where the power lies. In these situations, the people involved are seldom equals, and sometimes the power shifts. In the above example, the CEO owned the company and had the ability to fire the president, so initially the balance of power tilted in his direction. After a time, however, the company went public, making the CEO subordinate to a board of directors. Since the board shared the president's management philosophy, the balance of power changed.

2. Do not criticize the executives or imply that either one of them is doing something wrong. Top managers are used to being in control and usually do not react well to criticism. Do not take sides.

3. If the parties are friendly, invite them both to a meeting to discuss your department's goals. In the meeting, ask both executives to outline their organizational goals and point out any areas that appear to conflict. Keep the discussion of these contradictions focused on the need to clarify goals for your own department. (This situation may be a bit tricky if one of the people is your boss. Nevertheless, if you can manage the politics of the situation, having this conversation can be quite helpful.)

4. If getting the parties together is not a wise idea, prepare a written draft of your department's goals. Indicate how they relate to organizational goals as you understand them. Send a copy to both executives and ask for their input. (In deciding how to do this, be sure to carefully consider organizational politics, including the nature of your relationship with each person and their relationships with each other.) After receiving their feedback, revise your goals if necessary and repeat the process until you have a set of workable goals that both parties agree on.

5. If one of the people is your boss, and if your boss is a reasonable person, ask for help. Describe how conflicting goals are interfering with your ability to achieve results. Present suggestions for resolving the situation. Try to get your boss to agree to involve the other party. (If a major power struggle is under way, however, this strategy may be unsuccessful.)

Problem Three: The Organization's Environment Is Highly Turbulent

If you work in a frequently changing environment, where market demands are constantly shifting, technology is steadily advancing, or the political climate is highly unpredictable, then staying focused on goals becomes even more of a challenge. In high-change organizations, goals may need to be revised rapidly and often. This constant churning can be quite frustrating for managers, who like to see their plans concluded successfully and become easily discouraged if their efforts are constantly interrupted. A primary challenge in this kind of environment is keeping your management team motivated and on track.

Suggestions for action:
1. Help team members accept the fact that frequent shifts in direction are a constant in your work environment. One fast-paced company told all management applicants up front that if perpetual change frustrated them, they would not want to work there. Team leaders also need to make an effort to communicate the reasons for change, since members will adapt and react more effectively if the cause of a change is fully understood.

2. Develop effective networks to ensure that you have current information about critical aspects of your environment. (Networking, the third success factor,

is discussed in Chapter Four). Staying up-to-date with the latest trends and developments is a crucial survival skill in turbulent organizations.

3. Review your plans and goals frequently, making any changes indicated by recent developments. View your plan as a living document, always responding to new demands from the environment.

4. Create "islands of stability" for team members. Regular meetings and predictable communication channels can alleviate some of the uncertainty created by ongoing change. Helping one another cope with the frustration of constant change is important as well. Keeping a sense of humor and developing supportive relationships goes a long way toward preserving sanity in a high-change organization.

5. Teams below the top level should communicate frequently with upper management to stay abreast of any changes in their perspective or their goals. The group should discuss this information as a team to determine what actions, if any, are required to effectively react to these changes.

Problem Four: There Is Little Communication with Upper Management About Goals

This problem usually results from a breakdown in communication between senior management and the leader of the management team. When considering this dilemma, team leaders need to remember that communication is a two-way street. In one organization, for example, an extremely reserved vice president of finance reported to a very outgoing CEO. The vice president didn't particularly enjoy interaction, so she seldom initiated communication with her boss. The CEO was uncomfortable with the vice president's lack of responsiveness in conversations, so he too tended to minimize interaction with her. As a result, they seldom discussed the goals of the finance department—or anything else. Both were contributing to the problem, though either one could have taken steps to correct it.

The first question for team leaders, therefore, is whether the communication deficit lies with your boss or with you—or both. Are you part of the problem? Here are some questions for team leaders to consider:

- Do you like your boss? If the answer is no, you may be avoiding opportunities for interaction. And you may wish to consider the suggestions in Problem Five.
- Do you prefer to work with a high degree of independence and autonomy? If so, you may fail to seek input from those with organizational power over you. People with a high need for independence sometimes resent the involvement of authority figures.

- Do you tend to be unassertive and wait for others to initiate communication? If this is the case, and your boss is not a good communicator, you may have a long wait.
- Have you lost interest in your job? If you have, you may be unlikely to look for opportunities to discuss work. This may not cause problems in the short run, but eventually you'll find yourself with career difficulties. And this lack of communication is certainly not fair to your team.

On the other hand, the fault may lie with your manager:

- Does your boss enjoy talking to people? If not, interaction on any subject is less likely.
- Does your boss hold regular management team meetings? Lack of meetings usually indicates a low value placed on discussion and shared decision making.
- Does your boss arrange for regular progress review sessions with you and your coworkers? If not, your boss may be of the "no news is good news" school of management, in which case you are only likely to receive communication if something goes wrong.

Although it may be interesting to think about where the problem originates, the solution must lie with the team leader. If you fail to initiate communication, you will simply wind up waiting for your manager indefinitely.

All the solutions to this problem are addressed to team leaders and involve their taking responsibility for communicating upward.

Suggestions for action:

1. Schedule a meeting with your manager to discuss goals for your department. Few managers refuse such a request, since helping to set goals is clearly part of their job. Before the meeting, ask for a copy of organizational goals so that you can be sure your department goals are appropriate. (If no goals exist, refer to the suggestions under Problem One.)

2. In the meeting, ask for your manager's view of organizational goals. To get the conversation started, try asking questions such as "Where do you see this organization headed?" "What are the biggest problems facing us right now?" "What are your most critical priorities this year?"

3. Reach agreement with the manager on a specific set of goals for your department. Arrange for regular progress reviews.

4. Periodically, ask your boss or other members of upper management to attend team meetings to discuss organizational goals and anything else of interest. Encourage team members to ask questions.

Problem Five: The Management Team Leader Has a Poor Relationship with His or Her Boss

When bad feelings exist between people, constructive communication about anything is difficult. The natural tendency is to avoid interaction. However, relationship difficulties are seldom the fault of only one person. Team leaders need to carefully consider the questions below. If your answer to any of these questions is yes, then you may want to take a hard look at your contribution to the relationship problem with your manager.

- Do you resent the fact that your boss has authority over you?
- Do you feel that your boss is incompetent?
- Do you believe that your boss has an ineffective work style?
- Do you say negative things to others about your boss?
- Does the phrase *your boss* irritate you when applied to this person?
- Did you prefer your previous manager?
- Has your career taken a downward turn since you began working for this manager?
- Do you find it hard to respect this person?
- Did this person ever work for you?

In one government agency, the director answered yes to six of these questions about her boss, the commissioner. In this case, the problem was largely due to the fact that these two people were total opposites. The director was a city dweller with a Ph.D. from a major university, while the commissioner lived in a rural area and had attended a small college. The director had many years of management experience, but the commissioner had never held a management position before her appointment to her present job. The director was extremely proud of her professional credentials, while the commissioner took pride in his political connections. They had completely opposite work styles: she enjoyed research and analytical pursuits, while he preferred networking and solving people's problems. Both brought valuable skills and abilities to the organization, but they did not like working together and tried to avoid each other as much as possible. Needless to say, they had difficulty agreeing on a set of organizational goals (and eventually the director was fired).

The suggestions that follow are addressed to team leaders, since team members can do little to resolve this problem on their own.

Suggestions for action:

1. Even a boss who is incompetent or ineffective still has organizational power over you and your work. Life will be easier if you get along. Since you are unlikely

to change your boss, all possible solutions rely on changing your own perspective or approach.

2. First, try to think about the situation from the point of view of an outside observer and examine your role in the problem. Honestly consider whether you are doing anything to make the relationship worse. For example, do you constantly complain about your boss? If so, this is probably not helping. You not only run the risk that your comments will be repeated, but you are also focusing your energy in the wrong direction. Your complaints may make you feel better, but they are unlikely to improve the relationship. One executive in a large electronics company became so bold with his complaints that he could be heard insulting the CEO right outside the office of the CEO's secretary. His direct reports arrived at work one day to find their boss's office completely empty. He was never seen in the company again.

3. If you need to vent your feelings, talk with your spouse, close friends outside the company, or your therapist. Do *not* share all your frustrations with your staff. Managers often have an important role to play as a buffer between their employees and upper management, because employees seldom benefit from knowing everything that goes on at higher levels. If you use your staff as a dumping ground for your own anger, anxiety, or uncertainty, you only hurt their morale and raise their anxiety level.

4. Try to detach yourself from the situation, that is, reduce the emotional content of your reactions. This is easier said than done, but it is a big plus in working on a solution. One step toward detachment is to view this as an organizational problem, not a personal affront. To develop this perspective, you may need to talk with someone removed from the situation who can give you an honest reaction and not just reinforce your opinions. You must approach this conversation with a willingness to examine your role in the problem, not as just another opportunity to gripe about your boss.

5. Make a real effort to look at things from your manager's perspective, not your own. What pressures does your manager have to deal with? What needs of other departments does your manager have to meet? How is your manager's performance being evaluated? If your manager has a boss, how is that relationship going?

6. Try to look for your boss's strengths. We are usually quite aware of the ways that other people irritate us, but we tend to take their positive characteristics for granted. Reversing this perspective helps repair relationships. What does your boss do well? What organizational problems or challenges does your boss handle successfully? How has your manager helped the organization? What does your manager do better than you? Can you learn anything from this person?

7. Find areas of commonality that you and your manager share, related to either your work or your personal life. Look for opportunities to engage your boss

in conversation about shared goals, concerns, experiences, or interests. Focusing on similarities tends to build bridges between people.

8. Ask your manager's advice on organizational problems. Most people want to be helpful to others and feel good when they are seen as having useful expertise. Give a compliment when your manager does something well. Everyone likes to hear praise.

9. Create opportunities for communication. Invite your boss to your management team meetings. Ask a question after a staff meeting or when you see your manager in the hall. Share information that you know would be of interest. Have lunch together—or breakfast or dinner. The experience of eating together tends to set a positive tone for conversation.

10. Don't talk to your boss only when there's a problem or an emergency. Building a relationship must be done over time, through frequent and positive interactions. Bad relationships often result from a negative cycle: we decide we don't like someone, so we avoid them until there's a problem, thereby guaranteeing that we only communicate in unpleasant circumstances.

True Story: The Company with No Plan

Part Two: The Solution

The primary challenge faced by the management team described at the beginning of the chapter is getting the CEO to agree to and participate in the planning process. To address this problem, the group first looks for any aspect of planning that might attract him. They decide to capitalize on his interest in production.

To carry out this strategy, the operations manager meets with the CEO to discuss capital equipment purchases and turns the discussion to trends in manufacturing.

"You know, we have some critical decisions ahead about how we're going to make the next generation of our products," she says.

"We sure do," replies the CEO. "There've been some real changes in production methods since we set up this plant. It's kind of hard to know which way to go."

As they debate the pros and cons of various kinds of machinery, the operations manager suggests that some type of planning process might be useful in making these decisions.

"You're probably right," says the CEO. "Did you have something specific in mind?"

"Well, some of the other managers and I have done a little reading on the subject, and we think that a good first step would be to study all the changes that have taken place in this industry lately. Things move so fast that it's hard to keep up. And I think I know a consultant who could help facilitate the process."

The CEO agrees to this step, which proves so useful that he decides to continue the planning process. Working with the consultant, the management team is able to demonstrate practical results, turning the CEO into an enthusiastic proponent of strategic planning and establishing a clear direction for the management team.

Team Assessment: Does Your Team Have Clear Goals?

All teams need to establish a definite direction if they are to accomplish meaningful results. For top teams, the executive leading the group must take the initiative to establish direction for both the team and the entire organization. On lower-level teams, the team leader needs to develop and maintain positive communication with upper management in order to clarify goals and expectations. Strategic goals help the team make good decisions, work together cooperatively, and make wise use of resources. Without them, both results and relationships tend to suffer.

To determine whether a team is functioning effectively, input from team members is needed. This book provides two ways to get that input: written surveys for team members to complete and discussion questions to use in team meetings. These methods can be used separately or together. For example, the team may wish to complete the survey first and then use the discussion questions to explore problem areas. The surveys in the book are based on the TEAM instrument (Team Effectiveness Assessment for Management) that was used in the Management Team Research Project.

TEAM Survey: Strategic Goals

This survey helps determine whether management team members feel they have a clear understanding of goals. If you identify problems with goal clarity, you may wish to refer back to the appropriate sections of this chapter under "Strategic and Operational Planning" or "Overcoming Barriers to Establishing Goals."

For this chapter only, there is a separate survey for executive teams and middle management teams. Different surveys are needed because goals for middle management teams are driven by expectations of upper management, while executive teams must define their own direction. Surveys in subsequent chapters are the same for all teams.

Here are instructions for using the survey:

1. Give each team member a copy of TEAM Survey: Strategic Goals.
2. Tell the members *not* to put their names on these sheets.
3. Have them indicate their level of agreement with each statement and score their own survey.
4. Collect the survey sheets and add up the team score yourself or ask a team member to do so.
5. Determine a final team score using the formula under "Total Team Score."

6. To identify specific concerns, total the scores for each item and divide by the numbers of team members surveyed, as shown under "Item Scores."
7. Have a group discussion of the reasons for your scores. You may wish to use the discussion questions in the section following the survey scoring charts.

TEAM SURVEY: STRATEGIC GOALS

For each item, indicate your level of agreement by circling the appropriate number.

For Executive Teams

	Agree			Disagree
1. We understand the purpose of our organization.	4	3	2	1
2. We regularly evaluate how changes may affect our organization.	4	3	2	1
3. We have gone through a strategic planning process within the last three years.	4	3	2	1
4. We have an up-to-date operational plan, including goals and specific objectives.	4	3	2	1
5. The leader of our team clearly communicates expectations.	4	3	2	1
6. I understand the goals of other functions represented on the team.	4	3	2	1
7. In team meetings, we discuss progress toward individual and team goals.	4	3	2	1
8. I get regular feedback on my goals from the leader of this team.	4	3	2	1

For Middle Management Teams

	Agree			Disagree
1. Upper management clearly communicates organizational goals.	4	3	2	1
2. We understand the purpose of our department.	4	3	2	1
3. If upper management's goals change, we are informed about what is now expected of us.	4	3	2	1
4. We have gone through a strategic planning process within the last three years.	4	3	2	1
5. We have an up-to-date operational plan, including goals and specific objectives.	4	3	2	1
6. I understand the goals of other functions represented on the team.	4	3	2	1
7. We get feedback from upper management about whether our team is meeting expectations.	4	3	2	1
8. I get regular feedback on my goals from the leader of this team.	4	3	2	1

A. Individual Scoring

Add up the circled numbers and write your score below.

Total Score = _____

8–16	17–23	24–32
Goals not clear	Goals somewhat unclear	Clear goals

TEAM Goals Survey: Team Scoring

B. Total Team Score

Total of all team member scores = _____

Divide by number of team members = _____

Team Score = _____

8–16	17–23	24–32
Goals not clear	Goals somewhat unclear	Clear goals

C. Item Scores

Total for each item	Divide total by number of team members
1.	1.
2.	2.
3.	3.
4.	4.
5.	5.
6.	6.
7.	7.
8.	8.

Discussion Questions: Strategic Goals

These questions can start a discussion with your management team members about goals. They may be used alone or as a follow-up to the TEAM Survey:

Strategic Goals
For all teams:
- How well is our current planning process working? Do we need to update strategic or operational plans?
- Are we keeping up-to-date with changes affecting our organization? If not, what can we do to correct this?
- Do we have a good understanding of our organization's strengths and weaknesses?
- Are team members aware of one another's goals? If not, how can we share more information?
- In what areas do our goals overlap? How can we help one another meet goals?

For top teams:
- Have we reviewed and discussed long-range plans with our governing body (or board, or political official)? If not, how should we do this?
- Are the plans of lower-level management teams aligned with the overall strategic plan? If not, how do we involve them in planning activities for their functions?
- What are we doing to maintain ongoing communication with lower-level teams? How could we improve in advising them of changes or giving them feedback on performance?
- What have we done to exhibit commitment to goals through our actions? Do we ever send contradictory messages? How could we improve in this area?

For teams below the top level:
- How do we usually learn about upper management's goals? Could we improve communication in this area? If so, how?
- How do we usually get feedback from upper management about our performance? What could we do to get more feedback?
- When conditions change, does upper management tell us how we will be affected? If not, how could we get this information?
- Does upper management usually support our decisions? If not, why not? What could we do to get more support?
- Is there anything we are doing that hurts our relationship with upper management? What could we do to develop a better relationship?

CHAPTER THREE

EXTENSIVE NETWORKS

How to Connect with Sources of Information

True Story: The Isolated Library System

Part One: The Problem

The Marion County Library System has had the same director, Steve, for twenty years. When he began the job, Marion County was a sprawling, rural area dotted with small towns, twenty-five miles from a major city. The main library was located in the county seat, with a few branches in outlying areas. People usually went to work on the library staff because they loved to read and were longtime users of library services. The community felt the library system was quite modern and up-to-date.

During Steve's tenure, sleepy and rural Marion County got caught up in the nearby city's booming growth and has become one of the fastest-growing counties in the nation. The population has soared to more than four hundred thousand people. Construction projects of all types have become a fact of life; new roads, malls, subdivisions, and office parks are springing up everywhere. The booming business climate is attracting newcomers from all over the country and many parts of the world. At the same time, information technology has undergone a revolution, creating many alternatives to the printed word.

The library system has tried to cope with the increased demand for services by hiring more people, building more buildings, and ordering more copies of popular books. Few other changes have been made, however. The system itself operates much as it has for the past twenty years.

After Steve retires, a new director, Katherine, is hired from a large library system in another state. Slowly, the realization dawns that her staff, materials, information systems, and operating procedures are perfect for a county about one-third the size of Marion but are completely inadequate to meet this county's current needs. "Oh, dear," she thinks. "What have I gotten myself into?"

This library system has failed to progress because management lost touch with the surrounding environment. Although some changes have been made in response to the rapid increase in population, other environmental factors have been overlooked, such as advances in technology, the increasing diversity of library customers, the county's shift from rural to urban, and the growing influence of the business community. Like many organizations, the library has settled into a comfortable mode of operation, oblivious to the growing evidence that it is becoming outdated.

The Need for Networking Information

Organizations do not operate in a vacuum. They are embedded in a large and complex system of social, economic, and political influences. To succeed, they must become "learning organizations" (Senge, 1990), which can respond appropriately to change and take the actions needed to ensure future success. According to Senge, the ability to learn quickly may be the only sustainable competitive advantage in today's interconnected and complex world. Gareth Morgan (1986) stresses this point in comparing organizations to the brain, which adapts rapidly to almost any contingency because of interconnections among its hundreds of thousands of neurons. Similarly, "brainlike" organizations that foster connections among people are better able to deal with the demands of a complicated, ever-changing environment. Maintaining this flexibility requires that managers have ongoing access to reliable sources of up-to-date information. In fact, the need for outside information has escalated so dramatically that Kanter (1989) indicates managers may add more value by communicating at organizational interfaces than by managing their own functions.

Networking has been described as the process of gathering and moving information in organizations (Byrum-Robinson and Womeldorff, 1990). To make good decisions, a management team must develop networks that connect the group to the world outside the team. The Management Team Research Project revealed a separate, well-defined success factor reflecting team members' links to sources of information, including people in other departments, professional associations, conferences and workshops, publications, and other organizations (both inside and outside their own industry). These connections create "permeable boundaries" for the team, allowing unexpected and useful information to become available. To encourage this flow of information, many organizations today are intentionally creating both internal and external networks, linking separate departments through cross-functional teams and forming strategic alliances with suppliers, customers, and even competitors.

Because the ability to develop effective networks has become a key component of successful decision making, all management team members must be held accountable for maintaining accurate, up-to-date information about their areas of responsibility. Networks developed by team members help a management team in two ways: they provide information that improves decision making, and they build relationships that facilitate the implementation of decisions. In our research, networking was found to be one of the two significant factors affecting senior management's perception of a team's effectiveness. (The first factor, communication with upper management, was discussed in Chapter Two.) From a senior-management perspective, information access could be important for two reasons. First, teams with current information may indeed make better decisions than more isolated teams. Better-informed teams may also be able to provide senior management with new and helpful information.

Teams that isolate themselves risk becoming ineffective problem solvers and decision makers, since they are unable to stay abreast of changing conditions in their organization, their industry, or society at large. If the management team is not connected to critical information sources, significant events in the larger system are ignored. Research has found that teams isolating themselves from outside information become less effective over time, even if members continue to communicate with one another frequently (Tjosvold, 1988). The resulting tunnel vision can cause the team to fall into predictable habits and repetitive patterns, missing opportunities to respond to change or try new approaches. As a result, the organization may suffer the fate of a frog placed in a pot of cool water that is gradually heated to boiling: it may die without ever noticing that a change has occurred. This slow death can happen to a single department or an entire company.

Information needed by a management team is found both inside and outside the organization. Components of these internal and external networks are discussed below, followed by suggested strategies for developing these resources. As an example, the networking diagram in Figure 3.1 shows some of the connections that would be helpful to a human resource management team.

Internal Networks

Management teams need access to ongoing information from within their own organizations. For top management teams, all internal communication flows upward from lower-level managers and employees. One danger for top teams is that information may be filtered through several layers of management, causing executives

FIGURE 3.1. SOME CRITICAL CONNECTIONS FOR A HUMAN RESOURCE MANAGEMENT TEAM.

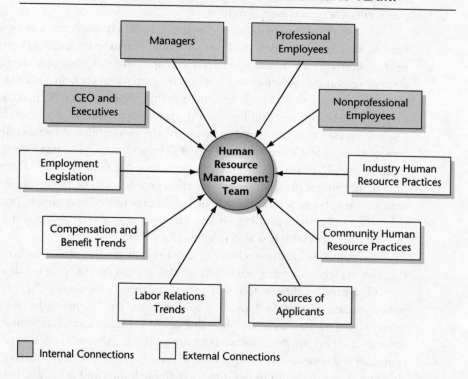

to lose touch with the people who actually do the work, that is, those who make the product or deliver the service. Executives often find that frontline employees communicate much more directly and honestly than managers, who usually have future career interests in mind whenever they talk with top management.

The president of one company found this to be true after he sent out several "motivational" e-mail messages copied from a book. Because he never made reference to the book in the messages, everyone assumed he had written them himself. Viewed from an employee perspective, some of these messages seemed to imply that the company had little concern for their welfare, and people began to get angry. Managers were aware of this reaction but never mentioned it, since none of them wanted to risk offending the president. Finally, during an employee meeting, one production worker said to the president, "You know, your e-mail messages are really making everybody mad." The president was stunned. After he explained that they had come from a book, the production worker said, "Well, we'd be much more interested in hearing what you have to say yourself." The president immediately changed his e-mails.

Frontline employees have valuable information about work processes and customer needs. They often can't understand why management doesn't change some obviously stupid procedure or practice. But a management team without good employee connections will probably remain ignorant of the many beneficial changes that employees could suggest. In many companies, for instance, help desk or customer service employees interact constantly with customers about problems. They represent an encyclopedia of information about customer wishes and concerns, yet management often redesigns products and services without ever tapping into this knowledge base.

For management teams below the top level, internal networks should include upper management and other departments, as well as employees. The importance of ongoing communication with upper management has already been discussed in Chapter Two. Good communication links between departments are becoming increasingly critical as the environment in which organizations operate grows more complex and departments become more interdependent. Unfortunately, walls just naturally seem to develop between departments or functions, causing valuable information to be lost. In one local department of transportation, for example, operations were divided into construction, which built new roads, and maintenance, which repaired existing roads. Because these two departments seldom communicated, maintenance workers wound up fixing roads that were almost immediately torn up for new construction. This obvious waste of time and money could easily have been avoided through better communication.

External Networks

If an organization is to survive and thrive, the management team must also connect with sources of critical information in the external environment, including customers, other organizations, the community, professional groups, the legal system, and political bodies. The relative importance of these connections varies from organization to organization.

Customers. In the business world, customers are clearly the most important source of information. Many government agencies have begun to realize that *customer* is not just a business term and that they too need to stay in touch with those they serve. Staff functions, such as the training or legal department, must be sure they communicate with their "internal customers": the people or departments to whom they provide services.

Managers often assume they know what customers want and are surprised when they learn otherwise. In one case, a package delivery company strictly limited the amount of time their truck drivers could spend on each delivery. Managers never imagined that customers might actually like to talk with the drivers. Much to their surprise, surveys revealed that customers wanted more time to ask questions and get information from drivers, who were their only contact with the company. Once the policy was changed to allow some interaction time, management actually began giving drivers a commission for any additional business developed through these conversations.

In another situation, a home health care company decided that paying nurses by the visit instead of by the hour would increase productivity. Predictably, visits became shorter; patients began to feel rushed, and some decided to switch to another company. Management noticed the decrease in business but did not understand the cause until they solicited feedback from customers.

Other Organizations. Contact with other organizations can also provide valuable information for a management team. The practice of benchmarking—studying organizations that excel in a particular area—is an excellent example of the value of organizational networks. Companies in the same industry can alert one another to important changes and trends. (Information that would hurt a company's competitiveness should obviously not be shared, however.) Government agencies can learn from their counterparts in other locations or at different levels of government. These contacts are often developed through trade or professional associations.

Management teams also learn from organizations that are quite different from their own. In one fast-paced technology company, the training director was asked to assume responsibility for internal communications, a newly created function in which he had no experience. To get up to speed quickly, he visited companies with well-established communication departments, including a soft-drink manufacturer, an electric utility, and a producer of paper products. Although none were in his industry, he learned a great deal from their experience and was able to help his management team do a much better job of communication planning.

Community. Organizations also need to stay in touch with the communities in which they operate. If "community" means a city or town, membership in local organizations and involvement in civic activities can be useful. For multinational corporations, community may encompass the entire world, since operations take place in a wide variety of countries and cultures; in this situation, managers need to develop connections with "the world" through many different communities. Government organizations (local, state, and national) must maintain connections with the taxpayer base that supports their existence. In the true story at the beginning of the chapter, the library system fails to respond to changing needs because managers have lost touch with their community.

Community connections provide one way to gather customer-related information, since this is where your customers reside. Community involvement also aids recruiting efforts, since companies with reputations as good corporate citizens are often more attractive to prospective employees. Information from the community may help to identify recruitment problems, allowing necessary adjustments to be made.

While attending a civic club meeting, the president of a company happened to sit alongside a self-employed accountant.

"You know," the accountant said, "people in the financial community don't want to work for your company."

"Why not?"

"Your vice president of finance is a maniac," the accountant replied. "According to the grapevine, he loses his temper and screams at people whenever he's upset—and he gets upset a lot!"

The president was thus alerted to a problem that employees had never mentioned because they were afraid to speak up.

Professional Groups. When success depends upon specialized knowledge, management teams must keep up with the latest developments in their field—and today most functions do require special expertise. Whether the team is responsible for manufacturing, sales, tax collection, human resources, information technology, finance, or social service delivery, the members have an obligation to know about new trends and techniques in their professions. Each team member has to maintain the individual expertise needed to add maximum value to the team. A human resource management team, for example, should be able to advise the CEO on such issues as compensation and benefit trends, changes in employment law, and recruiting strategies. They can only fulfill this function if individual team members stay up-to-date in their areas of responsibility.

Legal and Political System. Finally, management teams need to stay abreast of trends in the legal or political system that could affect their organizations. Awareness of such changes allows managers to avoid problems that may occur through ignorance of legal developments or political issues. If informed about trends in advance, a management team may be able to influence the direction of change to prevent future problems for the business.

Internal and External Networking Strategies

Networking requires ongoing contact with sources of information on critical aspects of your environment. The strategies below are intended to help your management team identify and connect with important information sources. These strategies are in three categories: general suggestions, internal networks, and external networks.

General Suggestions

Strategy One: Complete a Network Diagram with Your Team

You can use the network diagram in Figure 3.2 to identify the most critical connections for your team. Completing the diagram as a group exercise is likely to produce the best result. Team members may also wish to complete individual network diagrams for their own areas of responsibility, possibly involving their staff in the process. One way to get a lot of information out quickly is to use Post-it Notes to create the diagram by having everyone "post" ideas and then eliminate duplicates.

The remaining strategies can help your management team become more effective in developing and sustaining the critical connections identified in the

FIGURE 3.2. NETWORK DIAGRAM.

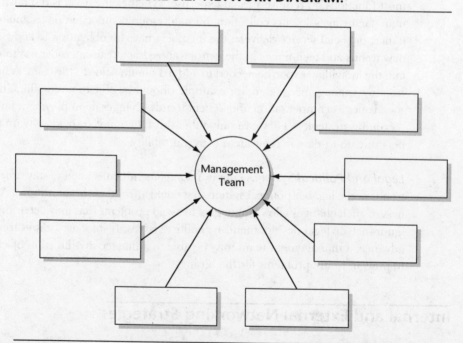

Note: List your team's critical internal and external connections in the boxes. You may add boxes if necessary.

network diagram. As you read through the strategies, you may think of new connections to add to your network.

Strategy Two: During Strategic Planning, Use the Areas Identified in Your Network Diagram as the Basis for Your Environmental Scan

One of the early steps in strategic planning is to conduct a scan to gather information about external influences on the organization, including customers, competitors, social and economic trends, legal and political issues, etc. (Environmental scans were discussed in Chapter Two.) This can be done in a number of ways. Some organizations create task groups to study each area, collecting existing information and gathering new data through surveys, interviews, or focus groups. Others hire consultants to conduct data-gathering projects and analyze the information collected. However you get information, the key is to learn about events outside your organization that may affect your future. The network diagram helps you identify critical sources of information.

Strategy Three: Have All Management Team Members Set Networking Goals

Every management team member has an obligation to contribute information to the team for good decision making. For this reason, each team member should be responsible for maintaining certain networking contacts (as outlined in the internal and external strategies below). These goals can be included in the manager's performance review and evaluated along with other job responsibilities.

Strategy Four: Share Information in Management Team Meetings

When networking contacts provide useful or interesting information, management team members should be encouraged to share their knowledge to promote group learning. Time can be set aside in meetings for members to discuss information from workshops, visits to other companies, readings, or any other source.

Strategy Five: Invite Outside People to Your Management Team Meetings

From time to time, bring in customers, employees, or people from other departments for question-and-answer sessions with the management team. This not only provides useful information but also helps build those relationships. You may wish to talk with team members in advance about the most useful areas for discussion.

Internal Networks

Strategy One: Develop Regular Communication Links with Employees

This is the primary internal networking strategy for executive team members, since everyone else in the organization reports to them. In addition to maintaining good communication with their own direct reports, top management teams in large organizations need ongoing two-way communication links with other managers and employees. Here are some communication tools that top managers have used to maintain this connection:

- Regular visits by top management to lower-level management teams
- Quarterly managers' meetings, with question-and-answer sessions
- A newsletter for managers that invites questions and comments through voice mail or e-mail
- A similar employee newsletter
- An annual opinion survey of employees and managers
- A quarterly breakfast with a group of employees from throughout the company
- Distribution of the top managers' e-mail addresses with an open invitation to use them
- Regular walk-throughs by top executives, with no management escort

These techniques help top teams keep their finger on the pulse of the workforce without having to rely on information filtered through several layers of management.

Members of management teams at all levels need to have good communication links with employees in their departments, because employees always have information about activities at their level that managers can use to make better decisions. In one human resource department, for example, a secretary alerted management to a serious sexual harassment problem. The people being victimized were afraid to talk with anyone else in human resources because they did not know them well, but the secretary (the person who usually answered their benefits questions) was a familiar and trusted figure.

For most managers, maintaining open communication with employees simply means creating circumstances that encourage dialogue: walking through a work area, visiting remote locations, having lunch with employees, stopping to chat with people about their work, allowing time for questions and comments in meetings. Because employees have contacts with so many people, you can greatly expand your own network by tapping into theirs. Remember that employees can choose whether or not to share information with you. Many factors influence that decision. If you want them to choose in your favor, you must sincerely listen to their comments, remain nondefensive, and never use information in a way that would harm the person providing it.

Strategy Two: Be Sure That Employees Understand Their Managers' Goals

Employees can determine what information might be useful if they know what managers are trying to accomplish, so be sure that management team members communicate their goals to employees. When one retail organization conducted an employee survey, the results showed that 90 percent of employees were quite clear on the goals of their own jobs but only 60 percent said they understood their managers' goals. The company began requiring managers to discuss their goals in staff meetings and give all employees a written copy.

Strategy Three: Have Employees Do Their Own Network Diagrams

Identifying critical connections also helps employees be more successful in their jobs. As their network expands, so does yours.

Strategy Four: Create a Yellow Pages for Your Organization

Computer technology has made it possible for almost any organization to create its own Yellow Pages: an internal data bank of employees' skills, talents, and knowledge. One maker of heavy equipment began such a system after a secretary simply compiled a list of "who knows about what" for a temporary receptionist to use in routing phone calls. This basic listing proved so useful that the company now has a database allowing any employee to enter a few keywords and retrieve the names of people who have the expertise they are seeking. Note, though, that once such a system is developed, you must be sure to keep it updated by entering new employees as they are hired and periodically gathering additional skills data on everyone.

Strategy Five: Determine Which Other Departments Are Necessary for Your Success

The remainder of the internal strategies offered here focus on networking among departments, which is critical to the success of management teams below the top level. Once agreement on goals is reached with top management, the group needs to determine which other departments affect their success. If your team has internal customers—departments that receive services from your group—they should be at the top of your networking list. Study the links among various functions in your organization to identify departments with useful information and those whose cooperation you need. In a company making and selling a product, for example, product design, sales, and manufacturing must all cooperate and share information if the customer is to receive the best result.

Strategy Six: Develop Relationships with People from Departments Listed on Your Network Diagram

Networking is most effective when people have ongoing, well-established relationships. Try to learn about the work done in your critical departments. Understand concerns, problems, and successes from their point of view. Indicate an interest in their activities by asking questions, visiting their work area, looking at their "products." Ask to attend some of their meetings and invite them to some of yours. Find opportunities for conversation: go to lunch, stop to chat in the hall, walk through their department occasionally. One unintended side effect of designating outdoor smoking areas has been the interdepartmental relationships that often develop among the smokers. In some organizations, nonsmoking managers have been known to tap into the "smokers' network" for the latest information.

Strategy Seven: Look for Opportunities to Help Other Departments

If people in other departments affect your life, then you probably also affect theirs. Ask how you can make their work easier. Share information with them that might be useful. One corporate human resource manager in a large company made a presentation to management team meetings in every division, describing her department's services. She included some interesting information on employee relations issues, discrimination charges and lawsuits, and training opportunities. The meetings not only gave managers some useful data but also created an opportunity for dialogue about how her department might be helpful to them.

Strategy Eight: Ask Others for Help

Ask for help when you need it—and sometimes even when you don't think you do. Most people like to return the favor of being helpful; this reciprocity can further strengthen relationships. People from other departments often assist in unexpected ways if you share your problem with them. A team of design engineers in a manufacturing company, for instance, decided to involve the production department in discussing plans for a new product. Much to their surprise, they found that their previous designs had greatly increased the cost of manufacturing. Collaboration on the new product line led to a design that was easily manufacturable and also improved the relationship between the two departments.

External Networks

Strategy One: Develop Mechanisms to Gather Regular Feedback from Customers

Whether your group primarily serves internal or external customers, you need to get ongoing feedback from them. Methods can be formal (customer surveys, comment cards, focus groups) or informal (visits, phone calls, lunches). You may choose to involve customers in your planning processes or ask their advice on specific problems. Sometimes, what you learn surprises you. One household products company that was trying to increase market share for its brands decided to survey customers for the first time. They asked for specific feedback about a pine-scented cleanser that had been on the market for decades. When the survey results came back, managers were shocked to discover that most customers did not like the smell of pine. After changing the scent to lemon, they saw an immediate increase in sales of the cleanser.

Strategy Two: Participate in Work-Related Groups

All team members should be expected to affiliate with appropriate work-related groups, to promote interaction with people from other organizations. Have your team identify the most useful groups and then decide which team members will join them. Most management teams fail to make conscious decisions about group membership and just let members go where their interests take them, thereby losing an opportunity to strategically develop networks. It is surprising that many organizations fail to encourage their managers to join any groups, since a team with no outside contacts easily develops tunnel vision.

Work-related groups generally fall into three categories: industry groups, civic organizations, and professional associations. The nature of your work determines which ones are the most helpful for your team. Industry groups, such as banking associations, technology groups, and hospital associations, focus on a particular type of business. *Industry* does not just refer to business organizations, however. Government agencies often have industry groups of their own, including associations of tax collectors, election officials, prison employees, and many others. Industry groups tend to be an excellent source of information about trends, new ideas, political issues, and legal developments. These organizations usually offer local meetings and national conferences, as well as written materials in the form of newsletters, journals, and legal alerts.

Civic organizations are based in a local community and include charitable organizations such as the United Way, clubs on the order of Rotary or Kiwanis, or such business groups as the Chamber of Commerce. Membership in civic organizations is usually most helpful to management teams with a local focus or those who want to create goodwill in the community. Participation in civic activities is an excellent way to develop relationships with a wide variety of people in a particular location.

Professional associations are composed of people who do similar work in different settings, such as engineers, human resource specialists, nurses, buyers, or lawyers. Management team members who are responsible for a particular area of expertise should belong to the appropriate professional association, since these groups help keep their members' knowledge current through newsletters, journals, workshops, and conferences.

Strategy Three: Read

Some of us like to get information from other people, while others prefer reading. Which category are you in? Just ask yourself if you would rather attend a professional association's dinner meeting or read its journal. Useful networking does not always have to involve direct interaction with people. Much industry and professional information can be obtained through newsletters, journals, books, magazines, or the Internet. Management team members should also be expected to keep up with management trends through such publications as *Business Week, Fortune,* or the *Harvard Business Review.*

Strategy Four: Visit Other Organizations

We all view the world through the lens of our own experience, which tends to limit the ideas and options we consider. Visiting other organizations provides a different view of our own work and broadens our perspective. Despite the frequent use of buzzwords like *benchmarking* and *best practices,* many management groups fail to recognize the benefits of learning how things are done in other places. The management team in one large government agency fell into this category. During a discussion of concerns about the information management system, one team member said, "Maybe we should find out how these problems are handled in other states." "Nah," replied another. "They wouldn't be anything like us anyway. We'd just waste our time." So the idea was dropped, and the team lost an opportunity to learn from others' experience. Had they pursued the idea, they might have found that someone else had already solved their problem.

Overcoming Barriers to Networking

Barriers to internal networking usually involve problems with relationships, while barriers to external networking often stem from lack of interest, time, or money. In this section, we consider problems that can prevent management teams from acquiring useful information:

1. Departments often act territorially.
2. Friction exists between staff and line functions.
3. Management and employees have an adversarial relationship.
4. The organization is too internally focused.
5. Limited time is available for networking activities.
6. There is a lack of money for networking activities.
7. Very few networking activities are available.

Problem One: Departments Often Act Territorially

Departments have a natural tendency to compete instead of cooperate. Conflicting goals, limited resources, or overlapping roles can cause departments to view one another as adversaries rather than as partners. In one company, for example, production and sales had ongoing battles over customized orders. Production felt that sales placed extra burdens on the manufacturing process by frequently requesting special features, while sales felt that production had little interest in the needs of customers. In another organization, the human resource and accounting departments fought constantly about payroll issues because both were involved in providing the information needed for paychecks. This kind of territorial attitude can keep any organization from reaching its full potential.

Suggestions for action:
1. All solutions to this problem require increased positive communication between departments. If relationships have deteriorated badly, an outside facilitator may be needed to direct the discussions.
2. Identify the goals that are shared by both departments. This should be possible at a broad level, since both are in the same organization.
3. Share information about each department's point of view. Discuss problems and pressures on both sides. Determine how each department contributes to shared goals.
4. Identify areas where each department could make changes that would help the other. This discussion should involve requests, not demands. Agree on specific actions to be taken by each department that will improve working relationships.

5. Invite representatives from the other department to your management team meetings to discuss ongoing concerns or celebrate shared successes. Regular communication can help break down barriers.

6. Hold joint planning or team-building sessions with the other department. Spending some extended time together can provide opportunities to build relationships and discuss work issues. In one university program, two departments that did not want to work together discovered during a team-building session that most of their concerns were based on complete misconceptions about one another.

Problem Two: Friction Exists Between Staff and Line Functions

Negative feelings between staff and line departments are quite common, because these two organizational components have very different perspectives. Line functions are responsible for delivering the organization's products or services. They are trying to serve the customer, ship the product, make the sale. Staff functions, on the other hand, provide professional expertise in a specialized area, such as law, accounting, training, safety, or compensation.

Line managers must deal with the demands of a variety of staff people, all of which seem to take time away from their primary purpose of delivering results for the organization. Staff managers are trying to ensure that the organization follows accepted practice in their area of expertise, so one of their goals is to keep line managers from creating problems. Staff managers are usually unaware of demands made by other staff departments but quite aware of problems related to their own area. So each line manager sees a host of staff people all conspiring to create more work, while each staff manager sees an array of line people all trying to do things their own way. Line managers typically feel overburdened by staff people, and staff managers typically feel ignored and unappreciated by line people.

Suggestions for action for staff departments:

1. Learn about the business or operational units in your organization. Visit them, interview people about their work, discuss their problems, understand how the world looks to them.

2. Try to be a helpful resource instead of a demanding monitor. Let line managers know how your expertise can help them solve business problems.

3. Explain the reasons why line managers need to give you information or comply with certain rules. Look for ways to make these requests less burdensome.

4. Don't impose unnecessary work on line managers. Always ask yourself whether this report or that request for information really adds value. Be mindful of the fact that many other staff functions are also making demands on line departments.

Suggestions for action for line departments:

1. Learn about the role of staff functions. Try to understand how they contribute to the organization's performance.

2. Understand how staff expertise can be valuable to you, and learn to use it when necessary. Any well-run staff function can benefit line managers. A good legal department helps you avoid future lawsuits. A good human resource department helps you recruit talented employees and legally terminate incompetent ones.

3. Explain to staff managers why certain requests cause you problems. Understand, however, that staff people may need information or compliance from you in order to do their job properly. Engage them in joint problem solving to identify ways to simplify requirements.

Suggestion for action for management teams composed of both line and staff people:

Provide opportunities to promote open communication, understanding, and appreciation among the different functions. Encourage line and staff departments to engage in joint problem solving.

Problem Three: Management and Employees Have an Adversarial Relationship

When management-employee relationships deteriorate, the cause is usually related in some way to unwise use of managerial power. Managers in organizations have power by virtue of their position, but they sometimes forget that employees have power as well—they always have the power, for instance, to choose whether to do only acceptable work or give their best effort. They also have the power to decide whether to share information with managers.

Managers who abuse power never have employees in their network. In fact, employees may sit by and chuckle while their manager rushes headlong into a problem that could have been avoided with shared information. In one company, the head of operations was famous for screaming, yelling, and cursing at employees. As problems began to develop in the production process, no one dared mention them to him. Eventually, the problems became more serious, production deadlines were not met, and the operations manager was taken to task by upper management. (The employees were most happy about it.) If employees had felt comfortable sharing their observations as soon as the production problems began, a quick solution could have been found and major shipping delays avoided.

Suggestions for action:

1. Employees never share information unless they feel that managers and employees are on the same team, so the first step is to determine the cause of adversarial relationships. Ask yourself the following questions about yourself and the other members of your management team:

- Do we talk with employees?
- Do we take time to listen to employees' problems?
- Do we consider employees' ideas?
- Are employees involved in our planning activities?
- Do we discuss problems with employees without getting angry?
- Do we consider the employees' point of view when making decisions?
- Do we give employees clear reasons for the changes that we make?
- Do we involve employees in planning how changes are implemented?

Try to cite specific examples in response to each of these questions. If you can't easily think of a specific instance, then the answer to that question is probably negative.

Since we tend to have a biased view of our own behavior, answering this type of question honestly can be difficult. The president of a highly successful company was surprised when an employee survey produced a low rating on the statement "The company has effective leadership." In subsequent meetings with employees, a consultant discovered the root of the problem: the president seldom spoke to anyone who was not a manager; he would pass people in the hall without talking or enter their offices without saying hello. Employees' interpretation of this behavior was that the president had little interest in them and was therefore not a very effective leader, despite the company's success. In fact, the president was simply a person who became easily absorbed in his own thoughts. He had no intention of being rude or unfriendly and had no idea that he was perceived that way. He had simply never developed the habit of speaking to people when he encountered them.

2. Solicit input from employees about how management-employee relationships could be improved. If employees are uncomfortable talking with you, use someone from human resources or a consultant with good facilitation skills to do interviews or focus groups. Conducting an anonymous employee survey also provides insight into people's feelings and attitudes.

3. Establish regular communication channels with employees (see strategy one under "Internal Networks"). Sometimes simply providing a forum for communication can help improve relationships—and also provide networking information. One organization instituted quarterly "listening meetings," where small groups of employees from each department met with a human resource representative

to discuss issues and concerns. Another company began requiring managers to hold quarterly luncheons with employees to share ideas and suggestions.

4. Make employee communication a priority. In the rush and bustle of daily work, talking with people is often the easiest activity to push aside. But as a manager, communication may be your most important task. In a company that had recently undergone a workforce reduction, the director of information systems said, "I have a lot more to do now and a lot less time, but I never turn away an employee with a question or problem. I figure that helping them succeed is my most important job. If I get behind on the paperwork stuff, then I just stay late."

Problem Four: The Organization Is Too Internally Focused

Organizations sometimes get so involved in their own work that they fail to encourage people to look outside their boundaries for information or ideas. This problem is often created by either size or success. Large organizations have many managers and employees who never communicate externally in the course of their daily tasks and are therefore isolated from the environment. An interesting analogy can be found in the centuries-old example of Hannibal crossing the Alps with elephants. Many people died on that incredibly cold journey, but the elephants survived, thanks in part to their large body mass. Apparently, their size insulated them from the environment, just as the size of a large organization tends to distance employees from outside influences.

Success also causes organizations to ignore the benefits of learning from others. The arrogance that accompanies success makes people believe that they have found the answers and no longer need to ask questions. The danger in this attitude should be clear from the long list of successful companies that died a slow death after failing to respond to changes in their environment. Makers of horse-drawn buggies had to adapt when automobiles came along. Typewriter manufacturers had to deal with the computer age. Companies that made mechanical scales and cash registers had to shift to electronics. Those that ignored the changes disappeared.

Departments within organizations must also look outside their own boundaries and respond to changes in their field. New methods of accounting, advertising, developing compensation plans, or organizing production operations all help companies remain competitive. If departments are too internally focused, they cannot help their organizations continue to learn.

Suggestions for action:

1. In completing your network diagram, be sure to identify all areas of the external environment that may provide helpful information.

2. When engaged in strategic planning, be sure to conduct a thorough environmental scan (discussed in Chapter Two and in the strategies section of this

chapter under "General Suggestions"). Internally focused organizations often over-look or minimize this step.

3. Survey management team members to identify their external connections, including organizations they have joined, people they communicate with in other companies, and publications they read.

4. Set goals for the management team to increase the number and variety of external contacts. Evaluate networking as part of management performance reviews.

5. Consider the suggestions in the strategies section under "External Networks."

Problem Five: Limited Time Is Available for Networking Activities

Most managers in organizations today feel rushed. Job demands seem to occupy most of their waking hours; if they're lucky they have a little time left over for family and friends. In this environment, networking activities are often cast aside. The director of human resources in a computer business was quite active in professional organizations, where she made contacts with others in her field and learned a great deal about HR programs at other companies. As her responsibilities expanded, however, she found that she had little time or energy left for external activities. She resigned from offices she had held and stopped attending professional meetings. "I know I'm missing out on valuable contacts," she said, "but you can only do so much in a day."

Suggestions for action:

1. Even if team members can't attend many activities, have them join outside organizations anyway. They will receive useful written material, and the membership directories are helpful. If you want to contact someone in another company, for example, saying that you are members of the same organization is a good way to introduce yourself.

2. Set modest networking goals for the team. Different members might plan to attend one meeting every quarter, read one article per journal, scan one trade publication a week, take someone to lunch once a month, or attend one workshop a year. Some contact is better than no contact.

3. Identify each team member's preferred way of getting information. Some people like talking, others reading. Divide networking tasks according to information preference, with the readers focusing on journals and books and the talkers going to lunches and meetings.

4. Have team members identify networking times that are least likely to interfere with other activities. Reading can often be done in the evening. Breakfast meetings still leave much of the workday intact. If you usually go to lunch, that time can occasionally be used to develop new relationships.

5. Prioritize networking activities and focus on those that produce the greatest dividends. Use a rating scale to rank the importance of areas listed on your network diagram, and be sure that the highly rated areas are covered.

6. Delegate networking tasks. Employees or lower-level managers may benefit from making new contacts, simultaneously saving their manager time and contributing to their own professional development. They may also enjoy the process. Just be sure that any useful information finds its way back to the management team.

Problem Six: There Is a Lack of Money for Networking Activities

Small businesses, nonprofit organizations, and government agencies are less likely to have money readily available for membership dues and workshop fees. Managers in these settings are often expected to pay for professional development activities themselves.

Suggestions for action:

1. Pool your resources. Get one membership or subscription and share it among all team members. Pass along written materials and rotate attendance at meetings.

2. Set aside a time and place to share information. If only one person can attend a meeting or workshop, establish the expectation that a brief presentation about it will be made to the team and that any useful materials will be shared.

3. Maximize no-cost networking. Get involved in volunteer activities in the community. Make visits to other organizations. Use resources at the library. Brainstorm other ways to get information without paying.

Problem Seven: Very Few Networking Activities Are Available

Not everyone lives in a city. Small towns and rural areas may have fewer resources available for networking purposes.

Suggestions for action:

1. Have managers attend workshops and conferences where they interact with people from other places. Set the expectation that attendance at a conference should include informal discussions with others who do similar work. Have them share this information with other team members when they return.

2. Join organizations that provide high-quality written materials in your field. Use library resources and the Internet to access a wider range of information.

3. Professional or industry groups become even more important if you have limited local resources. Encourage team members to join these organizations and develop contacts with people in other locations.

4. Make occasional trips to the nearest city to attend professional meetings or visit organizations.

5. Be sure to explore all local resources. Small towns often have active community and civic organizations, which can be a valuable source of certain kinds of networking information.

True Story: The Isolated Library System

Part Two: The Solution

Katherine, the new library director, immediately takes steps to make the Marion County library system more responsive to its environment. Despite some initial resistance from her management team and staff, she is gradually able to push them into greater involvement in the world outside the library walls. All managers are required to participate in at least one community organization, such as Kiwanis, Rotary, or the Chamber of Commerce. Employees are encouraged to get involved in community activities as well; many staff members go back to school to work toward a professional degree.

Katherine also begins to focus on customer service in the library, conducting surveys and asking the staff to learn more about customer needs and concerns. She initiates a quality improvement program and designates one member of her management team to learn what other organizations are doing in this area. Through her contacts in the professional association, she gathers data about new library information systems and designates another management team member to be responsible for upgrading this process.

The management team receives training in management techniques, using outside sources. To create a climate of continuous learning, a training team is established to assess ongoing training needs throughout the library system. Employees' ideas and suggestions are solicited, and employee teams are created to foster involvement in many aspects of library operations.

In a few short years, the Marion County library becomes a very different place. As the county continues to grow, the library system is able to grow along with it, engaging in a regular planning process that provides ongoing information about critical aspects of the environment.

Team Assessment: Does Your Team Have Effective Networks?

Management teams can only make good decisions if they have complete, accurate, and up-to-date information. This information is brought into the team by its members, who acquire knowledge and data from a variety of internal and external sources. All team members should therefore be expected to provide useful information related to their area of responsibility. If any team member fails to do so, then the team is weak in that area. Leaders of management teams should set clear expectations for networking responsibilities and include them in managers' performance reviews.

The survey and discussion questions that follow can help determine whether your management team is meeting its networking responsibilities effectively. The survey questions are based on those used in the Management Team Research Project.

TEAM Survey: Extensive Networks

This survey evaluates team member perceptions of the group's participation in networking activities. If you identify problems with networking, you may wish to refer back to the appropriate sections of this chapter under "Internal and External Networking Strategies" and "Overcoming Barriers to Effective Networking."

Here are instructions for using the survey.

1. Give each team member a copy of TEAM Survey: Extensive Networks.
2. Tell the members *not* to put their names on these sheets.
3. Have them indicate their level of agreement with each statement and score their own survey.
4. Collect the survey sheets and add up the team score yourself or ask a team member to do so.
5. Determine a final team score using the formula under "Total Team Score."
6. To identify specific concerns, total the scores for each item and divide by the numbers of team members surveyed, as shown under "Item Scores."
7. Have a group discussion of the reasons for your scores. You may wish to use the discussion questions at the end of the chapter.

TEAM SURVEY: EXTENSIVE NETWORKS

For each item, indicate your level of agreement by circling the appropriate number.

	Agree			Disagree
1. Team members are well informed about trends or new developments in their field.	4	3	2	1
2. We know a lot about what goes on in other organizations like ours.	4	3	2	1
3. Team members communicate with people who have similar jobs in other organizations.	4	3	2	1
4. Team members attend professional meetings or workshops in their field.	4	3	2	1

	Agree			Disagree
5. Team members stay informed about important trends in business or government.	4	3	2	1
6. Team members usually know what's going on in other parts of the organization.	4	3	2	1
7. Team members stay up-to-date on trends in our organization's field or industry.	4	3	2	1
8. When making decisions, team members consider current trends in business or government.	4	3	2	1

A. Individual Scoring

Add up the circled numbers and write your score below.

Total Score = _____

8–16	17–23	24–32
Poor networking	Moderately effective networking	Good networking

TEAM Networking Survey: Team Scoring

B. Total Team Score

Total of all team member scores = _____

Divide by number of team members = _____

Total Score = _____

8–16	17–23	24–32
Poor networking	Moderately effective networking	Good networking

C. Item Scores

Total for each item	Divide total by number of team members
1.	1.
2.	2.
3.	3.
4.	4.
5.	5.
6.	6.
7.	7.
8.	8.

Discussion Questions: Extensive Networks

These questions can start a discussion with your management team members about networking. They may be used alone or as a follow-up to the TEAM Survey: Extensive Networks.

- How can we improve our ability to get the information we need to react effectively to changing conditions?
- Do we need to learn more about trends in our industry? If so, how can we do this?
- Who are our customers? How do we learn about their needs and concerns?
- Does our planning process include a step for studying changes in the environment? If not, how can we build this in?
- Do we spend enough time communicating with employees? If not, what communication mechanisms can we develop?
- Which other departments are critical to our success? How can we improve relationships with them?
- What professional, industry, or community groups do managers belong to? Are there others we need to join?
- How can we get the greatest return from our investment in these group memberships?
- What trade or professional journals do we receive? Are there others we need? Are we making the most effective use of this information?
- Do team members regularly attend workshops or conferences to keep their skills and knowledge up-to-date?
- What contacts do we have with people in other organizations? Do we know which organizations are on the leading edge of our field? How can we learn from them?

CHAPTER FOUR

COLLABORATIVE RELATIONSHIPS

How to Develop Cooperation Among Departments

True Story: No Teamwork in the Finance Department

Part One: The Problem

Gail, the vice president of finance in a newly formed company, is frustrated.

"I am so tired of these managers coming into my office and complaining about each other. They're all supposedly intelligent, mature, adult human beings. Actually, I'm not so sure about the 'mature' part. Why can't they just get along?"

"What do they complain about?" asks JoAnn, her administrative assistant.

"Everything! Incomplete reports, information not being shared, managers stealing employees from other departments, who has the best office—you name it, they're unhappy about it."

"They're a competitive bunch, no question about that," says JoAnn. "And since they all came from different companies, they have different ideas about how things should be done. All of them are pretty young, too, and I think they're concerned about who gets that next promotion."

"True," replies Gail. "But what should I do about it? They're great with number-crunching and analysis, but ask them to work together on a project and you can be sure that within five minutes one of them will be in here complaining about the others. You could hardly call this a management *team*!"

"Why don't you talk with Jim in human resources?" JoAnn suggests. "He's done some pretty good work developing teams in other departments."

The finance department managers may be quite competent at their individual tasks, but when required to work cooperatively, they fail miserably. In this situation, several factors are operating to reduce collaboration. First, the managers were recruited from different companies and therefore have varying expectations about how work should be done. Since the company is new, there is no well-established organizational culture to guide behavior. Because their work emphasizes analytical abilities, these managers are less likely to have developed the interpersonal skills that build cooperative relationships. Finally, because they are all competing for promotions, the managers have little interest in making others on the team look good. Like many management groups, they are a team in name only.

The Foundations of Collaboration

Collaboration has not always been valued in organizations. Decades ago, management theorists viewed limited knowledge, skills, and abilities of individual people as the primary obstacles to good decision making. Their solution to this human failing, however, was not to encourage managers to collaborate and combine their perspectives, but to develop detailed policies and procedures that narrowed managers' choices to a small number of acceptable alternatives (Simon, 1960). Managers still have limited knowledge, skills, and abilities, but today's complex problems require them to explore many options and combine ideas from a variety of sources. Decision making needs to be team-oriented and cooperative, and this requires collaboration among people who may hold widely differing points of view. When combined with development of good information networks, a collaborative approach to making and implementing decisions helps an organization "learn" by expanding available knowledge and surfacing novel solutions.

To succeed in today's environment, management teams must develop the cooperative relationships required for effective group decision making. Since we have a natural tendency to communicate and cooperate with people we like and avoid those whom we dislike, the basis of successful group interaction is positive individual relationships. If people on a team have to expend energy dealing with difficult interpersonal issues, they have less energy to bring to their tasks. If team members fall into a competitive mode or simply operate independently of one another, the organization loses the benefit of shared ideas and perspectives. Poor relationships also affect accomplishment of individual goals, since the activities of different departments are usually linked. On the other hand, research has shown that teams whose members feel positively about one another are more likely to encourage cooperative behavior and accomplish successful results (Larson and LaFasto, 1989; Scott and Townsend, 1994).

A collaborative decision-making climate does not develop overnight. As with any important interpersonal relationship, team members require time and experience to develop familiarity, shared perspectives, and a common history. One study of group decision making found that the group's ability to make good decisions improved over time and that, as members became more familiar with one another, each person's knowledge was used more effectively (Watson, Michaelsen, and Sharp, 1991). Simply spending time together is not sufficient, however. If no effort is made to foster cooperation, or if a group's shared history consists largely of negative experiences, then a collaborative climate is not likely to develop. Our study of management teams found three factors to be necessary in developing collaborative relationships: respect, trust, and successful management of conflicts.

Respect

Two kinds of respect exist in work situations: basic respect, which should be shown to all people, and earned respect, which is given for demonstrated skills and abilities. In all work interactions, we should show basic respect to others by being courteous, listening to them, and considering their point of view. Earned respect, on the other hand, is only given to people who have demonstrated competence over a period of time. For a truly collaborative climate to exist on a management team, both basic respect and earned respect must be present.

Management team members should always be expected to behave toward one another with basic respect, regardless of their personal feelings. If basic respect is absent, collaborative relationships are unlikely to develop. We don't usually want to cooperate with rude, inconsiderate, and thoughtless people. One management team had a member who was sarcastic, critical, and hot-tempered. His coworkers tried to avoid him if at all possible, but they had to interact with him in meetings. Because no efforts were made to control his behavior, team meetings became increasingly unpleasant. As members began to find reasons to miss meetings, the entire team lost opportunities for communication and shared decision making.

For true teamwork to develop on a management team, earned respect is also important. Because team members are interdependent, competence is highly valued. Sometimes, earned respect can be increased simply by helping managers appreciate the value of different approaches, talents, or work styles. Incompetent team members pose a more difficult challenge. Since each member is responsible for an important function, poor performance by one person creates a team weakness. Collaboration also suffers because other managers usually try to avoid working with the person. If the manager's incompetence is caused by a skill deficit, the team leader should arrange for appropriate skill development activities. If the manager has the ability to do the work but is not performing, the team leader should set performance expectations and follow up to see that they are met. Sometimes a manager is simply in the wrong job and should be moved to another position. Whatever the cause, if a performance problem continues after sufficient efforts have been made to resolve it, the incompetent member should be removed from the management team.

Trust

Think of someone at work whom you trust. Exactly why do you feel that you trust that person? Here are some possible reasons:

- He keeps his word and follow through with commitments.
- He provides accurate information.
- She has the expertise needed to do her job.
- He tells the truth.
- She does not take credit for the work of others.
- Her words match her actions.
- He cares about you as a person.
- He looks out for your best interests.

Trust can be based upon any or all of these attributes. It is developed only over time and can always be quickly destroyed. How many times does someone have to lie to you before you conclude that you don't trust him? Probably just once. After that, how long would it take him to regain your trust? Probably quite a while, if ever. In one sense, saying that you trust another person means that you don't have to worry about what she will do. You can relax and not feel the need to be vigilant in any way.

On a management team, different levels of trust may exist. For team members to interact cooperatively, a minimal level of trust about work activities is required: being able to count on others to do what they say, tell the truth, and carry out tasks competently. Over time, a highly cohesive team may develop a deeper level of personal trust, with members caring about one another as people and looking out for each other's interests. Such close relationships are likely to be the exception rather than the rule on a management team, though. This higher level of trust is not necessary for effective working relationships.

If team members are not able to trust one another, cooperation tends to erode. One management team had a member who frequently told dramatic stories about her experiences at other companies, using the "lessons" from these tales to support her position on various issues. Then another manager learned that one of the stories was a clear fabrication, meant to help the person influence a particularly important decision. Word quickly traveled (as it usually does) to other team members, who became reluctant to rely on information she provided or share information with her for fear it might be distorted. She began to notice this change in relationships and started to feel excluded by the other members. As relationships deteriorated, cooperation declined, affecting the work of the entire team.

Conflict Management

No team can avoid conflict—in fact, no team should want to, since a team without differences of opinion is virtually useless. When conflicting views are expressed, however, the team needs to engage in a constructive problem-solving discussion instead of a destructive argument. In these situations, the challenge for management teams is twofold: first, to encourage expression of different opinions, and then to channel those differences into a helpful exploration of problems and solutions.

When conflicts arise, our natural tendency is to fall into a fight-or-flight mode. People who are uncomfortable with interpersonal tension have an immediate flight reaction, trying to avoid conflict by suppressing their own opinions or minimizing their differences with others. These team members quickly back down when challenged or sit quietly by while others disagree. As leaders, they try to promote harmony at all costs by denying that differences exist or cutting off arguments when they arise. If an entire management team is in flight mode, meetings are quiet and superficially friendly but relationships deteriorate through gossip and back-stabbing. Since differences cannot be worked out in the group, members begin to take action independently and make decisions without input from others. The leader is caught in the middle as members privately lobby for their own positions.

At the other extreme, people who enjoy engaging in aggressive behavior often leap into a fight stance at the first sign of disagreement. They like to verbally attack other opinions (and sometimes other people) and tend to quickly defend their own position rather than consider the merits of another view. These battles damage relationships with other team members, who try to avoid working with the aggressive person. Less feisty members become reluctant to bring up issues for fear of being attacked. As leaders, the fighters often unduly influence the group by strongly expressing or defending their positions, thereby destroying opportunities for valuable discussion. Since the leader of a management team has organizational power over the members, challenging that person is risky; many members opt to just go along. If an entire team is in fight mode, meetings tend to resemble a free-for-all. Decisions are difficult to reach without a facilitator, since everyone is adamantly defending his or her own position.

Fight and flight represent our natural biological responses to aggression. Whenever a saber-toothed tiger came upon our early ancestors, running or attacking were the most useful behavioral options available. With modern-day conflicts, though, our ingrained biological responses don't serve us too well. Attempts at reasoned discussion with the saber-tooth would have brought about our untimely demise, but reasoned discussion with work colleagues (or family members) is likely to lead to a more productive result than either leaving or yelling.

Members of one management team felt that the leader failed to listen when they came to him with problems. At a retreat led by a facilitator, one person was finally able to express this concern, which several others echoed. Although surprised, the leader did not brush off the comment (a flight response) or defend his behavior (a fight response). Instead, he asked questions that would help him further understand why team members perceived him as not listening. Through the discussion, the leader learned that concerns that did not seem serious to him were often important to his staff; team members came to realize that they often approached him while he was busy or distracted. The leader suggested that they bring him issues at the beginning of the workday, when he was least likely to be preoccupied by anything else. They also agreed that if people felt he wasn't listening, they would let him know by saying, "This is an important issue for me. Would it be better to talk about it another time?" This mutual problem-solving discussion improved both the work of the organization and the relationships on the management team.

In handling conflicts, a management team needs to develop skills, abilities, and habits that encourage expression of differences, respect for all opinions, and reasoned exploration of problems. If team members successfully engage in mutual problem solving, relationships tend to become more supportive and future cooperation is likely to increase.

Building Positive Relationships Among Team Members

The best predictor of collaborative relationships is positive intention. That is, if everyone on the team wants to work well together, they can usually overcome most problems. The strategies discussed in this chapter assume that intentions are positive. Difficulties caused by team members who try to sabotage relationships are addressed in Chapter Ten, "Fixing a Sick Team," under the section on toxic team members.

Strategy One: Be Sure That Common Goals Are Clearly Understood

For many years, research on teams has made it clear that cooperation cannot exist without an understanding of common goals. On a traditional management team, the lack of group goals usually creates tunnel vision within departments, causing them to act solely in their own interests without considering the effect on the organization. (Goals were discussed extensively in Chapter Two.) In one unusual situation, two universities offered a joint management development program run by a team of four managers, two from each school. During a period of scarce funding, the financial interests of the individual universities began to take precedence over the needs of the cooperative program. The two schools started competing for control of the money used to fund the joint program, causing relationships in the management group to erode. Both parties were now unwilling to share their best ideas, since they feared that the other school might steal them and reduce their competitive advantage. Having lost their focus on common goals, the managers also lost any reason to cooperate, and the joint program ultimately disbanded.

Strategy Two: Help Managers Identify Links Between Departments

To prevent tunnel vision, managers need to clearly understand how their departments affect one another. As illustrated in Figure 4.1, the relationships on a management team are complex. Although these connections may seem obvious, departments often happily pursue their own goals without considering how other functions are affected. Managers need to recognize that they are part of a complex system of interlocking goals, needs, and relationships.

FIGURE 4.1. DEPARTMENTAL LINKS
FOR A MANUFACTURING ORGANIZATION.

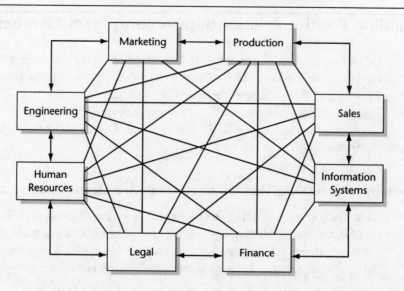

Strategy Three: Specify What People Need from One Another

In considering their links to other functions, managers should identify the information, reports, products, or decisions that need to flow from one department to another. By making requests and reaching agreements about these needs, managers increase both departmental and team effectiveness. Having all team members actually write down what they need or expect from the others is often more effective than just discussing the topic.

Strategy Four: Define *Trust* and *Respect* Behaviorally

Trust and *respect* are fuzzy words. They reflect a feeling rather than a behavior. When you say to someone, "I just don't trust you," the person probably understands that you feel negatively but doesn't know exactly how to correct the situation. If we want people to act differently, we have to talk about behaviors instead of feelings. Teams usually agree that trust and respect are important, but they need to define what those words mean in behavioral terms. One finance management team, for example, decided that trust included these meanings:

- I will receive information from you in time to complete my reports.
- Information that I receive from you will be accurate.
- You will not talk about me behind my back.
- You will not try to recruit any of my employees without telling me.
- You will share credit with me for work that we do together.

Strategy Five: Measure Internal Customer Service

Each manager's performance review should include a section on how well internal customers are being served, possibly using periodic surveys to gather this information. If, for example, the marketing communications department provides advertising materials to the salesforce, then the marketing communications manager should be held accountable for developing effective materials in timely fashion. Asking for input from salespeople may be the only way to find out if this is actually happening. As the old saying indicates, what gets measured gets done. Measuring interdepartmental cooperation is one way to promote collaborative relationships on the management team.

Strategy Six: Take the Pulse of the Group

Management team leaders are often unaware of the status of team relationships, in part because leaders are typically more focused on tasks than on relationship issues. Because team relationships usually develop outside the leader's view as members interact on various work issues and projects, the leader's information may be limited. Perhaps this is why our research found little connection between leader behavior and team member relationships. The leader does need to know how well people are working together, though, since member relationships largely determine how well the team functions. Individual meetings with team members, group discussions, or surveys all help provide this information. If relationship problems exist, the leader can then take the steps needed to improve the situation.

Strategy Seven: Help People Get Acquainted

Relationships are often enhanced by interaction outside of work. Happy hour every Friday isn't necessary, but an occasional lunch, dinner, or social activity is beneficial. Some managers view this as wasting time, not realizing that the relationships developed during nonwork activities are often fundamental to later cooperation. Social interaction is especially important for new teams, but even well-established groups need to get away from their work environment occasionally. The members of a management team in one government agency had worked together for ten to twenty years. When a facilitator suggested a get-acquainted activity during a retreat, they laughed and said they already knew everything about one another. Members agreed to talk about their early lives and work history, and the group was greatly surprised to learn that one had lived overseas, another had been to medical school, a third had taken a cross-country motorcycle trip, and a fourth came from a family of migrant workers. At work, we sometimes view our coworkers as a means to an end. The more we get to know them as people, the more likely we are to develop collaborative relationships.

Strategy Eight: Hold Management Retreats Regularly

In addition to building relationships through off-task interaction, management retreats help a team detach from daily demands and think more strategically about the work that members do together. Retreats are used to achieve a variety of objectives and can be held with or without a professional facilitator. Newly formed teams often hold retreats to define their initial goals and help members begin to get to know one another. One well-established team has retreats twice a year to discuss any issues that the group needs to resolve. Another group uses an annual retreat to review and discuss the goals of each department for the coming year. Whatever the purpose, retreats always offer the additional benefit of giving members a chance to build more collaborative relationships.

Strategy Nine: Discuss Differences of Opinion

An effective management team must be able to comfortably discuss different views and accept disagreement as a normal and beneficial aspect of decision making. When team members become aware of conflicts, they should bring them up for discussion at team meetings. Leaders of management teams must ensure that discussion of differences is conducted in a positive spirit and with a focus on common goals.

Strategy Ten: Resolve Interdepartmental Conflicts

Management team leaders are often frustrated by continually having to mediate conflicts between departments. But leaders only encourage this dependence if they continue to resolve these disagreements themselves. Teaching people to resolve their own conflicts is usually beneficial for both the team members and their manager. The leader should first help the parties agree on the goals to be achieved and then require them to work out a mutually acceptable solution. In one department, for example, managers constantly disagreed on the division of roles and responsibilities, frequently going to the director for resolution. Finally, the director called a team meeting and gave them a goal: within two weeks, develop a recommendation for a division of labor in the department. She said she would be available to the group to answer questions but would not discuss the issue with them individually and would not resolve disagreements. There were protests, but two weeks later the director had a recommendation; within two months she had a more effective department.

Strategy Eleven: Use an Outside Facilitator for Difficult Issues

Having an outside facilitator is useful when relationship issues or serious conflicts are being discussed. In these situations, people often feel anxious, fearing that emotions will get out of control and cause relationships to deteriorate further. An experienced facilitator helps make these meetings safe for the members by clarifying the goals of the discussion, allowing all points of view to be expressed and heard, seeing that negative comments are expressed neutrally and nonaggressively, and keeping the group on track. One caution: facilitators who simply encourage free and open expression of feelings as the solution to relationship problems are likely to do more harm than good.

Strategy Twelve: Teach Conflict Management Techniques

Outside facilitators or trainers can also help management team members learn techniques for expressing and discussing conflicts productively. Teams whose members are stuck in fight-or-flight mode often find this quite helpful.

Overcoming Barriers to Collaboration

Relationship difficulties are often attributed to individual interpersonal problems, while other factors—such as role conflicts, leadership behavior, or organization structure—are overlooked. As with most problems, correctly identifying the cause is instrumental to finding a solution. Barriers to collaborative relationships are grouped into three categories: individual relationships, group interaction, and organizational factors.

Individual Relationships

One-on-one relationships sometimes falter because the members have trouble getting along or avoid interaction altogether. Several problems can interfere with individual relationships on a team:

1. Team members have "personality differences."
2. Team members come from different cultures.
3. Cliques have formed on the team.
4. Team members prefer to work independently.
5. The team has a history of personal conflicts.

Problem One: Team Members Have "Personality Differences"

In fact, team members always have personality differences, since no two people are exactly the same. But there are certain common differences in work style that tend to result in predictable problems. Some people, for example, like to make plans well in advance and stick to them, while others prefer to make changes up to the last minute. Some people like to talk through a problem with a group; others prefer to think it through on their own. Some people like to focus on long-term goals and the big picture, and others prefer to work on details of implementation. These work style differences can be a strength since they provide different perspectives; but they are also a predictable source of conflict.

Suggestions for action:

1. Bring in an outside facilitator or trainer to conduct a session on work styles. There are many instruments or surveys to help team members understand these differences, such as the Myers-Briggs Type Indicator or the Communicating Styles Survey. Any valid survey that does not have right or wrong answers should serve the purpose. An understanding of work styles also pays additional dividends in

improved relationships with employees and customers. (Work style differences are also discussed in Chapter Five, under "Different Viewpoints.")

2. Use the neutral language provided by the work style survey to discuss differences and disagreements within the group. Terminology that does not label anyone's style negatively reduces defensiveness and makes it easier to focus on the issues. Encourage members to make requests of one another and reach agreements about how they can change their behavior to accommodate people with different styles.

3. Continue to reinforce the team's use of the neutral language to talk about working relationships. As team members observe style differences in meetings or work situations, they should point them out and encourage discussion about the benefits and challenges of having different styles on the team.

Problem Two: Team Members Come from Different Cultures

Misunderstandings also occur as a result of cultural differences, an increasing challenge as our world shrinks and people from different countries come together on management teams. One management team member, for example, came from a culture where it was considered rude to openly disagree with a superior. The rough-and-tumble style of management discussions in the United States appeared quite inappropriate to him. His fellow team members, on the other hand, perceived him as weak and unwilling to stand up for his ideas. Only after the team had a discussion of different cultural assumptions were they able to effectively address the issue.

Suggestions for action:

1. Be sure not to overemphasize differences between people. Regardless of race, gender, or nationality, all human beings have many more similarities than differences. If we suddenly found ourselves under attack by alien creatures from Neptune, we might find our similarities easier to see. Focusing only on differences without also discussing similarities actually widens the gap between people.

2. Provide a forum for open discussion of cultural differences, possibly bringing in a speaker to talk on the subject. Starting with examples of nonwork differences helps open up the discussion. Hand gestures, for example, can be quite innocent in one culture, very offensive in another. Words have different meanings that can cause problems. In one company, a British manager visiting corporate headquarters in the United States caused quite a stir with his parting words to a secretary: "Well, I'll knock you up the next time I'm over here." If you knock someone up in Britain, you get in touch with them, but in the United States it means to get someone pregnant. As your discussion moves to work-related topics, encourage team

members to ask about cultural differences they have noticed in working together. Combining the cultural discussion with an exploration of work style differences is also effective.

3. An experienced facilitator may be helpful if conflicts are likely to arise during a cultural discussion. Be sure to carefully interview and check the credentials of the facilitator. Some consultants who claim to do "diversity training" have been known to create hard feelings and damage relationships among group members.

4. Be aware of your own cultural blind spots, and learn from your multicultural team members. Make specific efforts to translate across cultural differences. If a team member's background causes her to feel that openly disagreeing with others is rude, for example, you may want to solicit her opinions privately and then encourage her to discuss them in the meeting.

Problem Three: Cliques Have Formed on the Team

Team members can cluster in subgroups for any number of reasons. Common interests, shared projects, prior work experience, work style similarities, even length of service all cause people to band together. Everyone tends to feel more in sync with some people than others, but problems arise if cliques make people feel excluded or form opposing coalitions during decision making.

The strategies offered here often work to resolve ordinary problems with cliques. If there are hostile cliques on your team, however, you may wish to refer to the discussion of this problem in Chapter Ten.

Suggestions for action:

1. Determine what effect the clique seems to be having. If no obvious problems exist with either task accomplishment or relationships, then there may be no need to address the situation.

2. Try to determine the reasons behind the formation of a clique. Are there any noticeable similarities or commonalities that some members share? Are there any obvious reasons why some members are left out?

3. Evaluate whether your own behavior is contributing to the development of cliques. Assessing your personal situation requires some honest self-examination, so consider these questions:

- Do you spend a lot more time with some team members than others?
- Are there some team members that you seldom talk to except in meetings?
- Do you regularly go to lunch (breakfast, dinner) with certain team members?
- Do you drop in to the office or work area of some team members and not others?

- When you want to talk over a problem, do you always tend to seek out the same team members?
- Are you involved with any team members in activities outside of work?

If you are the team leader, these questions are particularly important. Relationships among team members almost always suffer if the leader is part of a clique on the team, since it tends to become the in-group, thereby automatically creating a resentful out-group. Since only the opinions of certain members are heard, a leader in this situation begins to adopt a biased view of issues and problems. Leaders may also unintentionally discriminate against some members simply because they don't know them well or spend much time with them.

As you can see from the questions, the point here is not how you *feel* about team members but how you *interact* with them. If you answered yes to several of the questions about cliques, you may need to balance your relationships and spend more time with people you have been ignoring. A yes answer to even one of these questions can create problems if you are the leader. Leaders need to make particular efforts to communicate equally with everyone and avoid the appearance of playing favorites.

4. Provide interaction opportunities for the whole group, preferably away from the office. In one human resources department, the annual management retreat at a lakeside hotel was traditionally capped off by a houseboat cruise. Spending several hours together in a relatively small space encouraged social interaction among all team members and helped break down cliques that formed around work tasks, office location, or other factors.

5. Use people from different cliques to staff projects. The experience of working together on a task usually helps build or repair relationships. One director of a government agency was concerned that her division managers had split into two groups that often bickered with one another. When the management team went through a strategic planning process, she deliberately created planning teams that mixed the two groups, with the result that relationships greatly improved.

6. For firmly entrenched cliques, an outside facilitator may be needed. Before one management retreat, the facilitator sent out a questionnaire to poll the group about issues. Responses showed that about half the members felt cliques were interfering with teamwork. In discussion of the survey responses, the other half of the group was astonished to find that they were perceived as an exclusive in-group. The differentiating factor appeared to be length of tenure, since all in-group members had been part of the team for more than ten years. They had well-established relationships, knew one another's families, played golf together, ate meals together, and generally supported one another in group discussions. Having identified the root of the problem, the group was able to develop strategies to promote more interaction and a greater feeling of equality.

Problem Four: Team Members Prefer to Work Independently

People with an introverted, task-oriented work style often prefer to work on their own, seeking little interaction with others. Teams in which this style predominates have weaker relationships because members do not find interpersonal contact particularly rewarding and therefore spend less time together. Independent work styles are fine, as long as the team develops a foundation of positive relationships to draw on when they need to cooperate. Members of these teams don't need to become "touchy-feely" and engage in group hugs, but they do need enough positive interaction to prevent destructive conflicts.

Suggestions for action:

1. For people with this style, most opportunities for interaction should be related to work. Given a choice, they are not likely to show up for lunches, parties, or other social events. In one engineering company, the employee relations department was always disappointed by the low turnout for the annual holiday party and spring picnic. Unfortunately, they did not realize that their workforce had a high percentage of introverted, task-oriented people who simply did not think large social gatherings were fun. But they did turn out in great numbers for the engineering symposium.

2. Provide time in meetings for team members to share information with one another about their work. This not only promotes interaction but also alerts them to opportunities for helping one another.

3. Look for projects that members can work on jointly. Task-oriented people prefer to develop relationships through shared work rather than social interaction.

4. Hold off-site staff retreats where people have time to get to know one another. For this type of team, the retreat must have obvious practical value to their work. Group games and activities that seem silly to them are not likely to be well received (although they may develop a bond through shared complaints!).

5. Help team members identify areas where they might benefit from sharing knowledge and expertise. For example, one human resource director asked his training manager and policies and practices manager to determine how new policies could be communicated more effectively. In another company, the plant manager suggested that her production and sales managers develop a plan to have production workers talk with customers, who could help the employees understand how their products were actually used.

Problem Five: The Team Has a History of Personal Conflicts

Management teams with a long shared history may have had past experiences that interfere with present relationships. Competition for promotions, conflicts over projects and assignments, reorganizations, and relationships outside of work all create a difficult history for a team. On one government management team, most members had worked in the agency for more than twenty years. They had "grown up" together at work, competed for jobs, and managed one another in different capacities. Making it even more interesting, one of the men had dated three of the women. These team members had some strongly held opinions about one another and some firmly entrenched patterns of interaction—and avoidance!

Suggestions for action:

1. If you are the team leader, try to determine the source of conflicts, perhaps by talking separately with team members to get different perspectives on the situation. If you are the new leader of a well-established team and are not familiar with their history, individual discussions are strongly recommended. Keep in mind that surfacing issues can be difficult, so don't expect team members to share all their information with you right away. In the government management team that was just mentioned, an outside consultant worked with the group for three months before anyone told him about the history of dating relationships.

2. Consider holding a staff retreat to focus on group problem solving. Long-standing issues that require time for exploration and discussion can seldom be resolved in a regular staff meeting. Before the retreat, consider having team members complete a questionnaire to identify issues.

3. Bring in an outside facilitator to mediate discussions about serious issues. People often feel more comfortable raising controversial topics if they know someone is there to keep the process from getting out of hand. If long-standing conflicts provoke strong feelings, an experienced facilitator can help team members maintain productive dialogue. Structuring the discussion format and focusing on the issues instead of personalities often prevents the conversation from deteriorating into blaming and accusations. Just be sure that the facilitator knows how to help a group resolve issues. Simply expressing feelings is only likely to make the situation worse.

4. Train team members in conflict resolution techniques. Our natural, human reactions to conflict are usually not helpful: we either run away from the situation or get angry and defend our position. Learning specific methods for talking through disagreements helps team members become more adept at handling them in the future. Many workshops, tapes, and books on conflict management are available for this purpose.

5. While working on problems, be sure to emphasize strengths and accomplishments as well. Focusing only on weakness tends to sap energy and morale; celebrating success builds teamwork.

Group Interaction

For a variety of reasons, some groups fail to promote positive interaction among their members. In this situation, individual relationships are not necessarily a problem, but something about the group itself causes relationships to be less supportive:

1. Team members have no apparent common goals.
2. The group has few opportunities to interact.
3. Members have overlapping roles and responsibilities.
4. The team leader manages conflicts poorly.
5. Many team members are new to the group.

Problem One: Team Members Have No Apparent Common Goals

Some management groups are composed of diverse departments that seem to lack a common purpose. One team in a human resource department, for instance, was made up of people from training, internal communications, policy development, safety, and employment. The five functions operated quite independently and worked toward different goals.

Suggestions for action:
1. Use the process of creating a group mission statement to identify a common purpose. This HR group found that even though their activities were quite different, they were all trying to provide the company with a more effective workforce.

2. Share the goals of each department in planning meetings and identify areas where they might assist one another. The same group identified these opportunities to share their expertise:

- The internal communications department helped the others compose announcements and ads.
- The training and employment departments worked together on orienting new employees.
- Employment and policy development collaborated on hiring practices.
- All departments cooperated in creating an effective safety program.

3. Continue to share information about departmental activities in staff meetings, and encourage team members to be alert for possible areas of collaboration.

Problem Two: The Group Has Few Opportunities to Interact

As a group of people responsible for running an organization, management team members need to share information and collaborate on common concerns. If there is no need for a team to interact, then they are not really a management team. Teams may have limited opportunities to interact, for a variety of reasons. In certain work settings, autonomy is a natural outgrowth of the task. One research facility, for example, organized departments by scientific discipline, so each management team member focused exclusively on a particular type of research. In other situations, lack of time or conflicting schedules make attendance at meetings difficult. The leaders of some teams fail to see the need to have any meetings at all. Geographic separation, a serious obstacle to interaction, is discussed later in this chapter under organizational factors.

Suggestions for action:

1. Hold meetings to share information, even it is for just thirty minutes every couple of weeks. Be clear about the purpose of the meetings, and be sure that they are focused and organized. Even a small amount of interaction helps promote team communication. After a company survey revealed low scores on information sharing, the director of customer service told his three managers that there would be a brief informational meeting every Wednesday morning at nine. He said he would share any new business information with them and they would be expected to give a quick update on the week's activities in their departments. He assured them that these meetings would never last more than one hour and that longer meetings needed for planning or decision making would be separately scheduled.

2. If meetings are difficult to arrange, team members should try to develop the habit of communicating individually. As opportunities arise, they can share helpful information and consult with one another on projects. Team leaders should make every effort to encourage this behavior, pointing out areas for collaboration whenever possible.

3. Use shared projects to promote interaction. If people successfully complete a task together, they are more likely to communicate and collaborate in the future. In the research facility mentioned above, departments were encouraged to work together on projects involving more than one scientific discipline.

Problem Three: Team Members Have Overlapping Roles and Responsibilities

Overlapping roles and responsibilities usually create confusion and conflict. In one technology company, an advanced research group was created to study leading-edge technologies that might be used in future products. Management's original intention was for this group to deliver viable new product ideas to the product development group, which would then create a prototype. Over time, however, the advanced research group began to actually make the products themselves, putting them in competition with product development for resources. Until the issue was resolved, this situation seriously disrupted relationships on the management team. In another company, the human resource department was designing a new performance appraisal form. The three managers responsible for compensation, training, and employment law all had different views and opinions about the design of the form, but responsibility for performance appraisal had not been clearly assigned to any of them. The result was continuous bickering about every new draft of the form as each manager tried to control the issue.

Suggestions for action:

1. Identify the specific areas where job roles overlap; then outline a clear division of responsibilities. The team leader may choose to undertake this task, or the managers involved can work it out as a group.

2. If role confusion is likely to arise during a project, one person should be put in charge. Designating a leader avoids the "problem of equals," a common phenomenon in which leaderless groups have great difficulty reaching decisions. Not all groups need leaders, but it is helpful to have a leader when reaching consensus is likely to be difficult.

3. Reassign responsibilities that seem inappropriate. In one manufacturing organization, product inspection reported to the production manager. Whenever production was behind schedule, the inspection supervisor would become more lenient with product checks, knowing that his boss was anxious to meet production goals. As a result, more marginal products were released, causing friction between the quality assurance manager and the production manager. The solution was to move product inspection to the quality assurance function, where it more naturally belonged.

Problem Four: The Team Leader Manages Conflicts Poorly

As previously discussed, poor conflict management usually involves avoidance or aggression. Team leaders with an avoiding style may refuse to acknowledge conflict in a group, preventing open discussion of differences. Aggressive team leaders, on the other hand, often suppress conflict by imposing their will on the group and refusing to acknowledge dissenting views. In either case, unresolved issues tend to go underground and then surface as back-stabbing, gossiping, or power struggles. Damaged relationships and poor decision making are the likely result.

To assess your own conflict management style, ask yourself these questions about your reactions to conflict:

- Do you become uncomfortable when people are arguing in your presence?
- When something is bothering you, do you wait a long time to talk about it?
- Would you like for everyone to just get along and stop bringing you their problems?
- Do you get angry over small things?
- In an argument, do you try hard to come out the winner?
- If someone offends you, do you usually let them know about it?

A positive answer to the first three questions reflects an avoiding style, while affirming the last three indicates a more aggressive approach. Some people have a mixed style, avoiding conflict in certain situations and becoming aggressive in others. One common mixture is found in the person who acts subserviently toward people in power but becomes aggressive with subordinates and family members.

Suggestions for action:

1. All team members benefit from learning specific conflict management techniques. Many good tapes and books are available on this subject, but attending a workshop that allows you to actually practice effective behaviors is probably the best approach. If you are a management team leader, good conflict management skills are a necessity. If you are a member of a team whose leader handles conflict poorly, learning these skills helps you intervene effectively in conflict situations, even if the leader does not improve.

2. If you are the team leader and you believe you are not handling conflicts well, get some feedback from your team members. This can be done through informal discussions or formal surveys (often called 360 degree or upward feedback). Be aware, though, that honest feedback is difficult to obtain when you are in a position of power—especially if you have demonstrated an aggressive style in the past, since people may fear retaliation. Using your human resource department or an outside consultant to gather feedback produces more honest and accurate results. (The feedback process is also discussed in Chapter Ten under the section "Ineffective Team Leadership.")

3. Once you have defined your problem with conflict, ask team members to help you change. Describe the specific behavior you want to modify, and tell them what to do when you exhibit it. One manager who felt that he tried to avoid conflicts asked team members who noticed him brushing aside an important issue to say, "Do we need to talk about this further?" This became his signal to explore the matter in more detail.

4. Get individual coaching from a mentor, human resource development specialist, or outside consultant who gives honest feedback. If you feel that you have a serious problem dealing with conflict, you may wish to consult a counselor or therapist.

Problem Five: Many Team Members Are New to the Group

Management teams with many new members need to develop the relationships needed for teamwork. In one company, the vice president of marketing, chief financial officer, and vice president of operations were all new to the company and had been on the management team less than three months. Three other team members had been there less than a year. To develop the level of comfort required for effective group decision making, they needed to learn more about one another's goals, interests, and work styles. Unfortunately, the team had a rather autocratic leader who dominated most group discussions. As a result, the group took much longer than necessary to develop productive teamwork. If you have many new members, you may also wish to review the section "Starting a New Team" in Chapter Nine, "Managing Team Transitions."

Suggestions for action:

1. When a new team member is being hired, begin relationship building during the interview process by having the final candidates talk with other team members.

2. Shortly after starting work, a new team member should meet individually with the others to discuss their roles and functions. Having lunch together may promote more interaction than meeting in the office.

3. Share written information with new team members about the goals and responsibilities of other departments. Having a written summary allows them to refer back to the information later. New team members are taking in a lot of information at once and may have difficulty remembering it all.

4. Hold a staff retreat to identify work styles (discussed earlier in this chapter under "Individual Relationships," problem one), share information about goals, and engage in joint planning activities.

5. Develop a biographical profile on each team member, and share the profiles with the group. One company maintained a file of biodata sheets on executives for use in news releases. They found that simply giving copies of this information to new management team members helped relationships develop more quickly.

Organizational Factors

Sometimes factors outside the group affect relationships inside the group; however, when relationship difficulties develop, we seldom consider organizational causes. Our first reaction is usually to look for "personality problems," but closer examination may reveal that external circumstances are at least partly to blame.

Organizational policies, practices, and structures all affect interaction among management team members:

1. The organization structure discourages teamwork.
2. Unclear policies and procedures interfere with teamwork.
3. Team members are geographically separated.
4. Reward and recognition systems do not promote cooperation.

Problem One: The Organization Structure Discourages Teamwork

As discussed in Chapter Two, there is no perfect organizational structure. Each one has costs and benefits, but you should not adopt a structure that seriously interferes with teamwork. In one large government agency, each division had a director and an assistant director. Because there had been no turnover among division directors for at least ten years, all the new talent was at the assistant director level. The commissioner of the agency did not want to lose these fresh perspectives, so she put both directors and assistant directors on the management team. This arrangement had two drawbacks: the management team became too large for effective group decision making, and the presence of lower-level managers prevented strong relationships from developing among the directors. As a result, differences did not get worked out in the group but instead were all taken to the commissioner, who grew very tired of being involved in so many decisions. The relationships were influenced by the structure of the team.

A change in structure may initiate a change in the behavior of team members toward one another. In a large company with several divisions, the information systems function had been centralized for many years, with both corporate and division managers reporting to the same vice president. The corporate managers established policies that were then carried out by the divisions. When the information systems department was decentralized, divisional team members began reporting to division general managers but were still considered part of the information systems management team. Suddenly, these team members had much more autonomy, which radically changed relationships. Power shifted from corporate to division, so divisional team members no longer had to automatically follow directives from the corporate staff. Corporate team members now had to use influence and persuasion to achieve their goals. The point is not that one structure was better than the other, but that changing the structure also changed the relationships.

Suggestions for action:

1. Evaluate the structure of your organization and your team in light of the goals you are trying to accomplish. Keep in mind that no structure solves all

problems; alternative structures are simply more or less effective for accomplishing certain goals.

    2. Consider making the structural evaluation a group activity in order to hear various perspectives. Some management teams have found it useful to draw several possible organization charts and debate the pros and cons of each. During any such discussion, remember that structural changes usually shift the balance of power, so team members' opinions are likely to be influenced by whether they will gain or lose. Group discussion is helpful in assessing various options, but because of the bias created by self-interest, final decisions about structure need to be made by the team's leader.

    3. Make any structural changes that help achieve critical goals, both in terms of work and relationships. Clearly communicate the reasons for restructuring. Recognize that people naturally become territorial when organizational relationships are changed, so expect resistance from anyone who perceives a power loss.

Problem Two: Unclear Policies and Procedures Interfere with Teamwork

Sometimes conflicts develop because there are no clear guidelines for making decisions or resolving differences. At a staff retreat designed to address troublesome issues in a social service agency, participants complained about a problematic situation that was finally dubbed "squeaky people," to describe the problem of policy exceptions being made for people who complained. Over time, these exceptions had caused different departments to operate on widely varying sets of procedures, and charges of unfairness were rampant. As resentment increased, relationships in the group began to deteriorate. The basic problem was twofold: no guidelines existed for making policy exceptions, and the exceptions made were not communicated to everyone.

    Suggestions for action:

    1. Specifically define the work-related issues that are creating problems for your team, and explore the possible causes. This can be accomplished by having discussions at management team meetings, holding a staff retreat, or using a short survey.

    2. Determine whether changes in policies or procedures could prevent these problems in the future. These questions may be helpful:

- Do we need to standardize some of our practices by developing policies?
- Do some of our existing policies seem unclear?
- Are policies applied inconsistently in different situations or departments?
- Do we have policies or procedures that need to be eliminated?

3. Make any needed changes. Having a task force of team members work on these issues is often useful, since relationships can be developed while the problem is being solved.

Problem Three: Team Members Are Geographically Separated

Physical proximity increases informal communication, which in turn builds stronger relationships. If team members are in different buildings, cities, states, or countries, communication becomes more difficult and relationships suffer. Even a hallway can become a barrier. In the central office of a government agency, the operations section was on one side of the hall and the program section on the other. The two sections were led by people with strong personalities who were competing for promotion to division director. Whenever someone out in the field met a central office employee, the first question was usually, "Which side of the hall do you work on?" Managers from one side seldom ventured into the alien territory on the other, which prevented collaboration on many important subjects. The situation did not begin to improve until a building renovation forced people from the two sections to occupy adjacent offices.

The greater the distance separating team members, the greater the challenge in building and maintaining relationships. Management teams composed of people from different regions around the country or different countries around the world face many more obstacles than those who are simply in separate buildings.

Suggestions for action:

1. Recognize that layout and location of buildings do influence communication and relationships. Proximity encourages interaction. If you can locate managers closer to their coworkers, try to do so. One company with manufacturing plants on opposite sides of a busy highway improved productivity by moving them to the same side of the street. A not-for-profit agency with departments on two different floors of a high-rise office building relocated so that everyone would be on the same level. A fast-growing company leasing office space in widely separated locations throughout the city consolidated operations onto a suburban corporate campus.

2. If people are in different cities, states, or countries, encourage use of any available communication mechanism, including telephone, e-mail, or video, to help maintain relationships. One group whose members managed similar programs at different universities developed the habit of sharing all important information (and a good deal of news that was simply interesting) through their e-mail network. Interacting with distant team members through conference calls or videoconferencing, although not the same as having them physically present, is highly preferable to sending them memos.

3. Be aware of the hazards of e-mail. Many working relationships have been damaged by e-mail messages that were perceived as abrupt, rude, or hostile. E-mail conflicts usually develop for one of two reasons: senders are more likely to express negative feelings if they are not face-to-face with the recipient, and recipients are more likely to perceive negative intentions if nonverbal communication is not available to soften the words.

4. If possible, encourage team members to visit one another's locations. Seeing people on their own turf provides better understanding of their work situation.

5. Physical separation makes periodic gatherings even more important. Communication by video, phone, or e-mail is helpful, but nothing completely replaces the experience of talking with someone face-to-face. Meetings or retreats held quarterly, or even annually, provide the foundation for relationships that are then sustained through other means of communication.

Problem Four: Reward and Recognition Systems Do Not Promote Cooperation

Some methods of recognition do not promote teamwork. Employee-of-the-month programs, for example, stress competition and discourage group efforts. In one manufacturing company, executives wondered why their work groups showed poor teamwork. Part of the problem was that to give employees annual raises, each manager was allocated a certain amount of money to divide among team members. No consideration was given to rewarding team efforts. Competitive bonus plans, in which managers must compete for their share of a fixed pot of money, have the same effect. Developing teamwork among managers is a challenging task under the best of circumstances, but a competitive reward system makes it almost impossible.

Suggestions for action:

1. If possible, change the system to include recognition for group efforts. In the United States, people expect and are motivated by individual rewards, so these should not be eliminated—but teamwork should also be rewarded. Part of a manager's bonus can be linked to successful completion of interdepartmental projects or achievement of interdepartmental goals. Annual raises can be based in part on assessments from internal customers. Recognition programs can give awards for team accomplishments and group projects.

2. If you are not in a position to change the system, provide recognition within the group to convey the message that teamwork is valued. Praise team accomplishments in staff meetings, or go out for a group dinner to celebrate a milestone. Create a peer recognition program that allows team members to reward helpful people in other departments with a gift certificate.

3. If you are the team leader, ask your group to think of creative ways to reward teamwork. They will probably come up with ideas that never occurred to you.

True Story: No Teamwork in the Finance Department

Part Two: The Solution

Gail, the vice president of finance, calls Jim in human resources.

"I have a problem," she says, "And I understand that you may be the answer."

"I'll do what I can. What's the matter?"

"It's these so-called managers who report to me. I think they'd be fine if they could just work together for longer than five minutes."

"You're not the only vice president around here to have that problem," says Jim. "Let's talk about some things that might help."

After discussing the situation in more detail, Gail and Jim decide to survey the management team to identify specific problems and then hold a retreat to involve team members in working on solutions.

During the retreat, one event seems to have special impact on the group. As a warm-up activity, the six of them are given a box of Legos and told to work together to build something that symbolizes their department. They dump the Legos out of the box, talk for about sixty seconds about what to build, and then begin to work on four different things. At the end of the allotted time, the facilitator says, "Now, what has your team made?" The managers sit back and look slightly stunned as they survey their four different creations. Then they laugh. "That's exactly what we do all the time!" one of them exclaims. "We just go off and do our own thing because it's easier than trying to figure out how to work together."

This realization seems to set the stage for the rest of the retreat. Team members talk openly about the problems that pose a challenge to teamwork in their department and begin to reach some agreements about how to improve the situation. Over the next few months, they hold two more retreats to share their goals for the coming year, learn about their different work styles, and evaluate how well they have kept their agreements. By the end of the year, Gail finally has a true management team.

Team Assessment: Do Your Team Members Have Positive Relationships?

Collaborative relationships provide the glue that holds a management team together. If relationships begin to deteriorate, the group's effectiveness inevitably suffers because they can't function as a team. Too often, we assume that if we just focus on the work, relationships will take care of themselves. Unfortunately, this is not always the case. The leader of a management team needs to continuously monitor the status of relationships in the group and actively work to keep them healthy.

The survey and discussion questions that follow help determine whether your management team is maintaining positive working relationships. The survey questions are based on those used in the Management Team Research Project.

TEAM Survey: Collaborative Relationships

This survey helps determine whether management team members have collaborative relationships. If you identify relationship problems, you may wish to refer back to the appropriate sections of this chapter under "Building Positive Relationships Among Team Members" or "Overcoming Barriers to Collaboration."

Here are instructions for using the survey.

1. Give each team member a copy of Team Survey: Collaborative Relationships.
2. Tell the members *not* to put their names on these sheets.
3. Have them indicate their level of agreement with each statement and score their own survey.
4. Collect the survey sheets and add up the team score yourself or ask a team member to do so.
5. Determine a final team score using the formula under "Total Team Score."
6. To identify specific concerns, total the scores for each item and divide by the numbers of team members surveyed, as shown under "Item Scores."
7. Have a group discussion of the reasons for your scores. You may wish to use the discussion questions at the end of the chapter.

TEAM SURVEY: COLLABORATIVE RELATIONSHIPS

For each item, indicate your level of agreement by circling the appropriate number.

	Agree			Disagree
1. People on this team usually discuss their differences with each other openly.	4	3	2	1
2. People on this team trust one another.	4	3	2	1
3. People on this team have respect for one another's abilities.	4	3	2	1
4. People on this team are honest with each other.	4	3	2	1

	Agree			Disagree
5. People on this team like each other.	4	3	2	1
6. People on this team tend to see things the same way.	4	3	2	1
7. Team members treat one another respectfully.	4	3	2	1
8. Team members can disagree without getting angry.	4	3	2	1

A. Individual Scoring

Add up the circled numbers and write your score below.

Total Score = _____

8–16	17–23	24–32
Poor relationships	Moderately good relationships	Positive relationships

TEAM Relationships Survey: Team Scoring

B. Total Team Score

Total of all team member scores = _____

Divide by number of team members = _____

Total Score = _____

8–16	17–23	24–32
Poor relationships	Moderately good relationships	Positive relationships

C. Item Scores

Total for each item	Divide total by number of team members
1.	1.
2.	2.
3.	3.
4.	4.
5.	5.
6.	6.
7.	7.
8.	8.

Discussion Questions: Collaborative Relationships

These questions can start a discussion with your management team members about relationships. They may be used alone or as a follow-up to the TEAM Survey: Collaborative Relationships. For serious relationship problems, using an experienced facilitator may be advisable.

- What do we do well as a team? What team goals have we accomplished? What does this say about our strengths as a group?
- Do we know what our common goals are? If not, how can we identify them?
- Do we share enough information about what team members are working on? If not, what do we need to share and how should we do that?
- Do people on this team treat one another with respect? If not, how can we improve in this area?
- Do people feel comfortable expressing opinions on this team? If not, what would create more open communication?
- What happens in this group when people disagree with one another? Is this a constructive way to handle conflict? If not, how do we improve?
- Would it help us to have more formal meetings or off-site retreats? If so, what should be the agenda?
- Do people on this team have different work styles? What disagreements does this cause among team members? How does having different styles increase our effectiveness?

CHAPTER FIVE

EFFECTIVE INFORMATION PROCESSING

How to Make Good Group Decisions

True Story: Management Meetings from Hell

Part One: The Problem

"Have you figured out a way to escape that management team meeting tomorrow?" asks Jeff, the director of information services in a government agency.

"No, I'm still working on it," replies Julie, one of the regional directors. "I tried to schedule a dental appointment, but my dentist was all booked up."

Alex, a new team member, overhears the conversation. "What's so bad about management team meetings? Personally, I'd rather go to any meeting than deal with a dentist."

"Just wait!" exclaims Julie. "You haven't been to one yet. I'd be willing to bet that after tomorrow you'll be trying to schedule some dental work yourself!"

By the end of the following day, Alex understands. Never in his career has he spent such a frustrating day. The meeting was scheduled from nine to twelve but lasted till four-thirty. They started with an agenda, but people kept bringing up other topics. Bill, the agency head, took a very passive role and in fact delegated the running of the meeting to the director of operations, who had no authority over the other team members.

Of the fourteen people on the team, some talked constantly, often interrupting one another, while others spoke not a word. One person fell asleep, and no one bothered to wake him up. Alex understands why the guy dozed off, since much of the discussion involved trivial matters that could be easily resolved outside the meeting. In fact, half the issues only involved three or four of the people there. No one seemed able to make a decision about anything, so most matters were continued till the next meeting. Every new idea presented was viciously attacked by one of the regional directors, Ray, who clearly felt he was more intelligent than anyone else and should be running the show. At one point, when Alex ventured a comment, Ray turned on him and said, "What do you think you know about all this, anyway? You just got here."

The next day Julie sees Alex in the break room.

"So what did you think of your first management team meeting?" she asks.

"I think I'll be calling my dentist before the next one!"

These management team meetings are obviously out of control. The group is too large, the leader seems to have abdicated all authority, and the team is running wild. Members are becoming increasingly frustrated but feel helpless to do anything about it. Both the work of the team and the relationships among members are suffering.

Making the Most of Your Meetings

As the pace of change escalates and the world becomes increasingly interconnected, the amount and variety of information management teams must acquire, process, and evaluate increases dramatically. Since the primary function of a management team is to make decisions, having access to necessary information is essential for success. Without a productive decision-making climate, however, the best information is virtually useless. Most management team decisions are made in meetings—of either the whole group or of subgroups—so team members must be able to turn meetings into effective information processing discussions. Researchers have often found decision making to be a multifaceted process (Schein, 1986; Argyris, 1987; Zander, 1994). In our study of management teams, four elements appeared to be necessary for an ideal information processing environment:

1. Clear objectives
2. Complete information
3. Different viewpoints
4. New ideas

The performance of the team's leader is also critical. Our research results indicated that management team leaders had a greater impact on information processing than on any other aspect of management team effectiveness. The final step in decision making, the move from discussion to action, represents the fifth and final success factor; it is discussed in the next chapter.

Clear Objectives

The desired outcomes of a decision-making discussion need to be clearly defined. Some meetings seem to be held just for the sake of having a meeting—because we always have staff meeting on Thursday morning, or because we like to talk, or because we're in a panic and don't know what to do. Before a meeting is scheduled, someone needs to figure out what the group is trying to accomplish. Team members also need to understand how the desired outcomes relate to larger organizational objectives, creating a bridge between information processing and strategic goals (the first success factor).

Sometimes the problem is more fundamental. The objectives of a meeting may not be clear because the role of the management group is not clear. In one not-for-profit organization run by a board of directors, the executive committee met quarterly. They discussed staff vacancies, set the agenda for the full board meeting, and reviewed various projects that the organization was undertaking—but made few decisions. Their role as a governing body had never been clearly articulated, so the purpose of their meetings was vague.

Complete Information

To make good decisions, a management team must have all necessary information available for consideration; otherwise, decisions are made based on an incomplete picture of the situation. A beverage manufacturer lost market share when a new line of soft drinks was packaged in a bottle that appealed to consumers in market tests—but was too large to fit into automobile cup holders. Information may be overlooked because the team has not fully explored the problem to determine what is needed.

In a desire to move quickly, managers sometimes act on available data, without considering all the consequences. A company that had historically developed customized products for the business market decided to begin making a mass-production item. The management team based the decision on marketing projections alone, without considering their manufacturing capability and lack of experience with mass production. After two years of product recalls and losses, they finally contracted with an off-shore manufacturer to produce the product. The marketing projections had been so seductive that the management team completely overlooked other important considerations. The missing information could have been easily accessed through the networking process, but no one identified the need for it.

Networking alone does not guarantee that information is actually considered when decisions are made, since team members may have knowledge that they choose not to disclose. One rather discouraging study of group decision making found that people tend to be reluctant to share information that is not already known to most group members (Larson, Foster-Fishman, and Keys, 1994). Information may be suppressed for a variety of reasons. Team leaders who don't know how to invite participation inadvertently discourage input by doing most of the talking and failing to ask questions. If certain team members dominate meetings, knowledge possessed by quieter participants is never heard. When relationships on a management team are competitive rather than supportive, managers may hoard information to avoid helping a rival. If team leaders strongly state their own views at the beginning of a discussion, members may be reluctant to offer conflicting opinions for fear of offending the person in power. For effective decision making, the team must first identify the information needed and then ensure that it is gathered and discussed.

Different Viewpoints

To be most effective, a management team must consider a variety of perspectives. First, all major functions in the organization have to be represented on the team; otherwise, a serious knowledge deficit exists. One company failed to include the head of the legal department on the management team. As a result, decisions often had to be reconsidered when attorneys raised potential legal problems. The customer perspective also needs to be represented on the team, usually through departments that have direct contact with customers.

The group also needs to be able to see different aspects of an issue, which tends to happen naturally if the members have a variety of work styles. Work style is a reflection of cognitive style, which has been defined as the habitual thinking strategies people use to organize information from their environment (McKenney and Kern, 1979). Many frameworks have been proposed to describe different cognitive styles (Bruner, 1956; De Bono, 1985; Harrison and Bramson, 1982; McKenney and Kern, 1979; Myers and McCaulley, 1985; VanGundy, 1984). Regardless of the framework used, however, there is general agreement that individuals tend to repeatedly use certain strategies of problem solving and decision making and that these strategies can be grouped into categories reflecting important differences in approach. Whether people see the big picture or the details, whether they focus on the present or the future, whether they consider facts or feelings, whether they prefer to plan carefully or act spontaneously . . . all this varies with their preferred style.

Researchers have found that style preferences affect both problem selection and problem solution. That is, the way we think determines which problems we choose to address and the specific solutions we tend to prefer (McKenney and

Kern, 1979). In deciding how to focus their efforts, people naturally seek out tasks compatible with their style. One person starting a business, for example, might begin by going out and visiting potential customers, while another might start by writing a brochure. Individuals with opposite styles may also view the same project as an entirely different type of problem. Let's suppose, for example, that two management teams are facing workforce reductions. The first team is composed of managers with an analytical, structured style, while members of the second tend to be people-oriented and flexible. Team one plans the workforce reduction by developing detailed procedures for determining who is to be laid off, calculating severance payments, and distributing layoff notices and final checks. Team two plans the workforce reduction by asking for volunteers, working out job-sharing arrangements, and obtaining career counseling for those who are leaving. In short, the work styles of management team members often determine the kind of decisions they make.

A team whose members have different work styles can view a problem from a variety of perspectives. The challenge, however, is to maintain supportive relationships despite the conflicts that disparate opinions naturally produce. Studies of groups with diverse perspectives have found that if destructive conflict is to be avoided, the decision-making process must be well managed either by the members or the leader (Zander, 1994). Diverse teams should also expect decision making to take longer, since more differences have to be resolved.

Teams whose members have similar work styles often make decisions more quickly, but they run the risk of ignoring important considerations. On one manufacturing team, all five managers had a tendency to focus on facts and immediate concerns. As a result, the group was good at data gathering and solving short-term problems but overlooked the potential reactions of people to their decisions and the long-range implications of their actions. In an extensive laboratory study of management teams, Belbin (1981) found that successful teams required a balance in problem-solving styles. Whenever unbalanced teams were constructed, the predictable result was a shortcoming in performance. Teams composed largely of critical thinkers, for example, spent too much time in debate and did not develop creative solutions. Those made up of conservative, disciplined, and practical "company workers" lacked ideas and resisted change. If team members think alike, the group must make a special effort to bring in different perspectives.

New Ideas

When faced with challenges, management teams must avoid knee-jerk responses and consider a variety of solutions. To foster a culture of creativity, team members have to develop appreciation for novel ideas when solving both large and small problems. Unfortunately, new ideas often fail to thrive, for a variety of reasons. Management team members are often analytical thinkers, who have a natural talent for seeing what's wrong. This ability can prevent serious errors in judgment, but it may also kill off creative approaches before they can be seriously considered. On teams with highly critical members, new ideas may be attacked so strenuously that people are discouraged from expressing them at all. Ideas may also be suppressed if leaders consciously or unconsciously impose their own views. Finally, proposing a new idea may result in more work for the contributor. Suggesting a new approach to one CEO meant he would automatically ask for extensive data analysis to evaluate the idea. So his management team members, who were already overworked, never made any new suggestions. If management teams are to succeed in a rapidly changing world, members need to be sure that new approaches and suggestions are encouraged, shared, and, when appropriate, implemented.

Role of the Leader

In our research, management team leaders were found to have more influence on information processing than on the other four success factors, probably because they exercise a high degree of control over the setting in which decisions are made. Team leaders have more control over team meetings than they do over the organization's environment, upper management's goals, group networking contacts, team member relationships, or the manner in which decisions are carried out. In meetings, the leader can encourage or discourage discussion, welcome or criticize new ideas, invite or reject different opinions, clarify objectives or leave them vague, and keep the meeting on track or let it wander off course. Other studies have found that leaders help group members understand different points of view (Sessa, 1994) and provide "route markers" to help a group measure progress toward a goal (Leavitt and Lipman-Blumen, 1995).

Viewed in the context of the four components of an effective decision-making process (clear objectives, consideration of important information, expression of different viewpoints, and encouragement of new ideas), leadership seems to emerge as the central element. The leader is likely to be the source of goal definition for the team, and likely to control both the flow of information and the degree of open communication in team meetings. A leader's style and approach greatly influence any meeting—full staff meetings, conferences with upper management, or discussions with small groups of team members. Since most management team decisions are made in meetings, the leader usually has considerable impact on the decision-making process.

Strategies for Group Decision Making

Effective information processing occurs whenever objectives are clear, all important information is considered, different viewpoints are expressed, and new ideas are encouraged. Since most management team decisions are made in meetings, the strategies discussed in this chapter focus on ways to increase meeting effectiveness. Because team leaders have a great deal of influence over how meetings are conducted, many of the suggestions below are directed to them. Leaders are often able to improve their decision-making meetings through better planning, increased participation, and greater control of discussions.

Strategy One: Be Sure That Your Team Is Composed of the Right People

To have an effective management team, all necessary people must be included, and all unnecessary people must be excluded. Be sure that the critical functions in your organization are represented on the team. If not, then add team members from those areas that are missing. Also be sure that your customers' perspective is represented through team members whose departments have direct customer contact. This applies to teams with internal customers as well as those who serve external customers.

The ideal size for any decision-making team is no larger than seven or eight people. If your management team has more members than that, consider whether your organizational structure is too flat. Some consolidation of functions might be needed to reduce the number of people reporting to the team leader. Although unnecessary layers of bureaucracy are to be strenuously avoided, organizations should not be flattened to the point where upper-level managers have a cumbersome number of direct reports. If a management team gets too large, effective group decision making becomes almost impossible.

Should removing people not be politically or organizationally feasible, consider creating a two-level management team structure by appointing a smaller group to function as a decision-making body. In one organization, this small group is referred as the operating committee, while the larger group is called the management team. In other organizations, the small group is called the administrative team, the senior staff group, or the executive committee. This strategy allows decisions to be made or proposed by a group small enough to have thorough discussions in a reasonable time. But be sure that the smaller group shares information with and receives input from the larger group.

Strategy Two: Clearly Define the Desired Outcome of Your Meetings

Plan your meetings backwards; that is, focus on the desired results before preparing the agenda. If the goals of a meeting have not been clearly communicated, people tend to talk about whatever is on their mind at the moment, making the meeting less productive. For most management team meetings, the primary tasks are to make decisions and share information. To focus on outcomes, members need to understand exactly what decisions they are making and why information is being shared. Clearly separating decision making and information sharing on the agenda often makes the meeting more efficient.

Focusing on outcomes also helps clarify the type of meeting you need, since meetings with different goals need to be structured differently. If the primary purpose is to generate creative ideas, for example, the meeting should be held in a relaxed atmosphere where people are encouraged to blurt out any inspiration that comes to mind. A meeting to make a critical business decision would have a more structured format. To identify desired results, simply try to answer the question, "What do we want to accomplish by the end of this meeting?"

Finally, consider whether a meeting is actually necessary. Some outcomes can be achieved without the time and expense of calling a group together. One management committee charged with running a statewide training program met annually to plan the next year's offerings. They spent a full day creating the training schedule for the upcoming year—even though this task could have been easily accomplished by faxing all information to a central person, who would then fax back a draft schedule for review.

Strategy Three: Have an Agenda for All Formal Meetings

Determining desired outcomes—what information needs to be shared and what decisions need to be made—also makes it easier to develop the agenda for the meeting. An agenda provides a road map for the group to follow: a list of topics and the order in which they are to be discussed. The following suggestions can help team leaders create a useful agenda:

• List the desired outcomes of the meeting on the agenda. Team members need to clearly understand what you expect to accomplish. Phrasing agenda items in terms of desired results rather than topic is often helpful; listing "Budget reduction of 10 percent" conveys what is expected more clearly than "Budget issues" or "Budget discussion." Routine meetings usually have certain continuing objectives. Regular staff meetings, for example, often have an ongoing goal of providing members with up-to-date information about the business or the activities of other departments. This item might be listed as "Internal networking."

• Put the most important agenda items first. Some team leaders like to start meetings with "quick items that we can get out of the way," but this strategy hardly ever evolves as planned. At the beginning of a meeting, people are at a high energy level and ready to talk. Any topic brought up at this point, no matter how trivial, is likely to engender discussion. Use this initial energy for your most important topics and save lesser items for the end, when people are tired and ready to leave. In fact, if you want to limit discussion on a topic, putting it right before lunch or at the end of the day almost guarantees a short conversation.

• Give team members an opportunity to contribute items for the agenda. Surprise topics are then less likely to emerge during the meeting, and you can better control the timing of discussions.

• Omit any items that involve only a small number of team members. Meet with them separately to discuss these topics instead of wasting everyone else's time.

• Set a reasonable time limit for the meeting, and communicate it in advance. People are less likely to bring up unrelated topics if they know the time is limited.

• Distribute the agenda and any other important information before the meeting. Team members then have a chance to think about the upcoming discussion and determine what information might be useful. Those members with a more introverted and reflective style may particularly appreciate the opportunity to review information in advance.

Strategy Four: Relate Team Decisions to Larger Organizational Goals

Team leaders usually have a broader view than other management team members. The president of a company has more contacts with customers, shareholders, financial analysts, the media, and other external influences than anyone else on the executive team. The head of a department has greater access to higher management and to other department managers than the rest of the team does. To create an effective information processing climate, the team leader needs to use that broader perspective to help the group understand the context in which decisions are made and the consequences that decisions have. Team members need to know how the decisions they make contribute to their organization's success.

Strategy Five: Agree on Meeting Guidelines

For any group that meets on a regular basis, a set of meeting guidelines can make the time together more productive and pleasant. Meeting guidelines represent the group's agreement about how the members want to work together, including both task-related issues (such as having complete information before making decisions or showing up for meetings on time) and relationship issues (such as listening when others are speaking and treating everyone with respect). Meeting guidelines should be developed by the group and treated seriously. Post them in the meeting room so that the team can refer to them if necessary.

Strategy Six: Keep the Meeting under Control

No one wants a management team leader to become an all-powerful meeting dictator, but members do expect the leader to stay in control. The challenge lies in balancing efficiency and participation. Having identified desired outcomes for the meeting, the leader can employ them to gauge the usefulness of any discussion. If the conversation appears to be wandering, simply ask, "Is this discussion moving us closer to our goals for this meeting?" Having an agenda and meeting guidelines also helps in maintaining control, since they provide a reference point for the group. Referring to one of these documents is often all it takes to get a group back on track. These suggestions can help team leaders keep the meeting under control:

• Start on time. People learn quickly, so if you get in the habit of starting late, they get in the habit of arriving late. If your group has already developed a late-arrival habit, breaking it may take a little time. First, announce your intention to change your behavior, telling members that from now on meetings will begin at the appointed hour and that you expect them to be on time. Then stick with it! Keep in mind that they may not alter their behavior immediately, so you must start all subsequent meetings on time, even if only one or two people are present. You may feel a little silly talking with just one person, but do it anyway. During this transition, you probably want to make your first agenda item one that doesn't require everyone's participation.

• Follow the agenda, deviating only for important issues. An agenda should provide a road map, but not a railroad track; you should feel free to venture down unexpected side roads that could help you achieve your goals.

• Keep the discussion focused on one topic at a time. Staying on track is easier if your group is made up of linear thinkers, who usually prefer to discuss each item in order. Nonlinear thinkers quickly associate one idea with another and tend to jump from topic to topic. This makes for interesting, but not always relevant, discussion and presents a real barrier to reaching a decision.

• Create an issues list, where you can "park" topics for later consideration. If important matters arise that are unrelated to the topic at hand, list them on a white board or flipchart until they can be addressed. The issues list may include topics for a later meeting or matters to be discussed with people who are not present. This parking strategy is also useful in managing the freewheeling discussions of a nonlinear group.

• During long meetings, plan scheduled breaks to keep people from wandering in and out. Team members may be distracted by pressing phone calls, demands imposed by employees, or biological needs that must be attended to. If they know a break is coming, however, they can usually wait.

• If an issue involves only a small number of members, arrange a time to discuss it after the meeting. One human resource management team was held hostage in a staff meeting for thirty minutes while their vice president and director of safety debated changes in certain regulations. Since none of the other six team members were affected by the issue, this discussion wasted a total of three person-hours of work.

• End on time. Knowing that time for discussion is limited usually creates self-imposed discipline among team members. As with starting times, ending on time is a habit to be developed through consistent enforcement. Obviously, meetings should not be abruptly terminated if critical information is being discussed, but placing the most important agenda items first usually prevents this problem.

Strategy Seven: Identify All the Information Needed for a Fully Informed Decision

Whenever the group must make an important decision, determine in advance the information that should be considered. Constructing a decision tree can be a useful exercise. In its simplest form, the decision tree (shown in Figure 5.1) is a way for the group to list all information that should be collected and evaluated.

FIGURE 5.1. DECISION TREE.

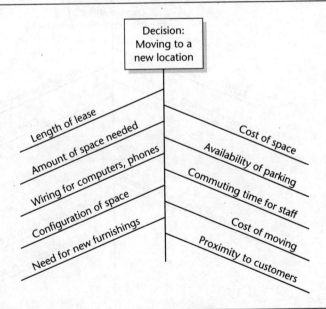

Note: This example shows information needed by a management team deciding whether to move to a new location.

An expanded format (shown in Figure 5.2) sequences the questions to be answered in the decision-making process and indicates the information needed at each step. By using large Post-its, a group can create the initial decision tree and then reorganize the information into categories.

The process of constructing a decision tree encourages all team members to thoroughly explore the problem and helps ensure that critical information is not overlooked.

FIGURE 5.2. EXPANDED DECISION TREE.

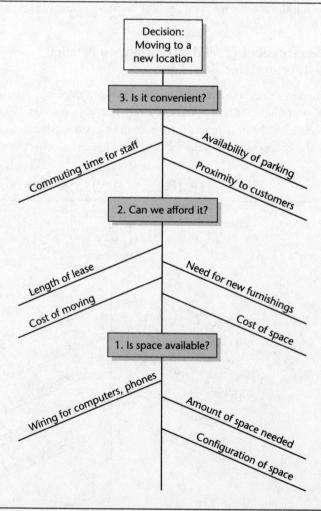

Note: This is the sequence of questions that need to be answered to make the moving decision of Figure 5.1.

Strategy Eight: Encourage Everyone to Share Information

To create an effective decision-making climate, the team leader must encourage participation by all members. First, leaders must avoid dominating the discussion themselves. Try to develop the habit of asking questions instead of making statements; be sure to wait long enough for people to answer. (If you habitually answer your own questions, people quickly get the message about whose opinion interests you most.) For some managers, making inquiries comes naturally, but others find it a difficult habit to develop. If you are not a natural question-asker, jot down some questions in advance for each topic on the agenda, and then use them to stimulate discussion during the meeting. It may take a while for questions to become part of your usual style, but the payoff is well worth the effort.

Once team leaders have their own talkative impulses under control, the next challenge is balancing participation by team members. Some people make decisions by talking them through, while others prefer to think about things quietly before having a discussion. In meetings, the talkers are more likely to control the conversation. If team members take too much airtime, the team leader can usually shut them down politely by saying something like, "I really appreciate your views on this subject, Fred. Now let me see how some of the others feel about it." If this approach doesn't work, the leader needs to take the talkative team member aside, express concern that some people are not being heard, and ask for help in encouraging others to participate.

People who talk too much can be a problem, but so can people who hardly talk at all. Several techniques help draw out quiet team members:

- Structure the discussion so that each person takes a turn sharing information or making comments.
- Have team members write down ideas before discussing them, giving quieter members a chance to think. Use large Post-its if you want to display the ideas.
- Watch quiet members for nonverbal signs that they have something they would like to contribute.
- Periodically ask quiet people for their thoughts or ideas. If they have nothing to say, however, don't make them feel uncomfortable.

Strategy Nine: Ensure That Different Viewpoints Are Considered

On a management team, all critical functions in the organization must be represented if the group is to make good decisions. Assuming that the team does include managers of all major departments, the viewpoint of certain functions may still be lost if those team members are reluctant to speak up. Leaders and members need to balance participation in discussions, making efforts to draw out quieter members and solicit their opinions in areas relevant to their function.

The team also needs to compensate for any cognitive styles that are not represented among team members. A work style analysis can help determine the degree of similarity in how members think and approach problems. (Work style analysis was discussed in Chapter Four.) Where strong similarities create weaknesses for the team, the group should develop strategies to compensate. Some teams modify their meeting guidelines to encourage thinking outside their usual style. This goal is often accomplished by asking specific questions during the decision-making process. The manufacturing team mentioned previously, whose members were all present-focused and factually oriented, forced themselves to regularly ask two questions and thoroughly explore the answers: "What could be the long-term results of this decision?" and "How will customers, employees, and others react to this decision?"

Strategy Ten: Encourage the Expression of New Ideas

Some teams generate so many new ideas that they have trouble deciding which ones to pursue, but most management groups have the opposite problem. The primary reason is that management work, as discussed earlier, tends to attract analytical people with a bias toward action. This is, of course, a broad generalization, more likely to be true in business organizations and less so in human service or creative environments. Teams whose members have an analytical, action-oriented style are less likely to produce novel approaches to problems. Analytical people tend to be critical thinkers who easily find flaws in new ideas and often discard them before they can be fully explored. People with a bias toward action want to move quickly, which usually means choosing a familiar path. Taking the time to explore the pros and cons of different ideas makes them impatient.

These suggestions help create a climate where new ideas can survive:

- Suspend critical comments during discussion of new ideas. For important issues, hold formal brainstorming sessions designed solely to generate as many new ideas as possible. Use brainstorming guidelines as ground rules in these meetings (quantity of ideas is better than quality; people should build on the ideas of others; no critical comments are allowed). Books on creative problem solving describe brainstorming and other idea-generation techniques in detail.
- Create a meeting guideline that requires members to say what they like about an idea before they can say what they don't like.
- Develop the habit of asking such questions as "What other ideas might work?" "How else could we approach this problem?" "What would be the benefits of that idea?"

- Turn problems around and ask the question backwards. For example, instead of asking "How can we get people to come to our store?" ask "How can we take our products where people are?" A similar technique is to explore the problem by discussing its opposite, in this case asking, "How could we keep people out of our store?" Answers such as "by building a fence" or "by putting bars on the door" highlight the importance of having an inviting and accessible entrance.
- See what you can learn from organizations unlike your own. One clothing company with a large chain of stores decided to study how products with well-known brand names, like soft drinks or toothpaste, were sold. "The most obvious thing," said the clothing company president, "was that you could buy these products in a lot of different places." The retail company decided to change its marketing strategy and supplement its own stores with other sales outlets.
- Look for best practices in your own industry. If someone has already solved your problem, there is no need for you to do so.
- Be sure to express appreciation for new ideas when they are presented. And be sure to use them whenever possible, since seeing an idea put into action is probably the greatest reward for the person who conceived it.

Strategy Eleven: Help the Group Reach Consensus on Important Issues

Use decision-making techniques to help the group reach consensus on important issues. Traditional voting is usually a poor decision-making strategy, since it easily polarizes people and splits the group into two camps of winners and losers.

One useful technique for consensus testing asks members to use a rating scale to indicate how close they are to agreeing with a decision. A point on the scale is chosen to represent sufficient buy-in for the group to proceed with the decision. On a 1 to 10 scale, for example, the buy-in point might be 7. Members then indicate their level of agreement verbally or in writing. Members below the buy-in point are asked to discuss their concerns, so that compromises can be made. When everyone reaches the buy-in level, the decision is considered final.

Multivoting is another method often used to narrow down alternatives and avoid traditional voting. These are the steps:

1. Generate a list of options or ideas on a flipchart or white board.
2. Have the group agree on criteria for narrowing down options.
3. Eliminate options not meeting the criteria.
4. Identify each remaining option with a letter.
5. Ask each person to vote for a specific number of options (always more than one).
6. Have members write down the letters of options they prefer.
7. Ask members to call out their letters in round-robin fashion.

8. Select the options with the most votes for further consideration.
9. Explore pros and cons of the remaining options.
10. To make a final decision, use another round of multivoting or a consensus rating scale.

A variation of this process has members use stick-on dots to indicate their votes. After options are written on flipchart paper, each member is given a certain number of dots and asked to put them under the preferred options. This method allows members to get up and move around, briefly breaking the tedium of prolonged sitting. These and other techniques help focus discussion and move the group toward a decision.

Strategy Twelve: End Your Meetings with Action Items

Meetings should begin with desired outcomes and end with actions to be taken. Having a list of action steps forms a bridge from information processing to the fifth success factor, focused action. One reason to be specific about plans at the end of a meeting is to avoid miscommunication. If we simply assume that expectations are clear when the meeting ends, we may be surprised when something important doesn't get done. Sometimes agenda items are discussed at length with no action ever agreed upon. Ending with action items forces a group to go beyond discussion and decide what needs to happen next.

Here are some suggestions for ending management team meetings productively:

- Summarize what happened during the meeting. Be sure that everyone has the same understanding about decisions that were reached.
- Create a next-steps list of actions to be taken as a result of the meeting. Designate the person responsible for each action item, and be sure that expectations are clearly described. Specify time lines where appropriate.
- If this meeting is one of a series, be sure everyone knows what must be done before the next meeting.

Action planning is discussed in greater detail in the next chapter.

Overcoming Barriers to Effective Information Processing

Most problems with information processing can be resolved through better management of meetings. In this section, we consider problems that can prevent management teams from using information effectively:

1. Discussions drift away from the agenda.
2. Meetings drag on and on.
3. Decisions are made too quickly.
4. A few members dominate group discussions.
5. No one talks much in meetings.
6. Team members think too much alike.
7. The group is too critical of ideas and suggestions.
8. The team is not very creative.
9. Managers tend to hoard information.

Problem One: Discussions Drift Away from the Agenda

If discussions consistently get off track, the problem is not with the group but with the leader, who has lost control of the meeting. Leaders often have a tough time deciding how much control to exercise, since they don't want to stifle discussion. The most effective leaders exercise moderate control: too much limits ideas and information, and too little prevents desired outcomes from being accomplished. If your group frequently wanders off the topic, the leader is probably erring on the side of too much participation in an effort not to become dictatorial. Even though team members are creating this problem, they may be quite frustrated and would probably appreciate being reined in a bit.

This problem may also indicate that the group has talkative team members with a nonlinear style of thinking, who naturally tend to jump quickly from one thought to another and meander down totally new paths. If the leader shares their style, changing the team's meeting habits may require considerable self-discipline.

Suggestions for action:

1. Continually refer back to the goals and agenda for the meeting if the discussion starts to stray off course. Consider posting this information where it can be easily seen by everyone. Asking "How does this discussion relate to our goals for this meeting?" often brings the group back to the topic at hand.

2. Refer to the meeting guidelines as a reminder of how group members said they wanted to work together. If none of the guidelines addresses the issue of frequent digression, the group may wish to add a statement about sticking to the agenda. If the group has not developed meeting guidelines, then do so.

3. Use the issues list to capture worthy digressions while encouraging the group to stay on track. A group member who is particularly good at structuring discussion might take responsibility for parking topics that get the group off track.

4. Cut off irrelevant discussions respectfully, saying something like "I know this is an interesting topic, but since we only have a limited amount of time, we should probably get back to our agenda."

5. If members are having side discussions, ask them to resolve the issue at a later time. If you get into a side discussion yourself, ask the other party to talk with you after the meeting, or arrange a later appointment.

6. If team members tend to spend too much meeting time on personal conversations, try to build some social interaction into the meeting plan, especially if these managers seldom have the opportunity to talk face-to-face. Scheduling a group meal before or after the meeting provides social time, helps build relationships, and reduces members' need to chat during the meeting. One management group that met quarterly always held a dinner the night before the meeting for this purpose.

Problem Two: Meetings Drag On and On

Some groups stay on track but discuss each topic interminably. Meetings can drag on for numerous reasons. Perhaps the group is too large; one management team of fourteen people could never complete a staff meeting in less than a full day. Or a leader who finds it difficult to eliminate alternatives and move toward a decision may not structure the discussion well. One CEO had a need for information that bordered on addiction. He found it almost impossible to stop considering possibilities and choose a course of action, so his management team meetings often lasted one or two days and produced few decisions. A clear case of analysis paralysis! Finally, some leaders do not want to appear rude by cutting off discussion, so they allow people to talk until they run out of things to say.

Suggestions for action:

1. If your team is too large, consider reducing the size. Ideally, a management team should have no more than seven or eight members. (See strategy one in this chapter for a discussion of team size.)

2. If team size is not an issue, assess the behavior of the team to determine the source of the problem. If team members are having interminable discussions, the leader needs to exercise more control in meetings. Leaders who contribute to the problem need to exercise more self-discipline. Doing an objective self-assessment is difficult, so consider having a professional facilitator or someone from another department observe your meetings and provide some feedback.

3. Set time limits for meetings and stick to them. Adhering to a schedule is difficult at first, but persistence is the key. (Refer to strategy six for a discussion of starting and ending on time.) You may also need to set time limits for the discussion of

each topic. Use longer intervals at first to help team members adjust to the discipline of a schedule while gradually learning to shorten their discussions. Actually writing the time limits for topics on the agenda makes them easier to enforce.

4. Get the group's agreement that everyone needs to help resolve this problem. Develop a list of solutions and incorporate them into your meeting guidelines.

5. Identify topics that tend to generate prolonged, unnecessary discussions and put them at the end of the meeting. People have less energy then and are getting anxious to leave.

6. Assign complex issues to a smaller group for further exploration. Ask this group to come back with the information needed to make a decision or a recommendation for what the decision should be. Once the group's work is finished, put the item on the agenda again.

7. If the group has difficulty reaching agreement, use the multivoting process to help the team narrow down options more quickly; then use a consensus rating scale to structure the discussion. These techniques are discussed under strategy eleven.

Problem Three: Decisions Are Made Too Quickly

Some groups proceed too slowly, but others move too fast. Rapid decision making is valuable in a crisis, but it can cause problems at other times if critical information is overlooked. Management teams fall into this trap for several reasons. Time pressures at work drive managers to minimize the amount of time they spend in meetings. Or the leader communicates, intentionally or unintentionally, that the decision has already been made, discouraging members from further discussion. Or team members share a strongly action-oriented work style, characterized by emphasis on activity and lack of deliberation or reflection. Whatever the cause, these teams sometimes find that their quick decisions lead to unpleasant surprises on implementation. If your group appears to be rushing through the agenda with undue haste, you need to slow down a bit.

Suggestions for action:

1. Separate critical decisions from less important ones. Discuss significant issues at the beginning of the meeting when people are less likely to feel time pressures. Allot a certain amount of time for discussion, and encourage the group to use it.

2. Use a decision tree (described in strategy seven of this chapter). This method forces the group to consider all categories of information that are relevant to the decision. Just be sure to spend enough time on the decision tree!

3. If your management team appears to have an action-oriented work style, try using a different approach when complex decisions need to be made. A work

style analysis (discussed in Chapter Four) can help the group understand the implications of the team style. First, team members should specifically identify the times when they need to shift "out of style." Then they must decide how to make the shift. Some of the other suggestions in this section can help, as does the habit of asking standard questions during decision making:

- What additional information would be useful in making this decision?
- Who will be affected by this decision? How are they likely to react?
- Who else needs to be part of the decision-making process?
- What might the long-term consequences of this decision be?
- Who needs to be informed about this decision? How should they be told?

4. Learn to ask questions. Learn to listen to the answers. Learn not to punish people for expressing opinions. These habits are important for all team members but especially critical for the leader. On one management team, the president, who had a rather autocratic style, would talk to managers in meetings without ever asking for their thoughts, ideas, or opinions. When he did ask a question, he would either answer it himself or give his own opinion before much discussion had taken place. People who disagreed with him often got blistered in return, so new team members quickly learned the value of agreement. Needless to say, there were few in-depth decision-making discussions on this team.

5. If you are the team leader, assess your leadership style in team meetings. Do you typically go into decision-making discussions with your mind made up? Could this be limiting discussion of alternatives? Stating your own opinion at the beginning of a discussion inevitably influences the response of your managers, so if you want them to explore a topic, reserve the expression of your own views for later. Don't even mention that you have an opinion until the discussion has ended. Who knows? By then, you may have changed your mind.

6. If you work in a demanding environment where people feel constantly pressured, go off-site to discuss truly significant issues. Getting away from phone calls, faxes, hallway conversations, and assistants with messages helps the team focus attention on the problem at hand and affords time to consider all aspects of a decision.

Problem Four: A Few Members Dominate Group Discussions

Balanced participation is an important part of effective information processing. If one or two people do all the talking, the result is lost information and biased decisions. In this situation, the group needs to reestablish balanced participation without being rude to the talkative members or intimidating the quiet ones. This change can be initiated by either the team leader or other team members.

Suggestions for action:

1. In a polite way, indicate that others need a chance to speak. Some sample statements:

- To a team member who wants to be an expert: "Joe, I know that you are very knowledgeable about this subject, but I think that we need to consider everyone's opinions."
- To a team member who shows intense emotional reactions: "Chris, I appreciate your strong feelings on this subject, and I believe I understand your point of view. I think we need to see how the other team members feel about it, though."
- To a team member who has told a long personal story: "Thanks for sharing that example, Jim. Now, what do the rest of you think about this situation?"
- To someone who seems ready to start a long personal story: "That sounds as though it would be an interesting example, Meg, and I hate to cut you off, but I'm afraid we're a little short of time."
- To two team members who keep exchanging opinions while ignoring the rest of the group: "Jane and Fred have certainly had a good debate on this issue, and I'm sure we've all learned a lot from their discussion. What do the rest of you think?"
- To someone who has spoken, but you have no idea what was meant and don't want to find out: "That's interesting, Andy. Thanks. Anyone else have an idea?"

2. You may need to be more direct if the dominant member continues after a polite warning: "Mark, I know that you have a lot of strong opinions, but I think we need to be sure that we hear from everyone on this issue. I'd be glad to talk with you further after the meeting."

3. If the problem persists, the team leader needs to discuss the issue with the talkative member(s) in private. Indicate that you appreciate their participation but fear that the ideas of quieter members are being lost. Ask them to please notice how much they are talking compared to others and to modify their participation accordingly. Tell them that if you observe a problem in the future, you will gently remind them by asking for others' opinions.

4. Lack of participation is a two-way street, of course. For some members to dominate, others have to hold back. Another approach, therefore, is to draw out the quiet members, keeping in mind that you just want to access their ideas, not put them on the spot. Several suggestions for doing so are listed under strategy eight in this chapter.

5. When making important decisions, consider having a more structured discussion to improve balanced participation. Numerous methods can be used. Have team members submit written ideas before the meeting and then present

a summary to the group for reaction. Or simply go around the room and have team members take turns giving their opinions. Breaking into small groups often generates more discussion. Each group can use Post-its or flipchart paper to write down the members' views.

Problem Five: No One Talks Much in Meetings

Some groups are simply quieter than others. If you have a strongly extraverted style and your group is more introverted, you may feel at times that you are babbling away to a sea of blank faces. One extraverted accounting manager had three introverted supervisors reporting to her. "Whenever I throw out a problem and ask what they think we should do, they all just sit there and look at me," she complained. "I don't know what to do with them!" Actually, they were just thinking about the problem before they talked about it, which is how introverts operate. The manager expected them to respond more quickly because extraverts tend to do most of their thinking out loud.

The group may also be quiet because the team leader is dominating the discussion. A college professor whose classes consisted of continuous lecturing once said to a group of students, "I'd like to have more class participation, but no one ever has anything to say." He didn't realize that they said nothing because he never asked them any questions. Some managers fall into the same trap.

Suggestions for action:

1. Get in the habit of asking questions to draw out other team members. After you ask a question, pause and wait for an answer. For talkative people, these pauses seem to last about half an hour, but wait it out anyway. If you get no answer after ten or twenty seconds, maybe you asked the wrong question. Try another one. And remember that open-ended questions tend to elicit more response than closed questions, which can be answered with one word.

2. Send out information to review before the meeting. Indicate the goals to be accomplished, specific questions to be addressed, and decisions to be made. Not everyone will review the information, but this gives more reflective members time to think before they have to talk.

3. If you have more than three people on the team, break into small groups for discussion. Most people who seldom talk in a large group participate in small groups. This tactic almost always generates more conversation.

4. Ask team members to write down thoughts and ideas individually before having a group discussion. Post-its can be used to organize or categorize comments. (You are probably beginning to see that Post-its are quite useful for people who lead meetings.)

Problem Six: Team Members Think Too Much Alike

The more similarities team members share, the more their views are likely to be the same. Managers who grew up in the same town, spent twenty years in the same company, have the same work style, and are all white men tend to see situations the same way. Even if they are brilliant, their decisions suffer from this limited perspective. One danger of too much similarity is that managers lose touch with critical constituencies. The top management team in one government agency fit this homogeneous profile almost exactly. Over time, they became so insular that they lost touch with their customers, their employees, the media, and the taxpayers. After a series of bad decisions, the head of the agency was asked to retire, two top managers were demoted, and the entire department was reorganized.

The management team is the central operating group in a complex system, making decisions that affect many people inside and outside the organization. If this central management team is not representative of the larger and more diverse system of employees, customers, and others, then the team is liable to make unwise decisions from the members' limited perspective. Imagine a group of men deciding on the content of a women's magazine, or a group of city-dwellers designing farm equipment. A management team needs to be as diverse as its major constituencies.

Suggestions for action:

1. Talk about the similarities in the group and identify possible pitfalls. If all members have spent their careers in the same company, they may lack ideas about alternative ways of operating. If everyone is female, the group may lack information about the reactions of male employees or customers. If the group members have spent their lives in the Midwest, they may not understand customers in other parts of the country. If everyone has a strongly action-oriented work style, the tendency may be to solve problems before adequately exploring them.

2. Develop some techniques to compensate for weaknesses created by the group's similarities. The all-woman team may want to solicit men's reactions to certain decisions or ideas. The managers who all grew up in the same company can visit other organizations as they consider a new project or a major change. On one management team, members identified themselves as people who liked to discuss long-range plans and big ideas. No one on the team was naturally inclined to focus on concrete details. This weakness in style was clearly illustrated when team members arrived at a hotel for an off-site meeting and found that no one had thought to book a meeting room. This is a group that needs to develop the habit of asking, "Are there any details we haven't covered?"

3. Stress the importance of networking contacts with outside groups. Broadening the team's perspective through interaction with customers, professional associations, other companies, and community groups helps them develop fresh ideas.

4. Invite outside people to meetings. Some management groups ask an employee representative (not in the union sense) to sit in on management team meetings. Customers are asked to participate in discussions of products or services. Experts in various fields can broaden a group's knowledge. People from similar organizations are invited to talk about a particular aspect of their operations.

5. Whenever you have the opportunity, fill management team vacancies with people who provide some diversity in background and work style. If your organization has a long history of promoting from within, recruiting managers from outside can bring an infusion of new ideas and perspectives. People looking at an organization with fresh eyes almost always ask useful questions and suggest new approaches.

Problem Seven: The Group Is Too Critical of Ideas and Suggestions

In both individuals and groups, every strength has a corresponding weakness. A management team with superior analytical ability finds that critical thinking skills are helpful for many tasks but harmful to development of new ideas. New ideas are somewhat like blades of spring grass: when nourished and given room to grow, they can produce beautiful results; but when starved and crushed, they die. Someone proposing a new thought may not be sure if it is really worthy. If the first response is, "Well, that will never work!" the person is likely to abandon the suggestion and may be reluctant to introduce ideas in the future. Overly critical groups run the risk of relying on safe, predictable solutions to problems and missing valuable opportunities.

Suggestions for action:

1. The first step is to help group members realize what they are doing. Share the observation that you fear useful ideas are getting lost in an overabundance of critical thinking. Be sure to stress that critical thinking is a valuable skill but one that simply needs to be suspended as new approaches are first considered.

2. Conducting a work style analysis (Chapter Four) helps the group understand their team style more clearly.

3. Hold meetings devoted solely to producing new ideas, with no criticism allowed. Attending entire meetings in which no negative comments are allowed helps team members break the critical-thinking habit.

4. Review the suggestions under strategy ten, "Encourage the Expression of New Ideas," earlier in this chapter.

5. Sometimes criticism is a symptom of deeper problems on the team. If you suspect that negative remarks reflect underlying anger among team members, then your real concern should be with the state of team relationships. Review the appropriate suggestions for improving relationships in Chapter Four.

Problem Eight: The Team Is Not Very Creative

When given encouragement, most people can be creative within their area of expertise. The director of a large organization once said to a consultant, "You know, I never have any ideas." "Of course you do," replied the consultant. "You just have them about things that you're familiar with." The director had plenty of ideas about how to change policies, procedures, and operations, but he never thought of these as "creative." We can't all be Picasso or Mozart, but most of us can think of ways to improve our work.

Suggestions for action:

1. If you are a natural "idea person" and other team members are not, some team discussions may be frustrating for you. Recognize that these managers have a different set of strengths from your own, so coming up with new concepts is not as natural for them as it is for you.

2. Sometimes less creative people are simply concrete thinkers: they relate more naturally to facts, figures, and objects than to concepts and abstractions. When working with concrete thinkers, be specific about what you want to accomplish. Asking them to draw three different plans for an office layout usually produces better results than saying, "OK, what do we want to do with the new office?"

3. Get a book or two on creative thinking and suggest using some of the techniques described. Recognize that for concrete thinkers this is work; don't expect them to share your excitement initially at the prospect of generating novel solutions.

4. Encourage people to make networking contacts that expose them to new ideas. Sometimes people find it easier to recognize a good idea than to think of one on their own.

5. To foster creativity, get away from the office. Spending the day at a conference center, especially one located in a natural setting, helps people relax and loosen up their thinking. Being creative is difficult when your mind is occupied with all the daily demands of your job.

6. If you are the team leader, be sure that you are not imposing your own ideas before giving group members time to develop their own. If your mind appears to be made up, they see no point in making new suggestions.

7. Use the suggestions of team members whenever possible. Actually implementing their new approaches is the best way to encourage people to share ideas.

8. Review the suggestions under strategy ten earlier in this chapter.

Problem Nine: Managers Tend to Hoard Information

If team members are intentionally keeping information to themselves, a relationship problem is the most likely cause. Typically, hoarding information means that a power struggle of some sort is under way. If managers are competing for raises or promotions, they may try to avoid aiding the competition. Angry team members hoard information so as not to help an adversary. One management team member felt that she was in danger of being eclipsed by a new arrival. To protect her position, she intentionally did not share any information with the newcomer about the company culture or the preferences of top management.

Suggestions for action:

1. If you can pinpoint the nature of the relationship problem, the suggestions in Chapter Four may be of some help.

2. If the team member hoarding information has useful expertise, acknowledge the value of this person as a resource to the department and discuss how sharing knowledge can make the entire department more effective.

3. If you are the team leader, talk with team members, as a group or individually, about the importance of complete information in making good decisions. Share your observations about information that has been withheld, and clearly communicate your expectations about information that should be shared in the future. Whenever you identify situations in which team members need to share knowledge or expertise, either direct them to do so or hold meetings where information sharing is identified as the primary goal.

True Story: Management Meetings from Hell

Part Two: The Solution

Bill, the leader of the dysfunctional management team, is ready to tear his hair out. After futile attempts to solve the problem himself, he finally calls in Lynn, a management consultant.

"I just can't take many more meetings like this!" he exclaims. "Can you do something?"

"Possibly," she replies. "I'll need some time to learn more about the problem."

For the next few weeks, Lynn interviews team members and observes team meetings. She meets with Bill to discuss her findings and presents her observations to the group, recommending a plan of action. To improve their meetings, she suggests that the team take the following steps:

- Have Bill run the meetings instead of delegating the responsibility to the director of operations.

- Develop a set of meeting guidelines to describe desirable behavior.
- Prepare an agenda for each meeting with time limits for each topic.
- Appoint the most structured member to help keep the team on track.
- Conduct a work style analysis to identify the team profile.
- Develop strategies to compensate for team weaknesses.
- Create a survey based on their meeting guidelines to evaluate their progress.

Privately, Lynn coaches Bill on how to deal with Ray, the aggressive team member, as well as the one who sleeps through meetings. Once the plan is implemented, team members complete surveys at the end of each meeting and send them to the consultant, who provides feedback on their progress. After six months, the group's perception of their meetings has improved by an average of two points on a five-point scale. Strangely, their need for dental appointments also seems to disappear!

Team Assessment: Does Your Team Use Information Effectively?

Effective information processing is central to the primary function of a management team: making the decisions that drive the organization. Knowledge possessed by team members and information gained through networking is easily lost in an unproductive information processing environment. Our research found that team leaders greatly influence this aspect of management team operations, because they control the meetings where most information processing takes place. Leaders therefore need to ensure that they use this power to improve the decision-making abilities of their team.

The survey and discussion questions that follow can help determine whether your management team has an information processing environment that encourages effective decision making. The survey questions are based on those used in the Management Team Research Project.

TEAM Survey: Effective Information Processing

This survey helps determine whether the management team is processing information effectively. If you identify problems with information processing, you may wish to refer back to the appropriate sections of this chapter under "Strategies for Group Decision Making" or "Overcoming Barriers to Effective Information Processing."

Here are instructions for using the survey.

1. Give each team member a copy of Team Survey: Effective Information Processing.
2. Tell the members *not* to put their names on these sheets.
3. Have them indicate their level of agreement with each statement and score their own survey.
4. Collect the survey sheets and add up the team score yourself or ask a team member to do so.
5. Determine a final team score using the formula under "Total Team Score."
6. To identify specific concerns, total the scores for each item and divide by the numbers of team members surveyed, as shown under "Item Scores."
7. Have a group discussion of the reasons for your scores. You may wish to use the discussion questions at the end of the chapter.

TEAM SURVEY: EFFECTIVE INFORMATION PROCESSING

For each item, indicate your level of agreement by circling the appropriate number.

	Agree			Disagree
1. The leader of this team clearly communicates what we are expected to accomplish.	4	3	2	1
2. Our leader encourages us to consider all relevant information when making decisions.	4	3	2	1
3. When problems are discussed, different types of solutions are usually considered.	4	3	2	1
4. Members of this team share information with one another.	4	3	2	1
5. Our team meetings are well planned and organized.	4	3	2	1
6. The leader of this team encourages people to express new ideas and different points of view.	4	3	2	1
7. In meetings, we talk about how our work relates to larger organizational goals.	4	3	2	1
8. In making decisions, we consider both the big picture and the details of implementation.	4	3	2	1

A. Individual Scoring

Add up the circled numbers and write your score below.

Total Score = _____

8–16	17–23	24–32
Poor information processing climate	Moderately effective information processing climate	Effective information processing climate

TEAM Information Processing Survey: Team Scoring

B. Total Team Score

Total of all team member scores =

Divide by number of team members =

Total Score =

8–16	17–23	24–32
Poor information processing climate	Moderately effective information processing climate	Effective information processing climate

C. Item Scores

Total for each item	Divide total by number of team members
1.	1.
2.	2.
3.	3.
4.	4.
5.	5.
6.	6.
7.	7.
8.	8.

Discussion Questions: Effective Information Processing

These questions can start a discussion with your management team members about information processing. They may be used alone or as a follow-up to the TEAM Survey: Effective Information Processing.

- Do we define the desired outcomes at the beginning of our meetings? Do we have a clear agenda?
- Do we need to do a better job of staying on track in our meetings? How can we do this?
- Do we make decisions without thoroughly discussing the problem or situation? How can we keep from jumping to conclusions?
- How can we ensure that all important information is considered in making decisions?

- Do we seem to think too much alike on some issues? How can we avoid the pitfalls this might create?
- How do we react to new ideas and suggestions? Are we too critical? What can we do to be sure new ideas are fully considered?
- Do we have balanced participation in our discussions? Do some people talk a lot while others are usually quiet? How can we improve in this area?
- Have we made decisions in the past that didn't turn out well? What could we have done to prevent this?

CHAPTER SIX

FOCUSED ACTION

How to Move from Discussion to Results

True Story: The Demise of the Human Resource Department

Part One: The Problem

On the grapevine, the upcoming planning meeting is known as the "survival conference" because everyone on the corporate human resource staff understands that their department is in trouble. The CEO seems to have little respect for Allison, the vice president of HR. She is left out of critical decisions and her meetings with him are often canceled. The vice president of finance has emphatically stated on numerous occasions that he thinks the human resource department should be dismantled. Managers in the operating divisions are particularly upset about the time required to fill vacancies, reclassify positions, and complete disciplinary terminations. To top it off, a recent company survey revealed widespread dissatisfaction with human resource activities. After seeing the survey results, Allison hurriedly scheduled a planning meeting to allow her management team to begin addressing the problem.

During the meeting, the HR managers carefully analyze the survey information, as well as the results of interviews with a sampling of managers. They pinpoint several areas where department performance needs to improve. Personnel transactions must be completed more quickly, and better relationships need to be developed with top management, both at corporate and in the divisions. Because their function appears to be poorly understood, group members feel they should try to help managers understand how the human resource department adds value to the organization. By the end of the meeting, the managers feel they have thoroughly explored the problem and reached several important decisions about the appropriate course of action. Allison is relieved and optimistic as she drives home that evening.

Six months later, all the managers in the company receive a memo from the CEO announcing the decentralization of the human resource function. In the future, all personnel transactions will take place in the divisions. Members of the corporate HR department will either be laid off or transferred to a divisional office, with the exception of a skeleton staff who will act as consultants in specific areas. Allison stares at the memo in shock. The CEO never mentioned this plan to her. When she calls her management team together, the mood is somber.

"I thought we had figured out how to avoid this at the planning meeting," says one team member.

"Yeah, we did a great job of figuring it out," replies another, "but we never did anything about it."

This management team is long on talk, but short on action. They identified a problem, gathered information, determined appropriate solutions, but never took the final step of implementing their decisions. After the planning meeting, their good intentions were lost in the daily demands of their jobs, with the result that all their discussion created absolutely no change in the workplace. Actually, if the team were able to take effective action, they might have avoided the problems that led to the dismantling of their department.

The Formula for Effective Action

Since the primary function of a management team is to make decisions, the team's true effectiveness must be determined by evaluating the results that the decisions produce. The first four success factors are necessary but not sufficient for a management team to achieve successful outcomes. Without action, the other four factors are meaningless. A management team with clear goals, comprehensive information, supportive relationships, and a good decision-making process is nevertheless totally ineffective unless the members are able to translate decisions into results.

Although the other success factors create the foundation for effective performance, results can only be obtained if the team moves successfully from discussion to action. In our research, focused action received a lower rating from team members than any of the other success factors. This result seems to indicate some dissatisfaction with the ability of management teams to translate decisions into meaningful outcomes. When team members in our study felt that a decision had not turned out well, they were likely to attribute the problem to a lack of necessary information (a factor in the decision-making process), delays in carrying out a decision, or failure to follow through and finish what they started.

Moving from discussion to action requires agreement on "what, how, when, and who" for every decision made by the team. These questions address aspects of implementation:

- Specific results: *what* is to be accomplished
- Action plans: *how* results will be achieved
- Time line: *when* actions will be completed
- Involvement of others: *who* will be part of the process

A fifth important question is "whether": finding out whether the desired results are actually produced. Answering this question requires a follow-up plan. This five-step process for moving from discussion to action applies to both long-term goals and specific projects.

Specific Results

Being specific about what you hope to accomplish helps to define success. What evidence will tell you that your efforts are worthwhile? When defining results, management teams often make certain mistakes:

- Focusing on activities instead of outcomes
- Failing to consider the customer's point of view
- Describing internal states that can't be measured or observed
- Using an inappropriate time frame
- Overlooking critical aspects of their work

Focus on Activities. Organizations sometimes measure activities instead of results; however, activities are not ends in themselves but are intended to achieve certain outcomes. In defining results, you want to identify the benefits that your activities are supposed to produce. For example, a company introducing a new product is clearly not interested in how many they can make but in how many people will buy. A training department shouldn't measure success by how many workshops they teach, but by whether people are using the skills learned in those workshops. The success of a company newsletter does not depend on the number of articles written, but on how many people read the articles.

Lack of Customer Input. The customer's viewpoint needs to be considered in deciding how to define results. How do we know if we are providing a useful product or service to our internal or external customers? A corporate finance department surveys internal customers to evaluate the usefulness and readability of their reports. An automobile dealership calls customers after a purchase to determine their satisfaction with both the sales process and the car. A county tax department decides that tracking the number, accuracy, and processing speed of tax documents is not sufficient to measure performance. Managers also need a measure of how well customers are being served in the tax offices, so they institute a customer service survey.

Internal States. Desired outcomes that describe internal states—such as "better morale," "increased understanding," or "higher customer satisfaction"—are virtually useless until we figure out how to measure them. People's feelings and perceptions are important to the success of any organization and should not be overlooked just because they are difficult to measure, but outcomes described only in these nebulous terms do not lead to focused action. Results can only be documented if they are measurable or observable, so managers have two choices: describe the feelings and perceptions in terms of observable behavior, or figure out how to measure the internal state directly. Either approach can be effective.

Limited Time Frame. Results can be measured at different points in time. We usually have more control over near-term results and less control over long-term outcomes, as shown in Figure 6.1.

An example of this relationship is found in the multilevel evaluation system that is often recommended as a comprehensive measure of training effectiveness. Figure 6.2 describes the four outcome levels of reaction, learning, behavior, and results. Trainers have much more control over the first two levels, but measurement at the third and fourth levels can help them evaluate the long-term impact of their work.

One government job placement agency defined success as a client remaining in a job for thirty days, at which point they closed the case. As a short-term measure, the thirty-day standard was useful; however, the agency knew little about the long-term success of its efforts. For a more complete picture, they might have also chosen to measure clients' job success at six months, one year, or three years. The agency would obviously have less control over these long-term results, since a client

FIGURE 6.1. RELATIONSHIP BETWEEN TIME OF MEASUREMENT AND CONTROL OVER RESULTS.

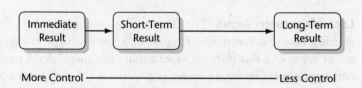

FIGURE 6.2. A FOUR-LEVEL METHOD
FOR MEASURING TRAINING EFFECTIVENESS.

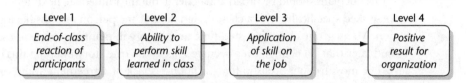

Level 1	Level 2	Level 3	Level 4
End-of-class reaction of participants	*Ability to perform skill learned in class*	*Application of skill on the job*	*Positive result for organization*

could leave a job because of health problems, layoffs, business failures, family relocation, or a host of other reasons; but even so, the agency would learn more about the ultimate value of its efforts.

Unbalanced Measures. To present a balanced picture, the results measured should reflect all critical aspects of the work to be done. If measures are not balanced, then one aspect of performance is emphasized at the expense of another. Manufacturing organizations that focus solely on technological excellence, for example, may create state-of-the-art products that are difficult for customers to understand or operate. The government team agency described above measured placement of clients but did not track job satisfaction, earnings, or tax dollars saved by the program. As a result, employees focused their efforts on getting clients into the first available job. These critical measures are sometimes referred to as "cockpit indicators," drawing a comparison with the array of gauges used by pilots to assess the status of their plane. Like airplane gauges, critical measures should provide you with sufficient information to accurately assess the status of your organization.

Action Plans

Action plans describe how results are to be accomplished. Three components are important:

1. A general outline of how the desired goal will be achieved
2. Specific description of initial steps to be taken
3. Assignment of responsibilities to specific people

For most goals or projects, the complete work plan should be outlined only in general terms. Trying to predict every detailed step of a complex undertaking is usually a waste of time, since later activities are often driven by earlier results. A more effective approach is to divide the work plan into phases, with detailed plans for the first phase only. Once the first phase is complete, you can evaluate progress and make detailed plans for the next phase. This combination of planning followed by action followed by more planning has been found to produce the best results.

Overall plans should be broad and general, but the immediate next steps should be described specifically with a clear designation of the person responsible for each action. Many groups have invested time and energy in planning discussions, only to find later that no change ever occurred (as in the true story opening this chapter). The most frequent reason for this failure is lack of agreement about exactly what action is to be taken and who is responsible for completion.

Many a strategic planning process has also foundered at the action planning stage. If the strategic plan is to be used to guide the organization, then the management team must make the transition to operational planning and agree on actions needed to move in the desired direction; otherwise, business continues as usual.

Time Line

Activities with no deadline tend to be postponed indefinitely. Preparing a time line forces the group to set expectations about when results will be delivered. At the end of any planning meeting, a general schedule should be established for accomplishing the goal or completing the project, with specific dates attached to all initial action steps.

Involvement

As action plans are created, the management team should consider how others need to be included in the process and then develop an appropriate involvement strategy. If a change is going to alter the work of another department, for example, then that department should be invited to participate in decision-making discussions. If employee acceptance of a decision is critical for success, then employee input should be solicited before the decision is made. If customers will be confused by a change in procedure, then they need to be given advance notice of the new method. Failure to consider these involvement needs can cause a team to act on inadequate information, increase resistance among important constituencies, or communicate unclear expectations.

Follow-up

Following up simply means getting feedback at appropriate intervals to determine if plans were indeed carried out and the desired results achieved. Building follow-up points into the time line prevents unpleasant surprises later on, when it may be too late to repair the damage.

Following up is particularly important when your results depend on the actions of others. This is particularly true for top management teams, since miscommunication easily occurs when expectations and feedback have to travel through two or more organizational layers. Pondering this phenomenon, one CEO exclaimed in frustration, "I'll never understand how I can tell someone to do something so simple, then a few weeks later I learn that it's turned into some huge, complicated project!" When information and instructions are delegated through several levels, more frequent follow up may be advisable, especially at the beginning of a plan.

Key Steps in Achieving Meaningful Results

Taking focused action is like planning a trip: you need to know where you are going, how you will get there, what the schedule is, and who will be going with you. As with any other journey, you must be able to deal with unexpected surprises, problems, and opportunities along the way, altering plans when necessary—and perhaps even changing your destination.

Strategy One: Clearly Describe the Results You Hope to Achieve

The first step in moving toward action is defining the *what*: the specific results you wish to accomplish. Whether you are discussing annual goals or one specific project, everyone on the management team needs to have the same understanding of what the group is trying to achieve. Desired results should not only be discussed in meetings but should also be formalized in writing with copies for all team members.

To direct action effectively, results must meet these criteria:

- Describe outcomes, not activities
- Include the customer's viewpoint
- Cover a time frame adequate to determine value added
- Include all critical aspects of the work

Outcomes. To focus on outcomes rather than activities, separate the end from the means. Try to describe the results that you want your activities to produce. These questions can help you identify desired outcomes:

- What change are we trying to create?
- How will we know if our activities are successful?
- What benefits are we trying to produce?
- If we succeed in our efforts, what will be different?

Customer Viewpoint. Be sure to view results from the vantage point of your customers. Put yourself in their place. What would success look like to a customer? To get into this mind-set, think of situations where you actually are the customer. What do you expect when you are buying a product, contracting for a service, or calling a government agency for information? In terms of internal customer relationships, what do you expect when you have to depend on information, decisions, reports, or completed work from another department? If thinking like customers is difficult, then you need to ask your customers directly. Use surveys, interviews, or focus groups to find out how they define success for your organization.

Extended Time Frame. To get a true picture of your organization's effectiveness, you may wish to focus on results at several points in time. Near-term results show the immediate effect of your actions, while long-term outcomes indicate your impact over an extended period. One government agency for the aging sponsors a series of workshops to train people in legislative advocacy. Their goal is to develop a group of committed advocates who will work to pass legislation beneficial to older people. To assess the effectiveness of the program, these time measures could be used:

- Short-term: Workshop participants agree to work as advocates.
- Intermediate: Advocates participate in legislative activities.
- Long-term: Legislation that benefits the aging population is passed.

When evaluating success over time, keep in mind that your control over results decreases as other factors intervene. In this same example, many factors besides the advocacy workshops influence the passage of legislation. If the workshops never help to create new legislation, however, then they need to be reexamined.

Balanced Measures. Finally, be sure that your targeted results balance all important aspects of performance. Success is usually defined by a combination of factors, such as quality, quantity, customer satisfaction, employee acceptance, accuracy, timeliness, and cost. Overlooking a critical factor usually produces negative results. An express delivery company, for example, put a great premium on speed. All their advertising and promotional materials emphasized how quickly a package or document could be delivered. Speed was also stressed in their performance measures, but it was not counterbalanced by a measure of accuracy. Needless to say, customers who quickly received the wrong package were not too pleased.

Each project undertaken by a management team should incorporate this balanced perspective in defining successful results. One executive team decided to revise the company's compensation plan. Under the new pay program, newer employees, who were lower in the pay range, were given a higher percentage annual raise than longtime workers, who were already receiving a larger salary. An employee who had been with the company for one year might receive a 5 percent raise, while a ten-year employee with the same performance rating received a 4 percent raise. Although the plan was quite logical from a compensation point of view, long-service employees were highly offended. As a result, this issue became the central focus of a union campaign in which organizers stressed the value of seniority under a union contract. In planning the compensation project, the management team had focused only on monetary aspects and neglected to consider employee acceptance as a critical aspect of the plan's success.

Strategy Two: Determine How You Will Measure Results

Once you have defined the specific results you hope to accomplish, you must decide how to measure them. Results that are not measured will probably not be achieved, since people naturally focus their efforts on areas that are being evaluated.

Measurement answers the question, "How will we define success?" Sometimes this is easy. If your results can be readily counted—such as number of products sold or amount of money saved—you just need to set a target. Measurement can simply mean assigning a numerical goal to desired results, as in the advocacy project described above:

- Short-term: *Thirty* workshop participants agree to work as advocates.
- Intermediate: Advocates participate in *ten* legislative activities during the year.
- Long-term: *Three* specific pieces of legislation benefiting the aging population are passed.

When desired outcomes are less concrete, measurement is more of a challenge. Describing results in terms of behavior rather than feelings or attitudes is often a useful first step in developing measurements. Organizations wanting to "improve employee morale," for example, should ask themselves what employees with high morale are likely to do. As an observer, how would we distinguish a low-morale organization from a high-morale organization? If we want to "enhance leadership ability," what do we expect people who are good leaders to do? How would we tell a good leader from a bad leader? Once you can define observable behaviors, you have taken the initial step toward measurement. In the above example, "developing committed advocates" means observing that advocates will be willing to actively participate in legislative activities. This is a behavior that can be observed and measured.

If your goal is to change customer or employee perceptions, you may have to create methods to measure these internal states. Surveys, focus groups, and interviews are all useful techniques for assessing perceptions, but they must be done properly to be effective. If your organization has no internal expertise in these assessment techniques, it is advisable to consult an outside expert.

Strategy Three: Outline the Overall Plan for Achieving Results

Once desired results are identified, the team needs to agree on a plan for accomplishing them. You do not have to determine each specific step from beginning to end, but a general work strategy should be developed. To generate an overall plan, have team members identify the principal phases that must be completed to achieve the goal. For example, if a management team wants to reduce the number of complaints about the company's customer service process, their overall action plan might include these phases:

Phase 1: Solicit feedback from customers to identify issues of concern to them.

Phase 2: Get input from customer service employees on customer concerns.

Phase 3: Analyze customer and employee information to identify critical problem areas.

Phase 4: Evaluate customer service policies and procedures.

Phase 5: Analyze the customer call-handling process.

Phase 6: Determine the primary causes of customer complaints.

Phase 7: Implement corrective action.

At this point, the team could not and should not try to specify exactly how every phase will be carried out, since initial results from the earlier phases will affect subsequent actions. They do, however, need a general road map to follow, which can be modified as needed.

Strategy Four: Define Action Steps for Each Phase

In most situations, combining planning with action appears to produce the best results: develop initial plans, take action, then do additional planning, followed by more action, and so on. Specific action steps therefore need to be developed at the beginning of each project phase. If the management team working on the customer service project plans first to gather information from customers, they need detailed action steps for accomplishing this goal. The information acquired during this phase is then used to plan subsequent steps.

Action steps must clearly describe exactly what is to be done. In this same project, phase one (soliciting feedback from customers) might include these action steps:

1. Draft a customer survey.
2. Locate an outside expert in survey design.
3. Have the expert review the survey.
4. Get a list of all customers who called the help desk in the past six months.
5. Consult the market research department about how to select a survey sample.
6. Mail survey to selected sample of customers.
7. Compile feedback from surveys and prepare report.

The customer information acquired through this process should be used in planning the next phase, in which feedback is obtained from customer service employees. For example, customer responses might be used to shape the questions that employees are asked. The team might also decide to modify the overall work plan for the project, based on customer feedback. If customers are complaining that products fail to live up to initial expectations, for instance, the team may want to add the steps of talking with the salesforce or reviewing product literature to determine how product expectations are communicated.

Strategy Five: Assign Responsibility for Action to Specific People or Groups

A specific person or group needs to "own" each action planned. In the customer service example, someone needs to draft the customer survey and send it to others for review; someone needs to identify an outside expert on survey design; someone needs to get the list of customer names; and so forth. It has been said that if everyone is responsible, no one is responsible. Unless specific people are charged with carrying out each action step, nothing is likely to get done. One executive board spent several hours discussing the organizational problems created by unclear division of roles and responsibilities. They all agreed that the issue should be addressed, and then they went on to their next agenda item. Six months later, board members were still wrestling with conflicts caused by poorly defined roles. Everyone understood the problem, but no one was responsible for taking action. (Eventually, the group appointed two members to draft role descriptions for the various components of the organization.)

Strategy Six: Determine How to Involve Others

Whenever team members are creating an action plan, they should consider whether to include others in the process. Customers, employees, upper management, other

TABLE 6.1. LEVELS OF INVOLVEMENT IN ACTION PLANNING.

Include in Decisions If . . .	Consult for Information If . . .	Inform About Actions If . . .
They have authority over something that you would like to change	Your actions have a significant impact on them in any way	The plan has some effect on their work or life
You cannot take action without their cooperation	They have information that you need in order to make good decisions	They are likely to have questions about your actions
They are critical to the success of the plan	Your actions make major changes in their work	They will feel excluded if they are not told about the plan
They have unique expertise needed so that effective decisions can be made	Their acceptance is critical to achieving your results	You are trying to develop a cooperative relationship with them

departments, and vendors may all have a part to play in implementing a plan. Unfortunately, managers often overlook the need to involve other people. Think about your own experience. Has anyone ever failed to give you information about a change that affected your work? Have you ever had knowledge that might have been useful to those making a decision, but no one asked for your input? If so, someone did a poor job of involvement planning.

People or groups outside the team may be involved in three different ways:

1. Included in making decisions
2. Consulted for information
3. Informed about actions or changes

Table 6.1 provides some general guidelines for determining which level of involvement is most appropriate.

For each phase of an action plan, you may wish to have the group develop an include/consult/inform chart listing the people or groups in each category. Table 6.2 shows such a chart for the customer feedback process outlined in strategy number four.

Strategy Seven: Develop a Time Line with Follow-up Points

Time lines should include the expected completion date for each phase and action step in the plan, as well as follow-up points for receiving feedback about progress. In developing a time line, consider which steps can occur simultaneously

TABLE 6.2. SAMPLE INVOLVEMENT CHART
FOR CUSTOMER SURVEY ACTIVITY.

Include in Decisions	Consult for Information	Inform About Actions
CEO: approve customer survey	Market research specialist: sampling procedures Outside expert: survey design	Sales representatives: content and timing of survey Help-desk employees: content and timing of survey

and which must be sequential. In our customer service example, steps one, two, and four (drafting a survey, locating a survey expert, and getting a list of customers) can be done at the same time. On the other hand, step three, having an expert review the survey, cannot be done until steps one and two are completed.

Be realistic about time! In their desire to progress quickly, groups often become too optimistic about schedules. Remember to consider the other demands on your time when taking on a new project. If others must review or approve some of your work, be sure to allow a reasonable amount of time for them to do so. Accurate time projections are especially important if commitments are being made to customers, employees, or upper management about when results will be delivered.

Strategy Eight: Create a Flow Chart to Summarize the Action Plan

Creating a flow chart often helps clarify the order of activities and calls attention to any steps left out of the process. This is a good summary exercise, since the diagram includes all the information required for a complete action plan:

1. Action steps
2. Order of activities
3. Persons responsible
4. Involvement of others
5. Completion dates
6. Follow-up points

For complex undertakings, project planning software can be used to order activities most effectively and efficiently. Figure 6.3 shows a simple flow diagram of steps needed to mail out the customer survey, including completion dates and the person responsible for each activity. In this example, follow-up points occur

FIGURE 6.3. FLOWCHART OF STEPS NEEDED TO MAIL OUT CUSTOMER SURVEY, WITH COMPLETION DATES AND ASSIGNMENT OF RESPONSIBILITY.

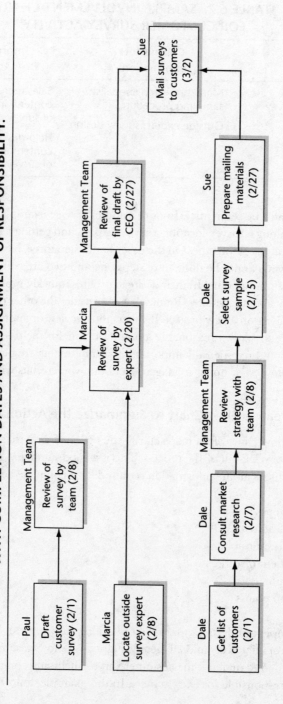

when completed work is reviewed by the team or the CEO. Constructing the diagram caused the group to realize that one critical step—preparing mailing materials—had been left off their original list. (If you use Post-its to create your flow chart, you can move the steps around easily should you want to make changes or additions.)

Strategy Nine: Modify Plans as Needed

Having a plan is important, but being flexible is equally important. As plans are implemented, feedback about how well the plan is working becomes available, either through formal plan reviews or through informal networking contacts. If you have built appropriate follow-up points into the time line, you should receive feedback at all critical junctures. Organizations ignore feedback at their peril. An alcoholic beverage manufacturer introduced a new product that was wildly successful during its first few months on the market. Distributors soon told the company that consumers were mixing the new beverage with fruit juice, but management paid little attention to this feedback. The underlying message, however, was that the stuff had a bland taste and needed more flavoring. Sales of the product quickly dropped off once competitors introduced tastier alternatives, and it faded into obscurity.

If feedback indicates a problem with the plan, changes are called for. A company that had always made products for the business market decided to venture into consumer manufacturing. As their new products found their way into customers' homes, the company quickly started receiving complaints. Realizing that the learning curve for this new market might be steeper than anticipated, the president decided to abandon the previous plan and contract with a consumer products company to manufacture the product. Had he stuck with the original strategy, the company's reputation among consumers might have been irreparably damaged before they solved their manufacturing problems.

Plan modification is also advisable when circumstances change. Market changes, company reorganizations, shifts in economic or political trends, and changes in top management can all render plans obsolete. One training department had invested considerable time, effort, and expense in working with an outside consultant to create a management development program. The initial program was well received by the target audience, but after two sessions the consultant had a heart attack and was unavailable for several months. Rather than wait for him to recover or locate another consultant, the department decided to change its approach and develop a cadre of in-house trainers to deliver the program. Although their original plan worked well, circumstances had taught them the danger of becoming too dependent upon one person.

Strategy Ten: Be Open to Opportunities

Plans may be modified in response to problems, but they may also change to capitalize on opportunities. When you identify a chance to increase profits, acquire resources, or develop relationships, consider altering your course to take advantage of these circumstances. A member of one state government management team learned that an aide to the governor was interested in a project being implemented by her agency. When she discussed this development with other team members, they decided to change their project plan to involve the aide, which gave them a chance to acquire a potentially valuable ally in the governor's office.

Strategy Eleven: Develop Communication Plans

Most action plans aim to create change. Managers who complain about resistance fail to realize that people's acceptance of change depends largely on effective planning and communication by management. Formal communication plans need to be developed for large-scale changes, but some thought should be given to the way any change is communicated. These questions address some critical factors in communication planning:

- Who needs to know about this change?
- How do we want people to react to the change?
- What messages do we want to convey?
- What might people get upset about?
- What information is needed by different groups?
- When do they need this information? In what order?
- What is the most effective way to share information?
- What questions might people have about the change?
- What is the most effective communication medium to use?
- Will people need information to keep for future reference?
- Should we give them information several times or in different ways?
- How can we get feedback about their reactions?

In one company, communication planning helped promote employee acceptance of an increase in insurance costs. Employee contributions for medical insurance had not been raised for seven years, so management knew that the upcoming rate increase would set off an outcry. Rather than simply send out the new rate schedule, though, the human resource department prepared an announcement describing how changes in the health care field had affected insurance costs. The announcement indicated that employee contributions would have to be raised in the near future but did not say how much the increase would be. People immediately assumed the worst and anticipated a much higher increase

FIGURE 6.4. DEGREE OF PERSONAL COMMUNICATION NEEDED.

Memos and e-mail Announcements Newsletters	Voice Mail Video	Individual Meetings Group Meetings
Use if information is short, simple, and low-impact	*Use if information requires a personal touch but not two-way communication*	*Use if information is long, complex, and high-impact*

Less Personal ——————————————————— More Personal

than the one that was planned. When they finally saw the new rate schedule, employees were quite relieved. Through communication planning, the human resource department avoided what appeared to be an inevitable negative reaction.

One important consideration in communication planning is whether the information should come with a person attached: should someone be available to give explanations and answer questions? As indicated by the chart in Figure 6.4, memos and written announcements are fine for routine, simple information with little impact on the recipient, but personal communication should accompany information that is important, complex, or of high impact. Some companies have actually sent layoff notices to employees through company mail, with no further communication. Similarly, one executive planned to leave a manager's disciplinary warning on her voice mail—until the employee relations manager intervened. Clearly, this kind of important, high-impact information should always be given personally. Personal communication usually involves individual or group meetings and often includes distributing written materials as well.

Strategy Twelve: Encourage Behavior Change

Taking effective action often means getting people to change the way they do things. People usually pass through three stages on the way to a behavior change: (1) giving up old behavior, (2) trying out new behavior, and (3) forming new habits. You might think of this as the "ice cube model," because the process is similar to changing the shape of an ice cube: first you melt the cube (give up old behavior); then you pour the liquid into a mold to form a new shape (try new behavior); and finally you freeze it into the desired shape (develop new habits).

People go through similar stages of melting, forming, and freezing. One management team wanted to simplify the purchasing process by eliminating purchase orders and issuing company credit cards. First, they had to get people to stop using purchase order forms; then they had to help them learn how and when to use company credit cards, and finally they had to put procedures in place to ensure that credit cards were the only method used in the future. Another company decided to adopt a quality approach that used process improvement teams extensively. But simply putting people into groups doesn't automatically create teams. First, employees had to understand why and how teams were being used, and then they needed to have the experience of working on a team. For this experience to be successful, however, they also had to learn teamwork skills and have an effective team leader. (If their initial "forming" experience had been negative, employees probably would have resisted future participation on teams.) Finally, policies and procedures were needed to freeze the change and encourage use of teams in the future.

Table 6.3 provides suggestions to help managers guide people through these three stages and create permanent behavior change. Keep in mind that when you are asking people to change their behavior, resistance is to be expected. Exploring the reasons for this resistance often provides useful information about employee reactions, problems with the change itself, or difficulties with the implementation process. Remember that if your goal involves behavior change, then your outcome measures should evaluate whether the change has taken place.

TABLE 6.3. STRATEGIES FOR BEHAVIOR CHANGE.

Melting (Giving up Old Behavior)	Forming (Trying New Behavior)	Freezing (Developing New Habits)
Explain reasons for the change	Clearly define desired behaviors	Recognize and reward new behavior
Give a dramatic demonstration of the problem	Be a role model	Communicate positive results of the change
Stress benefits of the new way and costs of the old way	Teach technical skills needed for success	Create systems to reinforce the new behavior
Recognize feelings about the change	Teach interpersonal skills needed for success	Change policies and procedures
Discuss reasons for resistance to the change	Provide resources for making the change	Change the reward system
Involve people in making the change	Remove obstacles to making the change	Change the organizational structure
Stop accepting the old behavior	Identify examples of appropriate behavior	Be consistent in your own behavior and your reactions to others
	Show appreciation for attempts to change	Don't accept relapses

Strategy Thirteen: Institute Feedback Mechanisms

To know whether actions are effective, a management team must receive feedback about results. Written progress reports, periodic updates at staff meetings, individual meetings with the team leader, review of draft materials, interim data collection, and development of prototypes are all forms of feedback. Some feedback mechanisms relate to a single project, while others become a permanent part of the system. The organization instituting company credit cards obtained regular purchase reports for each district office to determine which ones were successfully implementing the new system. The company wishing to begin using process improvement teams decided after the first year that they needed regular feedback about team effectiveness, so they instituted a semiannual survey of all team members. To get regular feedback about employee morale, an executive team created an employee satisfaction index, which was tracked quarterly. A department that published a company newsletter conducted regular readership surveys to learn which features attracted the most interest. Without feedback, a management team can never know if efforts are successful.

Strategy Fourteen: Learn from Experience

Some management teams make the same mistakes repeatedly. The reason for this is simple: they aren't paying attention to the results of their actions. When people or groups fail to learn from their mistakes, there are three likely causes:

1. Failure to solicit feedback
2. Ignoring available feedback
3. Denying the truth of feedback

The importance of soliciting feedback was discussed under strategy thirteen. Once feedback is received, the team needs to spend time reviewing it and learning from it. Developing the habit of review helps promote continuous learning. At the end of each planning cycle, for example, time should be set aside to discuss what was learned during the year that can help the group become more effective in the future. What problems occurred that might have been prevented? What should be done differently the next time? In what areas were we unsuccessful? Why? Of course, learning should also include reviewing accomplishments and celebrating successes. What did we do particularly well? What led to our success? How could we apply these abilities or techniques in other areas? In our fast-paced world, most people and groups have unfortunately lost the habit of reflection; but investing time in learning from experience usually provides a valuable return.

Reviews can be conducted for projects, meetings, staff retreats, or any other aspect of team operations. Every project should conclude with an examination of successes and problems. Retreats often end with a discussion of what was helpful about the program and what could have been better. On a staff meeting agenda, the last item might be a review of how effective the meeting was or how well the group is working together. In all aspects of our work (and our lives, for that matter), we should constantly ask ourselves what went well, what did not, and what we can learn from our experiences.

Denial is a more serious problem. If management teams consistently find reasons to ignore negative feedback, they are headed for failure. One management group in a government administrative services agency was frequently told that their processes were too slow. Team members would repeatedly explain the many reasons why their work took a long time, but they never acknowledged the problem or took any action to correct the situation. Ultimately, the head of the management team was asked to resign, several team members were replaced, and the work processes were redesigned. In the short run, denial often makes people more comfortable by allowing them to maintain a positive self-image while avoiding actual change. In the long run, however, denial usually causes people to develop harmful patterns in their work or relationships, which may eventually exact a heavy price. One CEO habitually ignored the concerns, opinions, and feelings of managers and employees in his organization and disregarded all feedback he received about this behavior. When he began to relate to customers and board members in this fashion, however, he was fired.

These questions can help you explore the issue of denial with your group:

- What complaints do we frequently hear about our work?
- From the point of view of our customers (internal or external), what do we need to improve?
- How would an outside observer describe our team? Does this reflect any bad habits that we need to change?
- How would upper management describe our team? Is this the image we want them to have? If not, how can we change it?

By definition, our blind spots are difficult for us to see. Just as discovering personal blind spots may require the help of a counselor, discovering your team's areas of denial may require assistance from an outside consultant.

In summary, you can help management team members learn from experience by seeing that feedback about their work is available, that time is devoted to discussing feedback, and that they are not allowed to develop blind spots by rationalizing away potential problems.

Overcoming Barriers to Focused Action

Some teams make decisions easily but fail to implement them effectively. In this section, we consider some problems that prevent management teams from successfully carrying out their intentions:

1. The results of our work are hard to measure.
2. The team is better at talk than action.
3. The group gets bogged down in details of implementation.
4. Some team members don't do their part.
5. Employees don't implement decisions as expected.
6. The team starts projects but fails to complete them.
7. Upper management interferes with our plans.

Problem One: The Results of Our Work Are Hard to Measure

Some organizations have "softer" results than others: the outcomes they strive for don't easily lend themselves to measurement. Counting the products you sold or the customers you served is simpler than figuring out whether you improved managers' leadership abilities or strengthened family relationships. Nevertheless, measures of success are important for all management teams. When managers make a decision or undertake a project, their goal is usually to create change. Without evidence that change is occurring, there is no way to know whether the effort is worthwhile.

Suggestions for action:

1. Turn your "soft" goals into specific observable behaviors. If you want employees to develop a "better attitude" toward customers, for example, ask yourself what employees with a good attitude would be doing: listening to customers? helping customers identify their problems? finding solutions for customer concerns? If your organization is dedicated to "improving family relationships," ask yourself what families with good relationships do: participate in activities together? eat meals together? resolve disagreements without fighting? Whatever the goal, if you can describe desired results in terms of behavior, you have taken the first step to making them measurable.

2. Find existing data that could reflect the results of your efforts. You may wish to create other measures as well, but useful information might already be available. If your department tries to help managers develop leadership skills, for example, look for existing indications of effective leadership. First, of course,

you should define *leadership* in behavioral terms, and then seek evidence that those behaviors are being demonstrated. If your company conducts employee or customer surveys, some survey items may reflect leadership effectiveness. If your definition of leadership includes community involvement, count the number of community activities in which managers participate.

3. Create your own measurement tool. If you are trying to create a change in people's perceptions, measurements of beliefs, feelings, and attitudes—even though less objective than results that can be counted—provide acceptable indicators of success. Developing a questionnaire or survey to solicit reactions is an effective way to evaluate these results. A state department of transportation measured perceptions of customer service by sending a survey to people who had called local DOT offices with problems. A human resource department assessed employees' feelings about their benefits by distributing an annual benefits questionnaire. Even counseling centers can measure results, by having their clients complete surveys before and after receiving services.

4. Find a short-term measure. If you are too focused on long-term results, you may be trying to measure outcomes over which you have little control. Training departments, for example, often have difficulty assessing whether participants use new skills on the job, but they can administer pretests and posttests to determine what was learned in a workshop. Of course, evaluating short-term impact does not mean that you should abandon attempts to measure long-term effects.

5. Use more than one measure. A more complete picture is usually gained from multiple measures. A counseling center may want to measure number of clients, number of visits per client, percentage of return clients, and clients' perceptions of service effectiveness. A customer help desk might measure number of calls, type of problem, number of repeat calls, length of calls, and customer service perceptions.

Problem Two: The Team Is Better at Talk Than Action

Failure to act sometimes grows out of fear. Action commits time, people, and money to achieving certain results, with the potential for negative consequences if expectations are not met. Some managers are so afraid of making the wrong decision that they do nothing. This inaction reduces their immediate anxiety, but it usually creates bigger problems, since taking appropriate action is the essence of management. One CEO spoke frequently of his desire to make strategic acquisitions of other companies. His management team devoted extensive time to locating and evaluating potential acquisition targets, but over a period of four years no new companies were ever acquired. The CEO could cite many reasons why none of the companies seemed to be an appropriate match, but the truth was that his fear of making a mistake completely paralyzed him. Eventually, he was fired by the board, in part because of his inability to grow the company through acquisitions.

Maximum discussion with minimum action is also a symptom of poor planning skills. Some people are born planners: they just naturally organize information into action plans, time lines, and implementation steps. Others have different talents and interests. If your group excitedly discusses one new idea after another but starts to doze off when details of implementation are mentioned, then you need to help them develop effective action planning habits.

Suggestions for action:

1. If your team frequently has to justify lack of action, perhaps team members need to explore their underlying feelings and motivations. If fear of failure is a predominant team personality trait, then the members need to force themselves to take the planning steps outlined in this chapter—recognizing that this will cause some discomfort. An outside consultant or counselor might also be helpful in identifying and resolving this problem. On the other hand, if the team is anxious because a number of plans have failed in the past, the group may need to work on some of the other four success factors. Taking action is the last step in a process that begins with clear goals, so problems earlier on can produce poor results.

2. When discussing a new idea or project, force the group to agree on action plans before moving on to another topic. Maintain their focus by writing action steps on a flipchart or white board. If they start to get off track, bring discussion back to the action plan and keep it there until all important steps are clearly outlined.

3. Set definite follow-up dates for each action step, and designate a specific person to be responsible for completion. Refer to suggestions in the strategies section of this chapter.

4. Include planning strategies in your meeting guidelines. Post meeting guidelines where they are clearly visible and refer to them as needed. (Meeting guidelines are discussed in Chapter Five.)

5. If one team member has particularly good planning abilities, ask that person to act as a monitor and ensure that the group moves from discussion to action steps. Be sure to pay attention anytime your monitor indicates a need to talk about *how* rather than *what*.

6. Develop the habit of summarizing decisions and actions at the end of each meeting. Agree on some standard planning questions, such as "What are our next steps?" "Who is responsible for carrying out that activity?" "When should that be completed?"

7. If the team will not sit patiently through group development of action plans, have one or two members draft plans after the meeting and bring them back for review.

8. For critical projects or decisions, use a facilitator who is skilled at guiding groups toward action.

Problem Three: The Group Gets Bogged down in Details of Implementation

Some groups waste valuable time discussing and debating every microscopic aspect of how a decision is to be carried out. This usually occurs on teams whose members have a natural talent for identifying the specific steps required to turn an idea into reality. When they overuse this strength, however, they get so lost in the details that nothing gets done. Time is wasted in debates about relatively insignificant aspects of a project, and the group pays too little attention to the bigger picture. This problem also arises in groups whose members tend to seek perfection; that is, they find it hard to stop improving the plan so that they can move on to action.

Suggestions for action:

1. Identify the subjects that tend to provoke discussion of trivia. Make a list of these seductive topics (groups with this style usually love lists) and agree to minimize such discussions in the future. One group, for example, recognized that they enjoyed discussing the logistical details of off-site meetings: where they would be held, what kind of food would be served, what kind of name tags should be used, how the tables should be arranged, and so forth. They agreed that in the future a committee would be appointed to make a recommendation on these matters.

2. Include a rule in your meeting guidelines that encourages the group to limit detailed discussions. Be sure that the guidelines are visible in the meeting room.

3. If you have a team member who naturally tends to focus on the big picture and long-range goals, ask that person to monitor discussions and speak up if the group seems to be wallowing in minutiae. When your monitor speaks up, pay attention!

4. Learn to delegate effectively, both within and outside the team. Select an appropriate person or group to create detailed implementation plans, and then agree on the goals they are to achieve and the parameters within which they are to work. Leave the "how to do it" questions for them to answer. Top management teams especially need to develop this skill.

5. Arrange for feedback about delegated projects at appropriate intervals. People who love detail are usually more comfortable with delegation if they receive frequent feedback, since they often want to have final review and approval of specifics.

6. Learn to let go. Managers who move up to higher levels in an organization must be able to focus on the larger picture and leave the less important details to others.

7. Encourage team members to notice when they have reached the point where further modifications and improvements are adding little to the effectiveness of a plan. With resource constraints and the presence of competing priorities, we seldom have the luxury of carrying out plans in their most perfect form. Management teams need to determine whether additional improvements actually add value or create an unnecessary delay.

Problem Four: Some Team Members Don't Do Their Part

If some team members aren't doing their fair share of the work, you need to wonder why. Consider three possible problems:

1. Communication: they don't *understand* what they are supposed to do.
2. Ability: they don't *know how* to do what they are supposed to do.
3. Motivation: they don't *want* to do what they are supposed to do.

Solving the problem depends upon correct diagnosis of the cause. The flow chart in Figure 6.5 and the suggestions that follow help you evaluate the situation and determine an appropriate course of action.

Suggestions for action:
1. Be sure that team members' roles and responsibilities are clearly defined and communicated. For any project, clarify who owns the various tasks and activities involved. At the end of planning discussions, summarize actions to be taken before the next meeting, and indicate which members are responsible. Distribute minutes or summaries that clearly designate responsibilities.

2. Be sure that expectations about how tasks should be done are clearly communicated. Sometimes team leaders or members make assumptions about how others will carry out assignments. If these assumptions are not shared by the person doing the work, the results may be disappointing. One management team member was responsible for completing a policy manual. His boss was not pleased with the initial draft, because she had expected the policies to be written in much greater detail. His belief, however, was that policies should be phrased as general guidelines, not detailed procedures. Had they agreed on the format in advance, the problem could have been avoided.

3. If failure to follow through might be due to lack of ability, the team leader needs to discuss the situation with the individual team member. Someone learning to do a new task may simply be in a developmental mode temporarily. Other people overestimate their abilities and take on tasks they are not equipped to handle, but rather than admit their incompetence, they simply fail to complete the

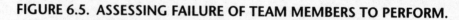

FIGURE 6.5. ASSESSING FAILURE OF TEAM MEMBERS TO PERFORM.

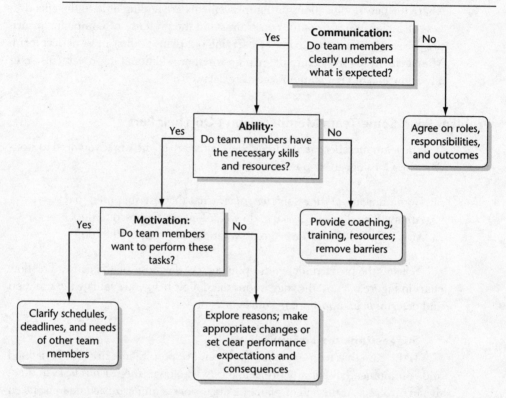

work. Whenever a task exceeds a manager's ability, the team leader needs to monitor the activities more closely, arrange for more frequent feedback, and provide more coaching. Pairing a less experienced person with a more experienced or talented team member often simultaneously increases learning and improves the quality of results.

4. Set deadlines for completion of tasks. Provide a written copy of the schedule to all members, stressing the importance of following the agreed-upon timetable. Many managers find that activities get lost in the daily shuffle unless there is a specific deadline to meet.

5. Be sure to check progress at follow-up points, especially for long-range goals or complex projects. Some people naturally develop and follow schedules, while others easily let time slip away from them. Knowing that there are interim check points helps motivate the less-scheduled people.

6. If a team member understands expectations, has the ability to do the work, has been given specific deadlines, but still doesn't complete assignments,

then the team leader should handle this like any other employee performance problem. Some suggestions for performance management are offered in Chapter Ten under the section on toxic team members.

Problem Five: Employees Don't Implement Decisions as Expected

Sometimes decisions are made by a management team but never carried out by their employees. In one computer company, for example, the new CEO was told to "get control of the engineers," who had a history of working according to their own goals and standards regardless of management's plans. If employees fail to carry out decisions, the first step is to diagnose the cause of the problem. Is their oversight intentional or unintentional? Is management contributing to the problem in any way? Do employees have information that managers lack?

Suggestions for action:

1. Spend some time as a team exploring the situation. First, list all the possible reasons why employees might not understand what they are supposed to do (they don't receive the information; expectations are not clearly stated; their role is not explained in detail, etc.). If this does not clarify the problem, list all possible reasons why employees may not be motivated to make the change (the old way is easier; there are no role models; the reasons for change aren't clear; the new way is hard to learn; etc.). If you can identify an obvious cause of the problem, then you should be able to take corrective action.

2. If you are not able to identify a communication or motivation problem, consider why employees might choose to actively resist the decision. Does it seem unfair to them? Do they have a bad relationship with management for other reasons? Or is it possible that this is a bad idea?

3. Talk with employees about the change, but be sure that you are not hostile or blaming during these conversations. Enlist the employees' help in solving your implementation problems, remaining open to the possibility that management is part of the difficulty. If employees have helpful suggestions, use them. Resistance to change always contains useful information, so taking time to explore resistance usually makes implementation easier.

4. In the future, solicit input from employees before making decisions that affect them. This not only aids implementation but is also likely to produce better decisions.

5. Once a decision is made, involve employees in planning implementation activities. If they are the ones who must put a decision into action, they probably have a helpful perspective to share. Participation in planning also helps them understand what is expected of them.

6. As part of any future change efforts, incorporate some of the suggestions for changing behavior and developing communication plans that are outlined in strategies eleven and twelve in this chapter.

Problem Six: The Team Starts Projects But Fails to Complete Them

Starting a project often generates interest and enthusiasm. Coming up with an idea, developing plans to make it a reality, and seeing the initial fruit of your efforts is exciting. Once the first rush of adrenaline is over, though, some management teams quickly lose interest and move on to the next appealing project, never following the previous one through to completion. The result is an organization littered with half-completed projects that produce little or no positive result. These intermittent efforts are quite frustrating for employees and lower-level managers, who put time and energy into implementing one set of directives and then are switched to another track before they have seen any payoff from the first one. The top management team in one health care organization suffered from this problem. The group began a strategic planning process, a management development program, a review of compensation plans, and an internal customer feedback system but never finished any of them. One of their weary lower-level managers complained, "Lots of things get started around here, but none of them ever get finished. We never know what we're supposed to do next."

Suggestions for action:

1. Be sure that your work plan for a project goes beyond the initial stages. Don't stop when you have outlined phase one; keep going until you have a general description of the entire process. With this kind of group, being specific about follow-up plans is particularly important.

2. Clearly define the measure of success for all projects, following the guidelines given earlier in this chapter. Identifying the specific results that you hope to accomplish helps maintain your focus on the project after the initial thrill has worn off.

3. Post a list of all current projects where it is readily visible during team meetings. Set aside time in every meeting to track the progress of all projects presently under way.

4. Carefully evaluate any proposed projects in light of those currently being implemented. Remember that organizations have a limited supply of time and energy, so you want to use these resources to their best advantage. Don't start new projects if people are already stretched to the limit.

5. Cancel projects that have outlived their usefulness. On this type of team, a project is often forgotten once the group has moved on to its latest enthusiasm, but people in the organization may still be working on the previous assignment.

Officially canceling an outdated project sends a clear signal that no more effort should be aimed in that direction.

Problem Seven: Upper Management Interferes with Our Plans

When upper management frequently overrules decisions or changes plans, the cause is likely to be poor communication or unclear goals. Sometimes, however, the source of the difficulty is an executive who is too focused on details. One CEO of a large company insisted on reviewing and rewriting every piece of advertising copy written about the company's products, causing two ad agencies to resign the account and one marketing communications manager to quit his job.

Suggestions for action:

1. Constant interference may reflect lack of agreement on goals, so be sure that you are clear about the expectations and priorities of upper management. Refer to Chapter Two for suggestions on goal agreement.

2. Share more information with upper management about your plans. Some executives want more information than others, so find out how much detail is desired regarding your work. Even if the executive's desire for data seems excessive, life may be more pleasant if you keep the information flowing. Many senior managers simply have a strong need to know what is happening in their organization and interfere less if they are given complete information.

3. In some situations, however, you benefit from providing less information to upper management. Knowing whether to ask for forgiveness or permission is an important management skill. By sharing every detail of your work, you may give the executive too many chances to interfere. Deciding how much information to share with top management obviously requires careful thought and sound judgment.

4. Know the hot buttons that are likely to irritate higher-level managers, and avoid them. Continually doing something that annoys upper management is usually not good for one's occupational health.

5. If you are the team leader, avoid getting into a power struggle with your boss or other top executives. If you have a high need for control, you may find yourself trying to win all disagreements with your boss. Unfortunately, many managers fail to recognize this weakness until they are cashing their severance checks— and perhaps not even then, if they are prone to denial. Realizing that you habitually engage in power struggles requires some honest self-scrutiny:

- Are you resentful of your boss's involvement in your work?
- Do you intentionally withhold information from your boss?
- Do you avoid responding to requests from your boss?

- Do you do things that you know irritate your boss?
- Do you complain to others about your boss?
- Are you stupid enough to complain to the boss's secretary?

If you think you may be perpetuating a power struggle, try to get over it. Usually, the person with the most power wins, and that's not you. Learning to manage your boss is a critical survival skill in organizations; trying to show that you can't be managed is usually suicide.

True Story: The Demise of the Human Resource Department

Part Two: The Solution

Shortly after the decentralization of her department, Allison resigns, feeling that she simply doesn't have the energy to cope with such a major transition. Following her departure, the CEO appoints Bob, a manager from the finance department, to the position of vice president of human resources. Bob knows little about the technical side of human resource work, but he has a good relationship with the CEO and a track record of getting things done.

Soon after coming on board, Bob meets individually with each of his managers to discuss their plans for successfully operating under the new structure. After these meetings, he decides that the managers have good ideas but need direction in carrying them out. He gives his management team the task of developing action plans to define and communicate their new role, improve ineffective work processes, and build better relationships with line managers. As a group, they establish a time line for completing the initial transformation and designate follow-up points to be sure they stay on track. Each team member is assigned specific responsibilities for implementing the plan. Within three months, they have made significant progress in creating the "new and improved" corporate human resource department. Morale on the management team is higher than it has been in years.

Allison, the former vice president, receives some career counseling during her job search and realizes that her strengths lie in innovation and planning rather than implementation and operations. As a result, she decides to join a human resource consulting firm instead of looking for another corporate management job. In a consulting role, she can assist clients with developing and planning new approaches, without having to be the person responsible for implementing the change.

Team Assessment: Does Your Team Produce Results?

A management team that does not act is useless, since without action the group cannot fulfill its primary function of guiding the organization with effective decisions. To act, the team must first make an informed decision and then determine the most effective implementation plan. Effective action requires agreement on specifics: what results are desired, how they are to be accomplished, when activities will be carried out, and who needs to be involved. Follow-up is required to ensure that the plan has been implemented successfully.

The survey and discussion questions that follow help determine whether management team members perceive that they are taking action effectively. (Of course, the true test of this factor lies in the perceptions of your internal or external customers.) The survey questions are based on those used in the Management Team Research Project.

TEAM Survey: Focused Action

This survey helps determine whether the management team is taking action effectively. If you identify problems with effective action, you may wish to refer back to the appropriate sections of this chapter under "Key Steps in Achieving Meaningful Results" or "Overcoming Barriers to Focused Action."

Here are instructions for using the survey.

1. Give each team member a copy of Team Survey: Focused Action.
2. Tell the members *not* to put their names on these sheets.
3. Have them indicate their level of agreement with each statement and score their own survey.
4. Collect the survey sheets and add up the team score yourself or ask a team member to do so.
5. Determine a final team score using the formula under "Total Team Score."
6. To identify specific concerns, total the scores for each item and divide by the numbers of team members surveyed, as shown under "Item Scores."
7. Have a group discussion of the reasons for your scores. You may wish to use the discussion questions at the end of the chapter.

TEAM SURVEY: FOCUSED ACTION

For each item, indicate your level of agreement by circling the appropriate number.

	Agree			Disagree
1. We can easily see the results of our work on this team.	4	3	2	1
2. Whenever we make changes, we develop good implementation plans.	4	3	2	1
3. We usually complete the projects that we start.	4	3	2	1

	Agree			Disagree
4. After we make decisions, we usually find that they are carried out effectively.	4	3	2	1
5. We usually include people in making decisions that affect them.	4	3	2	1
6. We receive regular feedback about the results of our work on this team.	4	3	2	1
7. All team members do their part to carry out decisions.	4	3	2	1
8. Our decisions are usually implemented without delay.	4	3	2	1

A. Individual Scoring

Add up the circled numbers and write your score below.

Total Score = _____

8–16	17–23	24–32
Lack of effective action	Somewhat effective action	Effective action

TEAM Focused Action Survey: Team Scoring

B. Total Team Score

Total of all team member scores = _____

Divide by number of team members = _____

Total Score = _____

8–16	17–23	24–32
Lack of effective action	Somewhat effective action	Effective action

C. Item Scores

Total for each item	Divide total by number of team members
1.	1.
2.	2.
3.	3.
4.	4.
5.	5.
6.	6.
7.	7.
8.	8.

Discussion Questions: Focused Action

These questions can start a discussion with your team members about effective action. They may be used alone or as a follow-up to the TEAM Survey: Focused Action.

- How do we identify success on this team? Are the results of our work clearly defined? How can we be more specific about what we want to accomplish?
- Do we create effective action plans for our goals and projects? Do we need to be more specific about responsibilities, time lines, or action steps? How can we improve in this area?
- Can we do a better job of involving others in carrying out our action plans? Are there particular groups of people we tend to overlook? How can we ensure that people are involved appropriately?
- Are our decisions implemented effectively? Do we usually find that our plans and projects have been carried out as we expected? If not, what seems to be the source of the problem, and how can we correct it?
- In meetings, do we have effective discussions about how to implement our decisions? Do we spend too much or too little time on details of implementation? How can we make our discussions more productive?
- Do we complete the projects that we start? Do lower-level managers and employees understand what is expected of them in relation to each project? If we have unfinished projects, what do we need to do to complete them successfully? How can we avoid this problem in the future?
- Do members of upper management often change our plans or decisions? If so, why does this occur? How can we improve our relationship or communication with upper management to prevent this from happening so frequently?

PART TWO

MANAGEMENT TEAM MAINTENANCE

CHAPTER SEVEN

KEEPING THE TEAM PRODUCTIVE

True Story: Tension on the Team

Part One: The Problem

Michael, the director of information systems, is concerned. The four managers who report to him are cordial to one another in meetings and have no open conflicts, but he always senses an undercurrent of tension whenever they are together as a group. Two of them have been with the company for more than ten years, while the other two joined the team within the last eighteen months. Since the four of them come from three different countries, Michael wonders if cultural differences may be creating some problems.

The immediate reason for his preoccupation with the status of relationships on the management team is a breakdown in communication that has temporarily halted progress on a critical project. Michael believes the problem could have been easily avoided if the managers of the operations unit and the system development unit had simply talked to each other about system requirements. So why didn't they? Michael decides that he probably needs to ask them.

"I wanted to talk with you about the project delay," Michael tells the two managers in his office. "How come you two didn't compare notes on system requirements in advance?"

The managers glance at one another and then look away. A few seconds pass before anyone speaks.

"I don't think the subject ever came up in staff meeting," says one manager.

"No, I'm sure it didn't," echoes the other.

"Anyway, I thought everyone knew the system requirements," says the first.

"Oh, give me a break," sighs Michael. "Do we have to have a meeting for people around here to talk to each other?"

Although this management team might not have serious problems, relationships appear to have gradually eroded to the point that the team's performance is now affected. A communication gap has developed between long-term employees and new arrivals. Diverse cultural backgrounds may have fostered differing assumptions about how work should be performed. Language barriers may also exist. Team members seem to have developed the habit of working on projects independently without consulting one another. If the current situation is not addressed, this team runs the risk of developing some critical difficulties. Problems of this sort often arise on management teams that fail to perform "routine maintenance" activities.

The Need for Regular Maintenance

Team effectiveness is not a goal to be attained, but a process to be managed. Just as you perform maintenance regularly on your car, home, or yard, you also need to follow a program of regular maintenance with a management team. We have discussed the five success factors necessary for a group to function as a leadership team: strategic goals, extensive networks, collaborative relationships, effective information processing, and focused action. This chapter suggests three types of maintenance strategies to help keep a management team in good working order:

1. Opportunities for group work
2. Team performance management
3. Having fun together

Opportunities for Group Work

The term *management team* implies a collection of managers who make and implement decisions together. To develop this skill, they need opportunities to operate as a group. The more practice managers have in group problem solving and decision making, the more effectively they function as a team. These opportunities are usually provided through shared projects, regular meetings, and staff retreats.

Shared Projects

Cooperative relationships can be developed by undertaking shared projects involving all team members or appropriate subgroups. The leader must clearly define the goals of the project and the parameters within which the group is expected to work. One chief operating officer who wished to increase cooperation on her management team told them to identify areas where they could work together to improve results. After they spent three months unsuccessfully trying to find shared projects, she realized that this was alien territory for them and that she needed to be more specific. She then told them they needed to identify $8 million dollars in budget cuts and bring her a recommendation within six weeks. After just two weeks, she had the recommendations for cuts on her desk.

Regular Meetings

Everyone complains about meetings, but management teams need to meet regularly for several reasons. First, a team approach to management requires that the group make collaborative decisions. If the team leader seldom finds a reason to call managers together, or if meetings consist primarily of information sharing, then the leader is making too many decisions without input from the group. Second, managers of separate functions need to have predictable occasions on which they share information with one another. Knowing that they are expected to provide regular updates helps managers develop the habit of screening information for its usefulness to other team members. Finally, ongoing interaction helps solidify relationships among team members. When the inevitable conflicts occur between departments, managers with well-established relationships resolve them more easily. Friendly feelings among managers also help promote similar working relationships among their employees.

Meetings should be scheduled at intervals frequent enough for your group to accomplish these purposes. Most management teams meet weekly, biweekly, or monthly. If you find that your meetings drag on until everyone is exhausted, you need to hold them more often. Meetings should occur at a predictable time to encourage regular attendance because routinely holding team meetings without everyone present defeats the whole purpose of having them in the first place. Even though some people truly loathe having to sit still for several hours, attending staff meetings should be a basic job expectation for all team members. Managers need to understand that the purpose of meetings is to increase interdepartmental collaboration, improve internal networking, and break down walls between functions. (For suggestions on improving meeting effectiveness, see Chapter Five.)

Staff Retreats

Although regular team meetings provide a valuable opportunity for ongoing dialogue, their structure, setting, and time constraints are not conducive to long-range planning, in-depth exploration of problems, or sustained interaction among team members. Staff retreats are valuable because they remove managers from their daily demands—usually for one to three days—and allow them to focus on targeted issues in a relaxed atmosphere.

Retreats are usually for planning, problem solving, or relationship building. At a minimum, every management team should hold an annual planning retreat to review the past year's results and agree upon goals for the coming year. During the year, the team may need to get away together to focus on important issues and make critical decisions. Teams that have had membership changes or interpersonal difficulties may choose to devote all or part of a staff retreat to building relationships and developing teamwork skills. At least once every three years, management groups should undertake a complete strategic planning process to review their overall direction and make any needed changes. Several retreats are usually required to complete various phases of the planning process.

When planning a staff retreat, consider the following suggestions:

- The key to a successful retreat is removing all normal work distractions. Get away from the office. Any gathering in the office is a meeting, not a retreat.
- Choose a location in a natural setting. Being in the woods and mountains, at a lake, or in any other natural environment tends to create a relaxed atmosphere and encourages people to spend time together.
- If possible, go to a conference center. For retreats, this is usually a better choice than a hotel because a conference center has more suitable meeting rooms and is more likely to be located in pleasant surroundings.
- Have everyone dress casually. Suits, ties, and high heels are not conducive to relaxed discussion.
- Be sure that the team leader is specific about the reason for the retreat and the goals to be accomplished.
- Use an outside facilitator under any of the following circumstances:
  The group needs help in structuring a planning or problem-solving process.
  Group members are hard to control.
  Relationship issues are being discussed.
  The leader wants to temporarily step out of that role in order to participate fully in the discussion.
- Allow time for socializing and having fun. If the group enjoys games, build in structured recreational activities. (A facilitator or conference center activity director can help with this.) Otherwise, simply allow time for people to socialize on their own. Leaders who view this as wasted time need to realize that social interaction promotes development of positive relationships, which set the foundation for effective teamwork.

In one company, a new president inherited a group of independent, autonomous managers. To develop a true management team, she decided to incorporate a series of retreats into their regular meeting schedule. During her first year on the job, the team participated in three retreats as part of their strategic planning process. They were held at a conference center two hours away from the office, which allowed team members to stay overnight and interact with one another outside of meetings. Each session included several hours of activities devoted to building relationships. During the year, four one-day retreats were held at a local hotel to focus on specific problems that the team needed to solve. In addition, the team had regular staff meetings every other week. Within her first year, the president created a real leadership team. In subsequent years, the team simply held an annual planning retreat, since the intense group activity during the first year had created a strong foundation for ongoing teamwork.

Team Performance Management

A second critical aspect of team maintenance is managing the group's performance. Performance management includes clarifying goals and expectations, monitoring progress, and evaluating results. This process is just as important for groups as it is for individual performers.

Updating Goals

With the pace of change in many organizations today, goals set at the beginning of the year are easily rendered obsolete by unexpected developments or changes in priorities. When major events occur, the team needs to update goals based on the new realities. To do so, a brief quarterly review of goals is a good maintenance habit to develop. During a recession, one small company experienced a downturn in business that forced them to lay off 15 percent of their workforce. No layoff had previously occurred in the company's fifteen-year history. When the workforce reduction became necessary, the human resource department was caught completely by surprise and had to put together a layoff policy quickly. Unfortunately, their first attempt contained several errors in calculating seniority and had to be redone, causing some employees to be laid off, then called back, and then laid off again. Had the company's executive team members reviewed their goals regularly, they might have anticipated the effect of the recession on their business and realized that they should be prepared for a possible layoff. Given additional lead time, the HR department could have tested the seniority calculations in advance and avoided the employee relations disaster created by the flawed policy.

If goals are not updated, teams may find that their accomplishments at the end of the year bear little resemblance to the original plan. For executive teams, revising goals in light of changing circumstances helps ensure that the team provides proper direction to the rest of the organization. Teams below the top level should use the occasion of updating goals to initiate communication with upper management about changes affecting their work.

Progress Reports

Team members should periodically share information about their progress toward individual and team goals. Regular progress reports serve several important maintenance functions: team members are reminded of actions that need to be taken, the leader receives ongoing information about members' activities, and networking on the team is enhanced through sharing information.

Both written and verbal reports are helpful. Having each team member regularly submit written progress summaries gives the leader a performance record for each manager. In addition, the discipline of writing down accomplishments encourages team members to focus on goals. Copies of these reports can also be shared among team members. For team maintenance purposes, however, verbal reports are also useful, since these discussions allow members to ask questions and share ideas with one another. Progress reports on individual and team goals should be a fixed agenda item for all team meetings.

Team Member Evaluations

Just as managers should receive feedback about their job performance, they should also receive feedback about their performance as a team member, including such behaviors as networking, information sharing, cooperation, participation in group projects, and implementation of group decisions. Because the leader only has access to limited information about team relationships, accurate evaluations must include input from other team members. Since people are often reluctant to express candid opinions about coworkers, team member input should be solicited anonymously, using a simple rating form that provides space for comments. Exhibit 7.1 shows an example of a team member rating form used by one management group. When discussing this feedback with managers, the leader should stress their positive contributions in addition to expressing any concerns about behavior. If managers have low ratings in some areas, the leader needs to help them identify specific strategies and behaviors that would be more effective and set goals for improvement. (Strategy twelve in Chapter Six provides suggestions for encouraging behavior change.)

EXHIBIT 7.1. EXAMPLE OF A TEAM MEMBER RATING FORM USED BY A MANAGEMENT TEAM.

Team Member Assessment

4 = Agree   3 = Somewhat agree   2 = Somewhat disagree   1 = Disagree

	Agree			Disagree
1. Involves others in decisions that affect them.	4	3	2	1
2. Takes time to listen to others' concerns.	4	3	2	1
3. Treats people with respect.	4	3	2	1
4. Asks people to share ideas and suggestions.	4	3	2	1
5. Can disagree without getting angry.	4	3	2	1
6. Demonstrates honesty in giving information and answering questions.	4	3	2	1
7. Responds in a helpful fashion to problems or complaints.	4	3	2	1
8. Shares useful information with other team members.	4	3	2	1
9. Gives credit to others for results they produce.	4	3	2	1
10. Follows through with promises and commitments.	4	3	2	1

Comments:

Team member performance can also be addressed during staff retreats, but the focus should not be on criticism. Encouraging people to simply air their complaints about one another is definitely not helpful. A more positive approach is to explore how managers can assist each other in accomplishing goals and achieving results. This feedback process should include two components: appreciation and requests. First, team members express appreciation to one another for helpful actions, behaviors, or characteristics. Next, they make requests for any changes in behavior that will help them work more effectively in the future. This exercise usually works well if relationships are fundamentally positive, but it should not be used if serious relationship problems exist. (See Chapter Four for suggestions on improving team member relationships.)

Group Process Assessments

In addition to considering the performance of individual members, management teams need to regularly evaluate how well they are working together as a group.

Some groups incorporate this assessment into team meetings by periodically reviewing the effectiveness of their discussions and decision-making processes. A more in-depth assessment can be conducted at staff retreats by using instruments and other activities designed to assess group processes. Exhibit 7.2 shows an example of a rating form developed by one management team to track specific aspects of their working relationship. The surveys and discussion questions in this book can also be used to involve team members in evaluating management team effectiveness.

Evaluating Team Results

Finally, performance management must include an evaluation of how well the group has accomplished its goals. The team should take time to assess results at the end of each project and the end of each year, determining what was done well, what could be improved upon, and what lessons were learned for the future. (Suggestions for evaluating and improving results are in Chapter Six.)

Having Fun Together

Having fun as a group is an important part of team maintenance. Humor and social activities help build relationships, improve communication, and reduce tensions. Celebrating accomplishments can reward outstanding performance and teamwork. Teams that have no fun are usually teams in trouble.

Humor

If no one ever laughs in your team meetings, something is wrong. Encouraging team members to tell jokes, share cartoons, or relate amusing experiences helps make meetings more enjoyable and relaxed. One extremely reserved company president who was never seen at work without a coat and tie kicked off a sales retreat by running into the auditorium wearing a toga and carrying an Olympic torch. In addition to providing amusement for the sales staff, his actions also conveyed the message that he didn't take himself too seriously (something people had never been too sure about). In contrast, the director of a counseling center was one of several managers subjected to a good-natured "roasting" at an annual staff party. But the following year, when he learned that similar activities were being planned, he threw a fit in the office on the day before the party, stormed out, and ruined the festivities for everyone. (Perhaps he was in the wrong profession!)

EXHIBIT 7.2. A TEAM RATING FORM
ADOPTED BY ONE MANAGEMENT GROUP.

Team Effectiveness Survey

1. Team members are willing to   Team members rigidly hold to
   consider different viewpoints.   their own views.

       1   2   3   4   5

2. Team members work toward the   Team members work only to
   achievement of group goals.   benefit themselves.

       1   2   3   4   5

3. Team members are familiar with   Team members are only aware of
   each other's work goals.   their own goals.

       1   2   3   4   5

4. Group decisions are supported   Group decisions are ignored by
   and implemented by everyone.   those who disagree.

       1   2   3   4   5

5. Team members freely share   Team members keep information
   information to help one another. to themselves.

       1   2   3   4   5

6. Team members participate equally Some people dominate discussions
   in discussions.   while others seldom talk.

       1   2   3   4   5

7. Team members share ideas and   Team members don't contribute
   suggestions in meetings.   ideas and suggestions.

       1   2   3   4   5

8. The team is willing to experiment The team sticks to familiar ideas
   with new ways of doing things.   and methods.

       1   2   3   4   5

9. Team members are willing   Team members seldom disagree
   to disagree with one another.   openly.

       1   2   3   4   5

10. Team members can disagree   Disagreements usually lead to
    without getting angry.   angry words or feelings.

       1   2   3   4   5

Socializing

Friendly interaction away from work helps keep teams running smoothly. Frequent socializing isn't necessary, but occasional get-togethers are quite helpful. Group lunches or dinners provide a break in the normal course of work and give people a chance to get better acquainted. In one department, for example, the managers would go out to lunch to celebrate each person's birthday and bring gag gifts. Social events that include families increase the feeling of connectedness among team members. For one team, social activities consisted of group dinners twice a year and an annual holiday party at the leader's house, to which families were invited. Another group held annual summer and winter parties. One management team attended a baseball game together each summer, while another formed a softball team and joined a local league. The athletic members would play while the sedentary types cheered them on. The type of activity doesn't matter; the key is to provide interaction that has nothing to do with work.

Celebrations

Taking the time to celebrate success is important. Savoring triumphs and accomplishments improves motivation, morale, and productivity. Celebrations can be small (a group lunch or a T-shirt with an appropriate slogan to celebrate the end of a project) or large (a group trip to a fancy resort to celebrate a highly profitable year). The owner of a travel agency took his entire staff to Paris for a week to recognize their success.

To be effective, celebrations need to be focused on a specific accomplishment and held without delay. In an information systems department, various functions worked together successfully to pull off an extremely complicated project. The head of the department took his management team to lunch to celebrate— but not until three months after the project was completed. Although the group appreciated the gesture, by this time they had moved on to other projects and had half-forgotten the previous one. The celebration would have been much more effective had it been held a week or two after the project ended.

Some managers feel that celebrations are a waste of time and that the only meaningful reward is money. Although money is almost always appreciated, a celebration provides the opportunity to talk about our success and savor it together, as a team. (Besides, who says that you can't hand out bonus checks during the party if you really want to?)

Providing opportunities for managers to work as a group, taking the steps needed to manage team performance, and giving members a chance to interact outside of work all help keep a management team running smoothly. Just as changing the oil in your car prevents engine trouble later on, maintaining your management team helps prevent eventual problems with work or relationships.

True Story: Tension on the Team

Part Two: The Solution

Michael is disturbed by the conversation with his managers. Why would they wait for a topic to surface on the staff meeting agenda before talking about it? Don't they know what information is needed by other team members without his bringing it up? And why would a longtime employee assume that new people are at the same knowledge level as he? Clearly, something has to be done.

Michael decides to take advantage of a feedback process offered by the company's training department. During the process, Michael and his five managers work together to develop criteria describing effective management in the information systems department and then evaluate the department's performance based on these standards. After identifying department strengths and weaknesses, they complete a work style evaluation to see how their individual preferences may be affecting department performance, and to develop a better understanding of their various communication styles. Because they come from three different countries, team members also spend time comparing the assumptions and expectations that grow out of their cultural backgrounds. Finally, the group develops an action plan for making the department and the management team more effective.

Three months after beginning this process, Michael reflects on his most recent staff meeting. "You know," he thinks, "I don't feel that sense of tension anymore. People laugh and joke with each other, and they get a lot of work done together. I see them in each other's offices more often, too. So I guess they must finally be talking when I'm not around!"

CHAPTER EIGHT

SELECTING NEW TEAM MEMBERS

True Story: The Union Expert

Part One: The Problem

John, the human resource vice president, is about to fill the newly created position of director of employee relations. His nonunion company has been identified by a national union as their major organizing target, and unfortunately John is the only one on his management team who has much experience in dealing with unions. The company has been through a few campaigns before, but nothing like this. He needs to hire an expert, fast!

A few weeks later, John feels quite relieved. He's just interviewed Murray, a candidate for the director position who has twenty years' experience working for a large unionized company. During the interview, the two swapped tales about labor contracts they have negotiated and union leaders they have dealt with. Murray really seemed to enjoy John's war stories—the interview was fun! "Clearly," John says to himself afterwards, "this is a guy who knows how to handle a union problem." He hires Murray immediately and puts him in charge of managing the company's response to the union campaign.

Soon the other members of the management team are feeling much less optimistic. In their initial dealings with him, Murray turns out to be arrogant and opinionated, frequently lecturing them on how they should be doing their jobs. Worst of all, though, Murray puts policies in place that could seriously harm relationships with the company's workforce—at a time when employees are deciding whether or not to vote for a union.

"The problem," says one of the human resource directors, "is that this fellow only knows how to deal with unions. He knows nothing about working in a non-union company."

"I know," replies another director. "And I'm afraid that under Murray's guidance, we'll be a unionized company before long. I wonder why John ever decided to hire him."

"I can't imagine," groans the first. "But we're stuck with him now."

This vice president selects a manager for a key position without carefully considering the responsibilities of the job. Most of the interview is spent swapping stories, with little exploration of the candidate's background—and the vice president surely does most of the talking. Unfortunately, this critical error in judgment can have serious consequences for both the human resource department and the company.

Common Pitfalls in Selecting Managers

Any team is only as good as its members. Every new hire or promotion into a management position represents a chance for the leader to strengthen or weaken the management team. Although filling any job is important, making a correct management selection is especially critical, since managers affect the performance of everyone below them. The higher the position, the more important it is to make the right choice. This chapter outlines an eight-step process for improving management selections. But first let's discuss some common traps to avoid in filling management positions.

Selecting First-Time Managers

When hiring or promoting first-time managers, you should assess candidates on their demonstrated potential for management work, particularly their ability to effectively supervise people. We frequently assume that an outstanding performer in a professional or technical job automatically becomes an outstanding manager. This is not necessarily true, however, because management work is likely to require a different set of abilities. The best salesperson, counselor, or engineer may therefore not be the most effective sales director, counseling supervisor, or engineering manager. In fact, employees who loved their previous jobs may find that they don't even like management work. Outstanding salespeople, for example, often find that management requires too much paperwork and time spent in the office. Technical employees who like working with machines or computers may get frustrated when they have to deal with the people problems that managers constantly encounter. Thus the organization loses an excellent employee, only to gain a mediocre manager.

Hasty Hiring

When a position is vacant—especially a management position—the hiring manager usually wants to fill it as quickly as possible. Paperwork is piling up, projects are left untended, people are coming in with problems, and the manager just wants a warm body to take up where the previous person left off. Unfortunately, hiring in haste only magnifies these difficulties if the wrong person is chosen. Should a truly poor performer be selected, the manager has to go through the pain of termination and the frustration of repeating the hiring process. Even worse, a mediocre manager may be hired, someone who is never bad enough to fire and who never voluntarily leaves, thereby creating a weakness in the management position for years to come. Considering the risks of hasty hiring, taking the time to make a proper selection is well worth the temporary pain of living with a vacancy for a while.

Random Recruiting

New hires obviously come from an applicant pool, but where do the applicants come from? In filling a management position, targeted recruiting is half the battle. Shotgun approaches like using general classified ads or Internet ads do nothing to narrow down the applicant group and usually generate stacks of unsuitable resumes. Getting referrals from employees often produces some excellent candidates, but this approach should not be overused as a recruiting strategy since employee referrals are likely to perpetuate the profile of your current workforce. This may be good in some respects, but it can also result in unintentional discrimination against racial, ethnic, or gender groups that are not represented. Managers need to take a strategic approach to recruitment, identifying the type of candidate they are seeking and developing specific recruiting strategies to locate suitable applicants.

Mirror Images

Some managers must really like what they see in the mirror, because they consistently hire in their own image. Candidates whose abilities—and personalities—match their own are more likely to be chosen. In some companies, a generic management profile seems to develop, and matching that stereotype becomes the primary qualification for promotion. Unfortunately, matching new hires to the manager rather than to job requirements often means that the best person is not selected. The eventual result can be an entire group of managers who think and act similarly and therefore have serious deficits as a team. To modify a mirror-image bias, hiring managers need to carefully assess the requirements of each management job and the needs of their management team.

Executives' Interviewing Skills

Executives are often poor interviewers. This is unfortunate, because the managers they hire have a tremendous impact on the organization. Failure to plan for interviews is one common problem. Because executives are so busy, they may give little thought to an interview until the candidate is walking in the door, and as a result they fail to focus their questions on critical skills and abilities. In most situations, however, lack of time is not a valid excuse, since executives usually have access to human resource professionals or search firm consultants who can help them identify position requirements and develop appropriate questions. The executive simply needs to be willing to ask for assistance.

A second problem is that executive interviewers often talk too much. Many management candidates leave their interviews wondering how they can be fairly evaluated when they hardly had a chance to speak. Some of these chatty interviewers are just talkative people who fail to curb their natural tendencies. In other cases, excessive talking reflects poor planning, since an interviewer who does not have questions ready often fills the gap by giving out a lot of information. Executives need to remember that the sole purpose of an employment interview is to get information for a good hiring decision. When you are talking, you are not learning anything about the candidate.

How to Hire the Best Person for the Job

The key to making good management selections is to fully understand the requirements of the job and assess candidates based on those needs. Following these eight steps helps improve your selection of managers:

1. Analyze the job.
2. Evaluate team needs.
3. Define the ideal candidate.
4. Decide on a recruiting strategy.
5. Develop effective interview questions.
6. Determine your interviewing plan.
7. Conduct a targeted interview.
8. Compare all candidates.

If you have never had interview training, consider attending a workshop where you can practice these skills, since interviewing is one of the most important tasks you perform as a manager.

Analyze the Job

To accurately assess a position, you must have comprehensive, current information about the work done in that job. When hiring managers, certain aspects of the work are likely to be predictable, since most management positions involve planning, making decisions, supervising the work of others, solving problems, and taking appropriate action. Specific requirements vary, however, depending upon the position, the department, and the organization.

Because most executives have only a limited view of the work done by those who report to them, you may wish to get other opinions about critical job requirements. Department employees, internal customers, and the manager leaving the position all have valuable perspectives. When you feel that your understanding is sufficient, prepare a brief job analysis: list major areas of responsibility, primary tasks for each responsibility, and important working conditions, such as frequent travel or management of geographically dispersed offices. A sample job analysis for a director of training is shown in Part A of the Interview Planning Worksheet in Exhibit 8.1.

Evaluate Team Needs

In addition to considering the needs of the position, you should also think about the needs of your management team. Would the organization benefit from new blood? Selecting an external candidate rather than promoting from within offers the advantage of bringing in fresh ideas and perspectives. Are there internal candidates who would improve the team's functioning? Choosing someone from a "customer" department, for example, might enhance that perspective on the team. Are team members too similar in background? If everyone is of the same age, race, gender, or nationality, then you may wish to add variety to the team. Do team members have similar work styles? If everyone naturally focuses on details, then you may want to look for a big-picture person. Do you have a successor on the team? If not, then you may wish to select someone with potential to move into your job. Specific issues vary from team to team, but executives should always consider team needs when filling management positions.

Define the Ideal Candidate

Describing your dream applicant begins to focus your thinking about the proper choice for the job. Consider the job requirements and team needs that you have identified; list the knowledge, abilities, and characteristics that help promote success in this position. Career interests may also be relevant. Even though the ideal candidate may be impossible to find, you can still use the profile to

EXHIBIT 8.1. EXAMPLE OF AN INTERVIEW PLANNING WORKSHEET FOR A TRAINING DIRECTOR POSITION.

Interview Planning Worksheet

Position: Director of Training

A. Job Analysis

Responsibilities	Tasks	Working Conditions
Provide direction to training department	Develop strategic and operational plans Assess company training needs annually Delegate appropriately to employees	Workweek routinely over 40 hours Expected to teach some management courses Travel approximately six weeks per year
Develop positive working relationships with line and staff managers	Maintain awareness of managers' needs and concerns Involve other departments in training projects Serve as a consultant to other departments	Some weekend travel required Training department located in separate building
Manage performance of training department staff	Develop annual performance plans with employees Provide coaching needed for employees to achieve results Give both positive and negative feedback to employees Resolve performance problems	

B. Ideal Candidate

Knowledge and Experience	Abilities and Characteristics	Career Interests
Knowledge about: • good management • adult learning • instructional design Experience in: • our industry • managing a training department • teaching adults • course design Prefer master's degree	Express ideas clearly Logically analyze problems Build good working relationships Work well as part of a team Handle difficult interpersonal situations	Likely to stay in job for minimum of two years Has potential to move into vice president position

(Continued)

EXHIBIT 8.1. CONTINUED.

C. Interview Objectives	Ask	Observe
At the end of the interview, I want to know whether the applicant:		
Uses effective management practices	X	
Has experience in our industry	X	
Has good relationship-building skills	X	X
Analyzes problems logically	X	
Writes and speaks clearly	X	X
Can handle difficult interpersonal situations	X	
Can conduct a training needs analysis	X	
Can teach adults	X	X
Can travel frequently	X	
Can be an effective consultant to managers	X	
Can be an effective management team member	X	X

D. Questions for All Applicants

1. What are some of the challenges faced by companies in this industry today?

2. How would your employees describe your management style?

3. Describe a difficult management situation and how you handled it.

4. Tell me about a team project that you worked on. What was most rewarding about working as part of a team? What was most frustrating?

5. What kinds of people do you find it irritating to work with? Give me an example.

6. Tell me about a training needs analysis that you conducted and describe the methods you used.

7. Suppose that you have just finished explaining a point in a workshop. Suddenly a participant says, "I think that's a stupid idea! We've never done it that way in my department." What would you do?

8. What are some important principles to follow in teaching adults successfully?

9. Describe a consulting project that you handled in your company. What problems did you encounter? How did you solve them?

10. How much do you travel in your current job? How much travel would be too much for you?

help screen your applicants. A sample description of an ideal candidate for the training director position is shown in Part B of the Interview Planning Worksheet in Exhibit 8.1.

Decide on a Recruiting Strategy

Having defined your ideal candidate, you can determine where such people might be found and how they can be reached. Identifying the organizations where ideal applicants work, the associations they join, the publications they read, the career fairs they attend, or the Internet sites they visit helps you determine the best recruiting strategy. One creative company found many good candidates at an annual home and garden show! This event attracted first-time home buyers who were successful young professionals in the area's predominant industry. Company recruiters mingled with the crowds, initiated conversations, and obtained business cards from likely prospects.

Another organization turned the traditional employee referral approach on its head. Rather than asking employees to supply names of potential applicants, the company ran job advertisements in movie theaters asking interested people to call and "make a friend" of one of their employees. Callers were then matched with an employee having a similar background, who phoned the prospect to tell them about the company. The program enabled the company to reach people who were not currently job hunting and resulted in many successful new hires.

Many management candidates are found through recruiters and search firms, but the success of this approach depends largely on good communication between the hiring manager and the recruiter. Once you have selected a search firm, you need to thoroughly explain your job requirements, team needs, and ideal candidate profile. The recruiter can be much more useful if you clearly specify the parameters of the search. Many executives have become frustrated with unsuitable applicants referred by a search firm, not realizing that they themselves were at least partly to blame for failing to clearly communicate their wishes and expectations.

Develop Effective Interview Questions

Deciding what to ask the candidates should be relatively easy if you have completed the previous steps. Use the information from your job analysis, team assessment, and ideal candidate profile to set goals for the interview; that is, what do you want to learn about each applicant? A sample set of interview goals is shown in Part C of the Interview Planning Worksheet in Exhibit 8.1. Based on the goals, develop a set of critical questions that form the core of your interview plan: the questions you plan to ask every applicant. Most questions should focus on past job experiences that help you evaluate the candidate's potential for success in the new position. You also need to be certain that your inquiries do not unintentionally discriminate against any legally protected group; if you are unsure of the ground rules in this area, consult your human resource department or labor attorney. A sample set of questions for the director of training position is shown in Part D of the Interview Planning Worksheet in Exhibit 8.1.

Finally, you need to review the resume of each applicant well before the interview to identify specific areas for exploration. If you pick up the resume only as the candidate walks through your door, you may overlook valuable information about the individual's background. Thorough resume review requires attention to detail, such as employment dates, job responsibilities, specific accomplishments, and so forth. Since your new manager needs to be an effective team member, prior experience on management teams or with other team activities should be explored.

Determine Your Interviewing Plan

First, you must decide whether to use multiple interviewers or conduct the process alone. Multiple interviews require more time and coordination but have the advantage of providing different perspectives on the candidates. Getting a variety of viewpoints helps correct for any unconscious biases of your own (and we all have some). Management team members, higher-level managers, employees, and internal customers are all useful interviewers. Although individual meetings are preferable, group interviews can be used if time is not available for one-on-one discussions. Just keep in mind that group interviews can be quite uncomfortable for candidates who are not used to being in this sort of spotlight, and this may affect the quality of their responses.

If multiple interviews are used, you need to determine the most effective sequence of interviewers. Remember that interviews are tiring for candidates, so try to avoid scheduling too many in one day. As the hiring manager, you usually want to place yourself first and last on the list, so that you can discuss the process with the candidate at the beginning of the day and answer questions at the end. You also need to designate specific areas to be explored by each interviewer, so the candidate won't be asked the same question four times in a row.

If your organization uses an industrial psychologist or an assessment center to screen applicants, incorporate these additional steps into the process. Finally, decide how many times you would like to see your top candidates. Is one interview sufficient, or do you need to bring them back for a second or third round?

Conduct a Targeted Interview

Keep in mind that the primary goal of an interview is to get the information you need to make a selection decision. This information transfer only occurs while the applicant is discussing relevant topics. If you are talking too much or if the applicant has strayed off course, then you are not getting useful information. During the interview, therefore, you must guide the applicant into productive areas of discussion and control your own urge to talk.

Your secondary interview goal is to make a positive impression on applicants that you may wish to hire, so always be mindful of how you and your organization appear to the candidate. One CEO lost many good management applicants because he was so disorganized that he kept them waiting for hours and constantly rearranged their interview schedules. Candidates quickly realized that this behavior was likely to be a reflection of the way he ran the company. (They were correct.)

Attending training in employment interviewing is the best way to sharpen your interview skills, but if you have never had such training, these suggestions are helpful:

- Don't give undue weight to your first impression of a candidate. Wait until you have actually asked questions and explored the applicant's background and experience before forming an opinion.
- Make the candidate as comfortable as possible. People usually provide more accurate information if they feel relaxed.
- For the most part, you should get information before you give information. Giving a candidate too much information about the job or the company at the beginning of an interview provides valuable clues as to how your questions should be answered. In addition, you waste time giving information to candidates who prove to be unsuitable by the end of the interview.
- Take notes during each interview so that you can review them later. After you talk with several applicants, people tend to blend together in your memory, so don't rely solely on recall.
- Ask all candidates your core questions, but probe for additional information based on their responses. Take time to go beyond initial, superficial answers. Develop specific questions for each person based on their resume.
- If the applicant will be seeing additional interviewers, provide a list of their names and titles. Remembering names during a lengthy interview process

can be difficult, so having a list avoids embarrassment for your candidate. For the person who is hired, the list will also be a useful reminder when these people are encountered on the job.

- At the end of the interview, answer any questions the applicant may have. If this candidate appears highly desirable, begin to "sell" the job and the company. You also need to let the applicant know what happens next. If you expect that reaching a final decision may take several weeks, say so. Most applicants anxiously await a phone call, so setting some expectations about how long the process takes is a kind thing to do.

Compare All Candidates

Creating a matrix similar to the one shown in Exhibit 8.2 helps structure the decision about your final selection. By this time, you probably have eliminated some candidates and narrowed down your decision to two or three potential hires (unless you are lucky enough to have one clear choice). Using the matrix, create a rating scale (1 to 5, 1 to 10, etc.) to compare applicants on the critical requirements of the job. If some requirements are much more important than others, give them greater weight (for example, multiply that factor by two).

Be sure to give balanced consideration to all of an applicant's qualifications. Don't be unduly swayed by one particular characteristic or type of experience. Try to be aware of your own biases and correct for them. If multiple interviewers are used, you should meet with them individually or as a group to discuss their reactions. You might also wish to have each interviewer complete a matrix. You may or may not decide to hire the candidate with the highest score, but the process helps you carefully think through the candidates' qualifications.

When making your final selection, remember that this new addition needs to be a positive addition to your management team. A candidate with outstanding intellect or technical abilities who cannot work successfully with others is not likely to be a good choice. Hiring or promoting managers is one of your most important activities, one with far-reaching consequences. Investing the time and effort needed to construct an effective selection process helps guarantee that your final hiring decision is a wise one.

EXHIBIT 8.2. EXAMPLE OF MATRIX USED TO COMPARE APPLICANTS FOR TRAINING DIRECTOR POSITION.

Criteria: Rating from 1 (low) to 5 (high)

Applicants	Management Skills	Industry Experience	People Skills	Logical Analysis	Speaking and Writing Clearly	Teaching Adults	Working with Management Team	Total
Jerry	5	4	4	5	5	3	4	30
Linda	3	3	4	2	3	3	2	20
Mallie	5	1	5	4	4	3	5	27
Larry	4	1	4	3	2	2	5	21

True Story: The Union Expert

Part Two: The Solution

John, the human resources vice president, gets lucky. After six months, Murray is offered more money to return to his former employer, and he decides to leave. The rest of the management team is elated and cannot believe their good fortune. They know all too well that most poor hiring decisions don't resolve themselves this easily.

Fortunately, John does not repeat his mistake. Because of his problems with Murray, he takes time to analyze the needs of the position and decides that an insider's knowledge of company culture is more valuable than experience with unions. In fact, if the company can halt the organizing drive, union experience won't be needed! Instead of looking for an outside "expert," John promotes a manager with a strong employee relations background. Working with the other management team members, the new director corrects many of the problems that led to the organizing drive in the first place. Several months later, a union election is held, and the company wins by a wide margin.

CHAPTER NINE

MANAGING TEAM TRANSITIONS

True Story: The Defeat of the Social Work Department

Part One: The Problem

Three managers from the social work department are glumly finishing their lunch in the hospital cafeteria. "So when did you hear about it?" asks Vivian.

"Sarah in accounting told me yesterday," replies Jake. "She said they were trying to figure out how to combine our budgets."

"Well, I think it's a crime," says Judy. "For eighteen years social work has been an advocate for patients, and now they're just dumping us into the rehabilitation department and shoving us out of the way."

Jake looks up from his lunch. "There's no way that this is going to work. These two departments just operate too differently. The rehab people know nothing about what we do, so how are they going to manage us?"

"They can't," says Vivian. "And I don't want to work the way they do. They're always rushing into new projects without thinking them through."

On the other side of the cafeteria, two managers from the rehabilitation department are talking excitedly over their sandwiches. "I can't believe we're taking over social work!" exclaims Bob. "It's about time that administration realized they aren't pulling their weight."

"I know," Rose answers. "They're so stodgy over there, never trying anything new. I can't wait to shake that place up. My experience with them is that they're just a road block."

"So who do you think will be on the management team? They surely won't leave that whole management group in place."

"I have no idea," says Rose, as she and Bob get up from the table. "But putting these two groups together ought to make for some interesting meetings. Thank heavens our boss will be running the show."

As Rose and Bob pass their table, the managers from social work stare intently at their plates and say nothing.

The rehabilitation department management team is about to get some new members; however, nothing seems to have been done to promote the success of this merger. People are hearing about the change through the grapevine, historical rivalries are in evidence, and people are falling into the roles of winners and losers. Unless appropriate actions are taken to ease this transition, relationships are likely to get off to a rocky start, possibly sowing the seeds of long-term conflict.

Critical Transition Points

Transition points represent a challenge for any management team, even one that is functioning quite well. Any significant alteration in the membership or function of a team creates a transition point. These changes cause a shift in team goals or relationships, the two most critical components of cooperation and teamwork. Taking steps to successfully navigate transitions prevents lost productivity and damaged relationships, possibly making the team even stronger than before.

Certain events are particularly important in the life of a team. At these junctures, actions taken by leaders and members affect the team's functioning for years to come. For each transition point discussed in this section, suggestions are provided for both leaders and members to help ease their passage through the change:

1. Starting a new team
2. Gaining or losing team members
3. Changing team leaders
4. Turnover in top management
5. Redefining the team's function
6. Working with constant change

Transition One: Starting a New Team

Building a team from the ground up is a rare opportunity. Since the leader is able to select every team member, choosing the right people is the most critical aspect of this transition. Technically, a start-up is not actually a team transition, since previously there was no team; however, all team members are simultaneously experiencing major personal change, so in effect this creates a transition point for the group.

Impact on the Team

Everyone on a new team is going through a learning curve at the same time, absorbing reams of new information and adapting to a new job, new organization, new boss, and new coworkers. As a group, they lack the foundation of shared experiences and assumptions that facilitates communication and decision making. As with any person or group on a learning curve, decisions take longer, and errors can be expected.

Members of new management teams are usually recruited from a variety of organizations or from different functions in the same organization. As a result, they may have conflicting expectations about how work should be done and how people should communicate. Such differences inevitably lead to disagreements among team members. At a new bank, the management team was recruited from large nationwide banking institutions, small community banks, and credit unions. Initially, these managers found they had very different operating assumptions; even their definitions of banking were dissimilar. Over the course of their first year together, the conflicting viewpoints were gradually resolved. But the first year was rough.

A new management group is like an expansion team in sports: players come from a variety of teams, where they have developed different habits and expectations. They need time to adapt to one another's strengths, weaknesses, strategies, and tactics before the team can function seamlessly.

Managing Group Stages

All new groups go through four predictable stages: organizing, arguing, blending, and producing.

Organizing. In the organizing stage, goals are established and relationships begin to develop. Members usually have many unspoken questions at this point: will they enjoy being part of the team, fit in with other members, find the group useful, achieve their personal goals, be able to make a contribution? The group needs to share information, begin to define its task, and start to form positive working relationships.

Arguing. As team members pass through the organizing stage and grow accustomed to working with one another, they start to feel more comfortable about expressing differences of opinion. The appearance of strong disagreements usually signals the beginning of the arguing stage, during which people express opposing views, debate goals and strategies, engage in power struggles, and test the leader's authority. For a group to become fully productive, they must learn to express these differences constructively. If team members come from different organizations, the arguing stage is likely to be prolonged, since they need time to share and compare their various perspectives.

Blending. As the group continues to work together, team members usually come to recognize that their personal experiences represent only one possible view of reality. During the blending stage, their separate perspectives begin to merge into a set of shared norms, expectations, and work patterns. By the end of this phase, they should develop a "group feeling," a sense that they are not just a collection of individuals but part of a larger whole. A primary challenge for new groups is to successfully navigate the arguing stage and blend into a team.

Producing. If the blending process is successful, the group enters the producing stage, during which they collaborate successfully on achieving their goals.

These four stages are outlined in Table 9.1, which describes team needs at each stage and suggests strategies to help the leader successfully guide the group through them.

Transition Guidelines for Team Leaders

1. When creating a new team, select your managers carefully. Keep in mind that they need to function not only as department heads but also as team members. You may find it helpful to follow the suggestions offered in Chapter Nine for selecting managers.

2. Provide written information to the new team members about the organization, the purpose of the team, members' work backgrounds, and anything else that helps people move along the learning curve more quickly.

3. Be aware that your new group has to go through an organizing stage. During this phase, you need to establish goals, clarify expectations, and share information about your own habits, preferences, pet peeves, and hot buttons. You should also allow time for people to get acquainted and begin to develop positive relationships, since friendly interaction during the organizing stage pays off when you hit arguing.

4. The organizing stage can be shortened by holding a kickoff retreat once all team members are on board. Engaging in the following activities helps move the group through organizing fairly quickly:

TABLE 9.1. STAGES USUALLY EXPERIENCED BY NEW TEAMS.

Stage	Team Needs	Leader Behavior
Organizing	• Understanding of purpose, goals, and expectations • Foundation for developing positive relationships	• Define and discuss mission and goals • Share your own expectations • Allow time to get acquainted • Encourage sharing of personal and work information • Generate enthusiasm for the future
Arguing	• Willingness to express differences of opinion • Effective management of conflicts	• Solicit different points of view • Encourage people to listen • Refer back to mission and goals • Look for points of agreement • Explore areas of disagreement
Blending	• Agreement on common goals • Accepting different points of view	• Help group develop shared objectives • Discuss value of different viewpoints • Help people see their similarities • Work toward consensus • Encourage development of group identity
Producing	• Support in accomplishing their work • Collaborative relationships	• Provide necessary direction • Share information • Obtain resources • Reward cooperation

- Agreeing on the overall mission and purpose of the team
- Establishing specific goals for the team
- Discussing members' backgrounds and work experience
- Learning about one another's work styles
- Defining criteria for positive working relationships
- Identifying valuable sources of networking information
- Developing meeting guidelines
- Holding social activities to help people get acquainted

5. Develop good meeting habits. The initial expectations you set are hard to change later, so create an effective decision-making climate from the beginning. (See Chapter Five for a discussion of effective meetings.)

6. During team meetings, encourage discussion, questions, and active participation in decision making. In addition to establishing a norm of open communication, this interaction helps members absorb information more quickly and move toward becoming a true team.

7. Help your managers develop the habit of working together outside of team meetings. Encourage them to share information and collaborate on joint projects.

8. Carefully manage conflicts as they begin to emerge during the arguing stage. Members need to learn that expressing differences is helpful as long as they treat one another with respect, listen to different points of view, and stay focused on common goals. During this stage, the leader needs to exhibit an appropriate amount of control: enough to keep the discussion focused on productive problem solving but not so much that disagreement is squelched.

9. Hold regular meetings with individual team members to address any questions or concerns they have about their new role. Frequent interaction between you and your managers helps all of you move along the learning curve more quickly.

Suggestions for Team Members

1. Develop a clear agreement with the team leader about your individual goals and the team's goals. Put goals in writing to ensure that you and the leader have the same understanding of what is expected.

2. Learn about your boss's expectations, preferences, and pet peeves. Arrange for regular meetings with your manager to discuss progress, accomplishments, and challenges.

3. Take time to get to know your new coworkers, since developing relationships now helps you work together more effectively later. Look for opportunities to collaborate with others by sharing information or helping with projects. Conflict is to be expected in any new group, so don't be surprised if other team members seem annoying or irritating for a while. Some of them probably find you annoying, too. Usually (though not always) these relationships improve with time.

4. Identify critical sources of networking information in your new role or new organization. Determine which people you need to get to know, and begin to make contacts with them.

5. Expect to experience a certain amount of disappointment and disillusionment. We often enter new situations with a high level of optimism and excitement but become discouraged as we begin to see the difficulties. Remind yourself that no situation is perfect; try to focus on the positive aspects of your new role.

Transition Two: Gaining or Losing Team Members

Management teams are fluid entities. Members leave for better opportunities, to begin retirement, or because their performance is not up to par. People are added to replace those who have left or to represent a new function. Each change in membership causes a shift in the dynamics of the group.

Impact on the Team

Departing team members take with them their unique abilities and strengths; this sometimes creates a deficiency in the group. On one team, for example, the departure of the member with the longest tenure left the group without a ready source of institutional memory. Another group lost the only manager with knowledge of specialized legal issues. If close relationships exist, losing a member may also mean losing a friend or confidant, creating a sense of personal loss for those who remain. If the person leaving served as the group's informal leader, members may initially feel abandoned and uncertain about how to operate. One team reacted with stunned silence when a respected and trusted member announced that she had accepted a job with another company; three years later, members of the group still occasionally reflect on how things would be "if Sue had never left."

If team members leave under negative circumstances, their coworkers may react with fear, anger, or relief. Fear is the predictable response if managers have reason to believe that they could suffer a similar fate. When a layoff or firing may represent the first in a sequence (because of reorganizations, cost cutting, or changes in leadership), team members naturally become anxious and worried. An angry reaction is to be expected if the departing team member appears to have been treated unfairly or if the reason for the dismissal is not clear. On the other hand, if a team member has been unproductive, incompetent, or difficult to work with, relief may be the predominant emotion.

New team members bring strengths, weaknesses, habits, and preferences to which team members have to adjust. When a position was previously held by a long-term incumbent, coworkers usually have definite expectations about how the role should be performed and may have difficulty adjusting to a different approach. One training director always addressed problems in an organized, analytical manner. If someone called her with a potential training need, she would interview the caller, gather a lot of information, and prepare a detailed written proposal outlining the best approach to the situation. After she left for another job, the training director position was filled by a more spontaneous and action-oriented manager. His approach, when someone presented him with a training problem, was to engage the person in a brainstorming session, identify several possible alternatives, and immediately select one to pursue. By the end of the meeting, an action plan was in place. Both of these styles had strengths and weaknesses, but the shift from one to the other was difficult for coworkers. For a time, until he established credibility with the group, the new training director's competence was seriously questioned simply because he performed the job differently.

If creating a new department or function adds a member to the team, people may initially lack a full understanding of the new role and its relationship to their own departments. The sales and marketing department in one company hired a manager to run the newly created marketing communications organization. Because no such function had ever existed before, management team members initially viewed the new department as simply a producer of brochures and did not understand that marketing communications would be instrumental in creating and shaping the company's image with customers. As this role began to emerge, team members initially felt that the new manager was interfering with their autonomy, but they gradually came to realize that she was a valuable resource.

Finally, if subgroups or cliques exist on the team, adding or subtracting members can shift the balance of power. On one human resource management team, for example, HR directors from the company's two largest divisions always presented a united front on issues at team meetings. When one of them left, the other found that his influence was somewhat diminished without the automatic support of his partner.

Transition Guidelines for Team Leaders

1. Whenever team members leave under positive circumstances, discuss their departure in a staff meeting or prepare a written announcement describing their reasons for leaving. Have some type of social gathering to recognize the person's contributions, and give members a chance to say good-bye.

2. If team members are laid off or fired, discuss the circumstances in a staff meeting at the appropriate time. Talking about their departure helps dispel negative emotions surrounding the event. If you are not able to elaborate on the reasons, say so, but give as much information as you can. One organization terminated a popular accounting manager after learning that she had been embezzling funds for several years. For both legal and public relations reasons, discussing the specifics of her firing was inadvisable. To head off rumors, the division director told his management team that there had been some serious problems with the accounting manager's performance, but he was not at liberty to discuss specifics. He said he knew she had been a popular member of the team, but she clearly could not continue in her position. He asked the managers to try to understand that he was in a difficult situation, since he would like to share more in-

formation, but doing so would be inappropriate. He encouraged them to try to calm the rumor mill by giving the same message to their employees.

If team members are angry over a coworker's termination, give them an opportunity to discuss their perceptions and feelings. Try to help them understand why the termination was necessary (if it was), why you can't discuss the reasons (if you can't), or why the group needs to accept what happened and move on (if it really was unfair). If the anger is directed at you, you may wish to have someone else facilitate the discussion.

When a termination causes members to fear they may be next, you need to be honest with them. Providing false reassurance is worse than saying nothing, since you will eventually appear to be a liar. If no further terminations are planned, say so. If you don't know or if you do know but can't discuss it, just say that you aren't sure what may happen in the future. If additional layoffs or firings are likely, acknowledge this reality but stress that work needs to continue despite the uncertainty; indicate that you will share information as it becomes available.

3. As new people join the management team, send written information about them to other team members before they arrive on the job. If the new person is from your own organization, provide facts about his work background. If she is from another organization, share information about her work history and previous employer. If a new function has been added, indicate the purpose of the new department and how it benefits the team. At their first staff meeting, give new team members time to talk in some detail about their background and work experiences.

4. Be sensitive to differences in the way people prefer to enter a new group. Some hit the ground running; they talk and participate from the start. Others like to observe quietly for a while until they get a feel for the group. This difference was clearly illustrated during one management retreat. The first day of the retreat was also the first day of work for two new team members. One had a comment about every topic and actively debated points with other members of the group, while the other said absolutely nothing for two days. Both became effective and well-accepted team members, but their initial approaches were quite different.

5. Provide written information to help new team members move along the learning curve as quickly as possible. Annual reports, marketing brochures, and newsletters all provide useful background information about the organization. A summary of the individual goals of other team members educates the new person about the various functions in the group. Resumes or biodata sheets about other people on the team help the new member begin to establish relationships.

6. Initially, you need to have frequent individual meetings with a new team member to answer questions and check out perceptions. Encourage the new person to bring questions or issues to you as they arise.

7. Share any important information about group or organizational history with new team members. In one situation, a new manager was puzzled by reactions and

remarks during his first joint meeting with another department. The interaction would have made more sense to him if he had been told in advance that people from the two departments had a long history of competing for funds and trying to stab one another in the back.

8. Promote interaction between team members and their new coworker. Suggest that the new member schedule lunches with individual managers to learn more about their departments. Identify opportunities for others to include the new manager in meetings or projects. You may want to appoint one person to serve as a sort of orientation mentor for the new team member, providing information, arranging introductions, and answering questions.

9. Begin the networking process by introducing the new team member to people in other departments or organizations. Provide a list of people for the new manager to contact.

Suggestions for Team Members

1. When you learn that a team member is leaving, determine what information you need to get before the person departs. Arrange a final meeting or ask for copies of relevant documents.

2. If you have questions about why a team member has left, ask your boss. Understand, however, that under some circumstances your boss may not be able to give detailed answers.

3. Get to know new team members soon after they arrive. Take them to lunch, explain your department to them, and help them learn about the organization. Information about your boss's preferred work style is also quite useful to a new team member.

4. Include new team members in collaborative activities whenever possible. Share helpful information, invite them to meetings, and involve them in projects.

5. Introduce new team members to other people, departments, or organizations that may be helpful in their new role.

6. Recognize that your new coworker may have a work style different from the one you are accustomed to. Look for benefits in the new approach to the job instead of assuming that the new person is less competent than the previous incumbent. Adjust your own style if necessary.

Transition Three: Changing Team Leaders

Team leaders, like team members, may leave for many reasons. Although getting a new team member may cause a shift in group dynamics, acquiring a new team leader is more like an earthquake. Replacing the leader means everything is open to change: individual and team goals, expectations about how work should be done, perceptions of team members' competence, relationships with other departments, communication with upper management. Power can also shift when leaders change. In one information systems department, the arrival of a new vice president signaled a complete reversal in influence. A manager who had been viewed as a performance problem was promoted, while the former "fair-haired boy" was let go. An additional complicating factor in some leadership transitions is that members of the team may have applied for the job and been rejected.

Impact on the Team

The advent of a new leader is often an anxious time for a management group, because the leader can change potentially every aspect of its work. Several months after a new and unpopular CEO came on board, one vice president was heard to remark that the change in the company was similar to having your mother's body occupied by an alien. It still looked like your mother and sounded like your mother, but in reality your mother had been replaced by an evil presence.

Initial reactions of team members depend on their prior knowledge of the new leader. If someone from the group is promoted into the leadership role, members already have preconceived opinions about the person's competence. When the leader comes from another department in the same organization, information travels quickly through the grapevine about the person's work history, habits, preferences, abilities, and weaknesses. But if the new arrival is a complete unknown, the ability of team members to predict the future suddenly drops to zero. Not being able to envision the future makes people highly uncomfortable, so they usually spend considerable time ferreting out information to help them figure out what to expect. Depending on their personal circumstances and their feelings about change, team members may be excited by the arrival of a new leader, or they may fear for their jobs.

Transition Guidelines for Team Leaders

1. Meet with your new team as soon as possible, for the members need to begin getting to know you. If they already know you, they need to get used to your new role. Talk about yourself: your work history, background, work style, leadership style, preferences, and hot buttons. If you knew the former leader, talk about differences that you perceive in your work styles and how they might affect team members. If you were promoted from within the group, talk honestly about how the change in role may initially be difficult for both you and others.

2. Have individual meetings with members to get acquainted, review goals, and learn about their work. Encourage them to ask questions about you and your approach to management. If you used to be one of the group, ask for their reactions to the change. Don't expect complete honesty, however, since your change in position means that you no longer get such candid information from your former coworkers.

3. If people fear that your arrival signals a round of dismissals, demotions, or reorganizations, be honest. If you plan to leave things as they are, say so, but if you are considering reorganizing or replacing some managers, don't offer false assurances. Simply state that you plan to assess the effectiveness of each operation and there may be some staffing changes as a result. If you do need to change functions or replace managers, get this phase over with as soon as possible. Working under the ongoing threat of termination reduces people's effectiveness, and building a team is impossible if the cast of characters is constantly changing. Once your restructuring is complete, announce the end of the process so that everyone can relax a bit. But never say that a reorganization or layoff is over until you are certain of it. If your statements are proven false, you will be considered a liar and lose people's trust forever. Someone who is not trusted cannot be an effective leader.

4. Hold meetings with all the employees in each department that you manage. Help them begin to feel comfortable with you by talking about yourself and encouraging questions. Since you also need to learn about them, you may wish to have people briefly tell you about their jobs (if the group is small enough). In some situations, formal presentations are appropriate, but be sure to allow time for informal discussion as well. Even if you were promoted from within the department, employees still need to get comfortable with you in this new role, so consider discussing your approach to the job and any ways that you are likely to differ from your predecessor. To reduce employees' anxiety, these meetings need to be held as soon as possible. One new vice president disappeared into his office at the end of the hall and did not talk with anyone except his direct reports for several weeks. This aloofness hardly created a positive impression among the troops.

5. Meet with your boss to clarify goals and expectations for yourself and your department. Discuss your boss's expectations with your management team.

6. Establish a regular schedule of staff meetings and individual conferences. Hold individual meetings more frequently at first to move along the learning curve that inevitably comes with a new position. Even if you came from within the department, frequent interaction is still needed to encourage mutual adjustment to your new role.

7. Get to know your peers, that is, people on the management team of which you are a member. Start to develop the networking connections you need for success in your new role. Consider having lunch with other managers to encourage informal conversation. (If you think this is beginning to sound like a lot of meetings,

you're right! Meeting people is the most important thing you can do in a new leadership role.) One newly appointed corporate vice president failed to make any visits to the manufacturing plants during his first year in the job. Not surprisingly, he came to be viewed as an ivory-tower type and encountered considerable resistance as he began trying to make changes that affected manufacturing operations.

8. If you are new to the organization, you need to learn about the business, history, and culture of your new employer. Read all available written materials, talk to knowledgeable people, and visit offices and operations. Learn about products, customers, suppliers, and competitors. Understanding your new organization helps you avoid the mistakes that might result if you operate on an old set of assumptions. One new CEO took steps to slash the pay of production workers shortly after he joined a nonunion company. He had previously headed a consulting firm, had no experience running a manufacturing operation, and failed to realize that this action might stimulate a union organizing campaign. Fortunately, the CEO listened to one of his division presidents, who suggested that cutting pay might not be the most effective approach to cost reduction if the company were to become unionized as a result.

9. Recognize that people were accustomed to your predecessor and developed habits of working and communicating based on that person's style. Don't expect them to read your mind and know instantly how you want things done. If you knew the previous manager, discuss the difference in your styles with team members. If not, learn about your predecessor and determine how you are different. Realize that a change in style can be quite confusing for team members, so help them adjust. One department had an outgoing, talkative vice president who liked to make fast decisions. Her successor was quiet and reserved, preferring to consider many alternatives before choosing a final course of action. Management team members soon found that talking about an issue and then quickly reaching a decision was no longer the desired way of doing business with the boss. They now were expected to present proposals in writing, provide several alternatives, and wait for a decision to be made at a later date.

Suggestions for Team Members

1. Recognize that the change to a new leader requires some adjustment on your part. You may need to alter your work habits or communication style to effectively "manage" your new boss.

2. Get to know your new manager. If the new person makes no effort to have an in-depth discussion with you, then take the initiative yourself. Schedule a meeting to discuss your department, your goals, and your staff. After all, understanding your function is part of your manager's job, so provide any information that would be helpful.

3. Be sure that you and your new boss agree on goals and expectations. With a change in leadership, you can no longer operate on assumptions that were valid under your previous manager.

4. If your new manager is from outside the organization, provide helpful information and insights about your organization's business, culture, and political landscape. Just be sure that you don't appear to be lecturing your boss.

5. If your new leader was formerly a coworker, recognize that this relationship has now changed. You will not be able to interact with each other in exactly the same way as before. If you feel some resentment about this change, realize that this is a natural reaction, but do not let it poison the relationship. This person is now your boss and therefore has power over you, whether you like it or not. One sure way to torpedo your own career is to resist being managed by a former peer and thereby gain a reputation for being difficult and uncooperative.

6. Don't get into a power struggle with the new leader. In a power struggle, those with less power usually lose; in this case, that means you. One executive disagreed with the approach taken by a new CEO and continued to blatantly disregard his wishes, frequently making comments to others about how much better things had been under the previous management. The executive was soon fired.

Transition Four: Turnover in Top Management

Just as team leaders and members come and go, so do executives. The higher the position, the more widespread the impact of an upper management change. Strategies, goals, or the entire direction of an organization may be altered. New CEOs have been known to break up companies and sell the component parts, initiate major workforce reductions, change the business focus, relocate operations to another state or country, eliminate the entire executive team, and make other such drastic changes. People who developed positive relationships with the former executive must start over in establishing their credibility. With the arrival of a new president, one manager said she felt like a slate that had just been wiped clean. Under a new leader, perceptions of departments and people may shift. When a CEO with a financial background replaced one who came from marketing, the power positions of those two functions were suddenly reversed.

Impact on the Team

Regardless of whether the change in upper management is good or bad for the organization, the change itself is likely to have an impact on all management teams. In one electronics company, a new president brought more order to the business by instituting policies and procedures that required all managers to operate in a more structured fashion. In another electronics company, a new CEO created chaos by alienating customers and delaying important decisions. Though the specific changes were quite different, both situations required every management team in the organization to make major adjustments.

For the top team, an upper management change means that the team members are getting a new boss, with all the effects described in the previous section. For lower-level teams, the change may signal a shift in the direction or influence of their department. When one small company acquired their first computer-literate CEO, for example, the information systems department received a sudden elevation in status. If the new president or CEO wants to bring in a new team, other high-level managers may be replaced. Knowing that this often occurs, management team members may begin to anticipate the possible departure of their leader. In one midsized company, thirty-one of the thirty-two top managers were dismissed during a new CEO's first year on the job.

Transition Guidelines for Team Leaders

1. Determine how this management change affects the goals and objectives of your function. Regularly discuss possible shifts in direction with your boss until you are sure you understand any new expectations. Share this information with your team members, specifically clarifying how they may be affected individually.

2. Help your managers get to know the new executive. Invite the executive to a team meeting where members can ask questions and provide information about their departments.

3. Share perceptions with your team members about how the new executive's style compares with that of the previous manager. Discuss how they can most effectively relate to the new person. In one government agency, a commissioner who wanted to know every detail of a project or problem was replaced by one who preferred to be briefed only on general goals and action steps. Managers quickly learned to alter their style of making presentations.

4. If this management change has given you a new boss, review the suggestions for team members under transition three above.

Suggestions for Team Members

1. Look for opportunities to interact with the new senior manager. If you have no legitimate business matters to discuss, try to have some casual conversation with the new person in the hall, in the break room, at the coffee machine, in the

parking lot, or in the restroom (if that's gender appropriate, of course). This is not to suggest that you should try to go around your boss, just that you should become familiar to the person at the top. An old saying holds that the person who really protects your job is not your boss, it's your boss's boss. If your boss's boss has no idea who you are, that's not much protection.

2. When you see the new executive, be prepared with questions to ask or information to share. Your goal is to be seen as a bright and useful person.

3. Expect things to change, since they usually do when top management turns over. Resisting the wishes of a new top executive is not likely to help your career, so be adaptable. If you are seen as someone who wants to help implement the new direction, your credibility is likely to increase.

4. If this change has given your boss a new boss, realize that the adjustment may be difficult for your manager. Empathize.

Transition Five: Redefining the Team's Function

Management teams are sometimes required to change the way they do business. They may begin a new venture, centralize, decentralize, change their focus, adopt a new structure, combine with other units, or split off from other units. When a management team experiences a major functional shift, members often have to adopt a new method of operation rather quickly.

Impact on the Team

A major shift in function means that prior goals and strategies are now outdated. In this situation, a management team is like a ship without a compass: moving forward but uncertain of the proper course. Until a new direction is clearly defined and specific goals developed, the team is unable to function effectively. In one medical center, three patient services departments were combined into a single unit. The new management team had to determine the proper relationship among the three functions, identify services that were being duplicated, and develop an effective organizational structure. In another situation, the people in a human resource department were told that they must immediately abandon their regulatory stance, become customer-driven, and adopt a consulting approach. The HR management team needed to quickly determine what *customer-driven* and *consulting approach* meant in behavioral terms and establish goals and strategies to move themselves in that direction. Redefining the function of a management team essentially means going back to square one and asking, "What are we here to do?"

Transition Guidelines for Team Leaders

1. Help your team understand why the change is necessary. If you are initiating the change yourself, thoroughly explain your assessment of the situation and the reason for your actions. If the change is being thrust upon you, be sure that you understand the thinking of upper management. Even if you don't agree with the new direction, avoid griping and complaining to your team members. Try to open a dialogue with upper management about your concerns, but if the change becomes inevitable, then you need to help your team members accept and cope with the situation. Be realistic about any challenges presented by the change, but also try to identify the potential benefits. To some degree, team members adopt your attitude (that's why you're called a leader), so if you can't be positive, try at least to be neutral. Let's face it: even changes that we don't want often have positive repercussions.

2. Be as specific as possible about new expectations of the team and of individual members. If you are the initiator of the change, describe exactly what you hope to accomplish and how you will evaluate success. (If you find this difficult to do, then you probably need to give more thought to the change.) If the change is coming from above, talk with your boss or other appropriate people about the outcomes that are expected. Ask them to describe the criteria they will use to determine if the change is successful.

3. Go through a formal planning process. Conduct an environmental scan to identify factors that may either impede or facilitate the change. Determine whether you have new customers and whether the needs and interests of former customers have changed. Review your mission, vision, and values to determine if they need to be revised in light of the new reality. Identify new strategic directions and goals. Define the results you hope to accomplish. Decide if you need a new organizational structure. In short, go through the process described in Chapter Two to establish your new direction and provide your team members with specific goals.

4. Determine whether this change requires your managers and employees to develop new skills and abilities. The existing staff was hired to meet expectations that are now outdated, so you may need to help them make this shift. The human resource department described above, for example, needed to develop customer service and consultation skills in order to successfully implement the functional change. Another example can be found in government organizations that privatize some of their operations. To make this change succeed, agency managers need to acquire new skills in negotiating and managing contracts with private vendors.

5. Clearly describe any changes in behavior that are required of managers and employees. Don't be surprised if you encounter initial resistance, since behavior

change is usually uncomfortable for people. (You may wish to review the suggestions for changing behavior in Chapter Six.) Remember that everyone is on a learning curve, so don't expect perfection at first. Use mistakes as opportunities for education, not punishment.

6. Be sure to involve employees in the change process. Executives sometimes invest time and effort in guiding managers through a change but neglect to communicate with and educate their employee groups. In one company, for example, all the managers received several days of training on how to use a new and radically different performance appraisal system, but employees—who constituted the other half of the appraisal process—received only a memo.

7. Follow up frequently at first to monitor progress in implementing the new direction. Feedback mechanisms include surveys, group and individual discussions, establishing outcome measures and collecting data, holding conversations with customers, and any other strategy that yields information about the change. If you are naturally a hands-off leader, you need to become more involved for a while, until the new direction is firmly established.

Suggestions for Team Members

1. Reach a clear agreement with your boss on what the change means for your department. Agree on a set of specific goals and outcomes.

2. Because your staff is also going through this change, most of the guidelines for team leaders in this section apply to you as well. Recognize that their acceptance of the change depends largely on your behavior, so try to be both realistic and positive. Empathize with any difficulties the change may cause, but encourage employees to focus on possible benefits and develop strategies to overcome obstacles.

3. If you are unhappy about the change, recognize when resistance is futile. Being seen as a road block by upper management does not help your career or reputation. Realize that you have a choice about whether to adjust to the new reality or find a more comfortable working environment. If you choose to stay, you are doing so because something about your current situation (pay, benefits, coworkers, whatever) is better than the alternative. You may feel locked in, but in reality you are making the choice to keep some present benefit.

Transition Six: Working with Constant Change

Many organizations experience periods of rapid change, but for some change is a constant. This is especially true in technology companies or any other industry with constantly shifting markets and products. In a turbulent environment, nothing is stable: customers, competitors, products, structures, managers, employees, procedures, and programs all tend to shift frequently. Referring to a turbulent environment as a transition is not exactly accurate; constant turbulence really means that transition is a way of life.

Impact on the Team

If the environment is constantly changing, managers can never relax or rest on their laurels. Today's accomplishment is immediately replaced by tomorrow's challenge. In this atmosphere, a management team needs to be highly adaptive; the members must be able to make quick decisions, begin new projects frequently, and implement rapid shifts in direction. Managers must stay up-to-date with changes both inside and outside the organization, increasing the need for frequent contacts with important sources of information.

Transition Guidelines for Team Leaders

1. If you are the leader of an executive team, you can only provide effective leadership by staying abreast of external changes and implementing appropriate shifts in organizational direction. You therefore need to maintain strong connections with sources of information about changes affecting your industry. You must also be willing to let go of the past. The CEO of one computer company was so committed to existing technology that he dismissed acquisition targets that would have prepared his organization for the next wave in computing. The result was that the company lost market share, became a niche player, and the CEO was asked to retire.

2. If you are the leader of a middle management team, you need to maintain frequent communication with upper management about changes in organizational needs and priorities. Frequently assess plans and projects to be sure they are meeting current needs, and update your goals regularly.

3. To develop a successful management team in a turbulent organization, you must hire flexible people who enjoy change and hate routine. Look for candidates whose work preferences are compatible with these demands and who have past experience in this type of setting.

4. Be flexible yourself. Expect and prepare for change. Being a leader in a turbulent organization requires special skills in rapid planning, quick implementation, and frequent communication with key constituencies. You must also be able to help your direct reports cope with the stress of constant change.

5. Maintain frequent communication with team members and encourage them to share information on an ongoing basis. Emphasize the need for everyone

to be aware of events and changes in different parts of the organization. In one rapidly changing health care company, managers complained that departments frequently duplicated programs and projects because they lacked information about activities in other areas. Two departments discovered that they were both providing customer service training to employees, which meant that two separate groups had gone through the same process of identifying needs, developing a workshop, and training trainers. Had they collaborated, half of this energy might have been available for other purposes.

6. Encourage team members to develop good internal and external networks to stay abreast of changes related to their functions. If they do, you may find that you and your team are regarded as a valuable source of information. If not, you may quickly become outdated. Knowledge is power, especially in the midst of rapid change.

7. Maintain some islands of stability for team members. Regular meetings, reports, newsletters, group activities, and planning sessions all help people cope with a turbulent workplace. In this setting, predictable avenues of communication help people retain their sanity.

Suggestions for Team Members

1. Be adaptable. If you hate change, you may be in the wrong organization. One federal government manager who went to work in a technology company found after six months that the increased pace of change was causing him extreme anxiety and frustration. He kept trying to impose order through detailed policies, procedures, and forms, but he found that these mechanisms were consistently ignored by people who were focused on taking quick action. Finally, he left for a more predictable environment. Both his experience and his temperament were ill-suited to a turbulent organization.

2. Develop good networks in your area of expertise. As a management team member, you have an obligation to bring current knowledge into the group.

3. Build an effective internal network. Your department will be most successful if you are able to coordinate and communicate with others in the organization. Encourage your employees to do the same.

4. Be a source of stability for your employees. In an atmosphere of constant change, people need to have their manager readily available to answer questions and help make decisions. You therefore need to be easily accessible. Employees count on you to help them cope with stress, so don't get in the habit of constantly complaining to them. This may relieve your frustration temporarily, but it just demotivates your staff.

Managing transition points is an important skill for both team leaders and members to develop. At these critical junctures, goals become unclear and relationships shift, which creates anxiety, frustration, and conflict. A poorly handled transition can impede a team's progress for months or even years. Successfully managing these changes requires extra time and effort, but the return is usually well worth the investment since taking effective action quickly reestablishes a cooperative, productive work environment.

True Story: The Defeat of the Social Work Department

Part Two: The Solution

Fortunately, while the managers are lunching in the cafeteria, a meeting takes place between Donna, the director of rehabilitation services, and Jerry, the director of social work. They are making plans to ease the transition of social work into the rehabilitation department.

"I know this is kind of awkward," says Donna, "But I really do think that our two functions can work well together."

"Well, I can't say that I'm happy about it," replies Jerry. "I guess I can see the logic in it, though. What worries me is how our work is going to be affected. We don't operate the same way you do, and our goals are different."

"True. But the missions of our departments ought to be compatible, and we may really be able to serve patients better by coordinating our efforts."

Jerry sighs. "I guess so. My managers are totally down in the dumps about this, though. I'm not sure how they found out, but they're already acting as though somebody died. They feel it's a real slap in the face, and of course they're worried about their jobs."

"So let's talk about what we need to do with both our management groups," Donna offers. "I guess the first step is to decide what the new organizational structure should look like, and then work with our combined management team to do some planning for the new social work and rehabilitation department. Let's talk about your role first." As Donna begins to draw options for the new department's structure on a flipchart, Jerry relaxes a bit. *Maybe,* he thinks, *this isn't going to be so bad after all.*

CHAPTER TEN

FIXING A SICK TEAM

True Story: Warfare on the Board

Part One: The Problem

Eight members of the board of a not-for-profit agency are seated around the conference table. The atmosphere is tense. "I don't see why we have to continue to fund this project," says the treasurer. "It's just sucking up money, and I can't see that it's producing anything."

"Because," the chairperson sighs, "as I've already explained three times, the school initiative is a pet project of our largest donor. You go tell him that we decided education wasn't important."

"It's not about education. It's about politics," answers the treasurer.

"Of course it is!" the secretary chimes in. "Everything is about politics. That's how the world works. Where do you think you're living, Fantasyland? How exactly do you think we get the money to run this organization?"

"Oh, please," says the treasurer. "I'm getting just a little tired of your lecturing me on how things work."

"Now, children, just behave," says the chairperson. "We have work to do."

"Behave?" replies the secretary. "Don't talk down to me. I've had a lot more management experience than you'll ever have. I don't know how you wound up running this outfit anyway."

The chairperson frowns. "I was elected. And if I remember correctly, you were the person that I beat. Which reminds me, I wish you'd stop trying to get back at me by spreading rumors about my social life. I got a call the other day from someone who accused me of having an affair with one of the board members. Now I'm pretty sure I know where that rumor got started."

"Who are you supposed to be having an affair with?" chimes in the program committee chair.

"I'm sorry I brought it up, and I'm not having an affair with anyone. Could we just get back to work? We need to talk about our new executive director. I asked her to skip this meeting because I think we need to discuss her performance."

"What's wrong with her performance?" asks the treasurer. "I think she's doing a great job. Contributions are up, the staff is happy and productive, and she's really pleasant to deal with."

"Pleasant?!" exclaims the secretary. "I think she's cold and unfriendly. She always acts like she wants to get off the phone as fast as possible. Doesn't she realize that she works for us?"

"She wants to get off the phone so she can do some work, not spend her time chatting with you about your golf game," says the treasurer.

The program chair speaks up again. "Well, I think she's fine, but some of those staff members are a problem. I'm not sure they're really qualified for the kind of work we do."

"As usual," sighs the chairperson, "we seem to be going around in circles. Do any of the rest of you have an opinion?" The other four members continue to sit in silence. "Okay, then. Let's take a break."

Clearly, this board is indeed going around in circles, and rather nasty circles at that. Members seem to be angry or withdrawn, direct verbal attacks are the norm, and no one seems focused on the work to be done. These people are incapable of running a meeting, much less an organization. Unless they are able to put aside their personal agendas and focus on common goals, the agency for which they are responsible is in serious trouble.

How to Identify a Sick Team

Some management teams are unpleasant, destructive groups. Unlike the "normal" problems discussed in earlier chapters, the illnesses plaguing these teams are deep-seated and chronic. Sometimes this dysfunction reflects the members' personalities, while in other situations the problem mirrors the larger organizational culture. Whatever the cause, these groups are not teams in any sense of the word. They are simply collections of people bound together by a particular organizational structure. Just as some serious illnesses are impossible to cure, so some team problems are beyond remedy. Others, however, may respond to appropriate treatment. In this chapter, strategies are suggested that may help improve teamwork in these difficult situations.

Is your team's problem like a cold, or more like a cancer? If your group exhibits any of the behaviors below, you may be dealing with a truly sick team:

- Open, hostile conflict breaks out in meetings. Members' remarks to one another are angry in tone and destructive in intent. While some managers vehemently argue, others completely withdraw and say nothing.
- Group members seldom interact outside of meetings. Team members don't share information, consult one another, talk informally, or eat lunch together. Attendance at any planned social function is poor. People hate team meetings and look for excuses not to attend.
- The group is clearly divided into factions. Team members interact only with certain people and avoid others. Established subgroups always eat lunch or take breaks together and never try to include other members.
- Managers are extremely apathetic. No one seems to have energy for starting new projects or coming up with new ideas. People appear to be trying to just get through the day.
- New people seem to quickly lose their initial energy and enthusiasm. They often leave for other jobs within a year or two.
- Team members try to sabotage one another's efforts and projects. They openly criticize each other to their boss or to higher management. Questions and comments in meetings seem designed to put others in a bad light.

Any of these behaviors should be viewed as a signal that something is seriously wrong with the management group. If someone tries to talk about addressing the problem, other members usually react with sighs, groans, and comments about what a waste of time it all is. In part, this reaction stems from the fact that members of sick teams have no emotional investment in the group's success and therefore have little interest in spending time to improve it. They have learned to adapt to the current situation, which is unpleasant but at least familiar.

An apathetic response also reflects fear about what may happen if long-standing problems are discussed openly. Most of the time, the issues troubling a sick team are not addressed directly: members simply act them out through their behavior. The prospect of actually talking about these problems is quite frightening for the group. Managers often fear that they will be personally attacked or expected to openly criticize others and that the attempted cure will ultimately leave the team in worse shape than before. This fear is not totally unrealistic, since poorly facilitated discussions can indeed have this effect.

Usually, the most important factor in determining whether a sick team can improve is intention: whether or not the members want the team to be more effective. When members have positive intentions, they work to resolve problems and make positive changes. If one or more members do not want the team to work more effectively, however, improvement is much less likely. In these situations, steps must first be taken to deal with the difficult individuals.

The remainder of this chapter presents strategies that may be used to fix—or at least improve—a sick team. In some situations, the team itself can take steps to move in a more productive direction. In others, progress requires the assistance of an outside facilitator. The problems of some groups are so entrenched that they cannot be solved and can only be managed; a few unfortunate teams are probably beyond all hope unless the members are removed or the organization's culture changes completely. Many of the suggestions in this chapter are directed to the team's leader, since members often find it difficult to resolve these problems on their own without strong direction or outside assistance.

Characteristics of Dysfunctional Groups

Although sick teams suffer from a variety of problems, certain difficulties appear most frequently:

1. Toxic team members
2. Hostile cliques
3. Intense rivalries
4. Autonomous managers
5. High turnover
6. Problems with upper management
7. Ineffective team leadership

Team difficulties arise on three levels: individual, group, and organizational. Individual problems stem from the behavior, intentions, or personal characteristics of one or more team members. Group factors reflect issues related to team dynamics: goals, structure, direction, problem-solving processes, and interaction patterns. Organizational issues reflect circumstances outside the team that affect how members interact and work together.

Problem One: Toxic Team Members

A sign on an office bulletin board says, "Some people are alive simply because it is against the law to kill them." This sentiment was undoubtedly inspired by interaction with a toxic person. Toxic team members represent a problem on the individual level. The presence of even one toxic person usually keeps a group from working together effectively.

Symptoms

Some people are simply unpleasant, while others are truly poisonous. Toxic people like to promote conflict, have a strong need to get their own way, enjoy criticizing others, and have a personal agenda that is incompatible with team goals. They focus only on their own needs and interests, have poor interpersonal skills, and make no attempt to see issues from different points of view.

Conflicts stirred up by a toxic person may be open or hidden. Open conflict arises in team meetings in the form of arguments, personal attacks, or derogatory remarks. Assertive people in the group attempt to debate or reason with the toxic person, while others shut down, withdraw, and say nothing until the storm has passed. Whenever the toxic person is absent from meetings, the whole atmosphere is more relaxed, productive, and friendly.

Hidden conflicts are more subtle but equally destructive. The toxic person spreads rumors, misrepresents information, undermines efforts of other members, and tries to pit one person against another. Conflict with the leader is often expressed covertly. One government manager spread false information to political officials about the director of his agency, trying to have him replaced. Another person put a voodoo doll on her desk; although not labeled it was clearly meant to represent her boss. The paradox of hidden conflicts is that they are never completely hidden; although the specifics may not be known, everyone is usually aware of the feelings involved.

Toxic team members focus solely on their own agenda and have no interest in helping the team become more effective. Groups with toxic members therefore lack the most basic ingredient for improving teamwork: positive intentions. Even if everyone else really wants to improve the situation, no progress can be made until the behavior of the toxic person is controlled.

Suggestions for a Cure

There are two routes to managing toxic behavior: the group approach and the individual approach.

Group Approach. Other team members can help control a toxic person. In fact, groups usually have a lot more power in this regard than they realize. Teams often complain loud and long about a toxic member, not realizing that they are actually permitting this behavior to occur. One management group held a retreat with a facilitator to focus on improving teamwork. When their toxic member failed to show up, the managers began complaining about his effect on the group. "What do the rest of you do when he acts that way?" asked the facilitator. The members were silent. Finally, one of them replied, "I guess we don't do anything."

For less severe problems, a group approach is often sufficient to control the situation. Try these steps to involve the team in managing difficult members:

- The group should agree on a set of meeting guidelines to help them be more productive. (Meeting guidelines are discussed in Chapter Five.) In drafting these guidelines, be sure to include prohibitions against the troublesome behavior, such as "We will treat one another with respect" or "We will listen when others are speaking." Because toxic behavior is not socially acceptable, the toxic person is unlikely to argue against these sensible rules. Post the guidelines in an obvious place in your conference room.

- The team leader should tell group members that they are expected not only to abide by the meeting guidelines but also to work together to enforce them. Indicate that should someone act inappropriately, group members need to help change this behavior by pointing out that it is not in accordance with rules that the team has adopted. The purpose of this instruction is to give members permission to openly discuss behavior that was previously tolerated in silence.

- When the toxic person engages in harmful behavior (which will inevitably happen), the team leader should wait to see if anyone addresses the issue. At first, team members may be reluctant to openly discuss something that has been ignored for so long, so the leader may need to be a role model. If no one else points out the inappropriate behavior, say something like, "Mike, I think we agreed that people need to listen to one another and try to understand different points of view. Your comments don't seem to be in line with that agreement. What do the rest of you think?" Asking the rest of the group for their opinion is important, because it sends the message that they have a responsibility to help the team function effectively. If the team leader does not involve the group, members may come to expect that the leader alone is responsible for monitoring the toxic person.

- Another tactic is to have the group create an assessment instrument based on the meeting guidelines to evaluate progress in becoming more effective. Attach a rating scale to each of the meeting guidelines, and have team members periodically evaluate the group's compliance with the rules they have established. Administering this survey at regular intervals allows the leader to monitor progress over time and provide feedback to the group. If the team is not improving, have a group discussion to explore the reasons. Remind everyone that they share responsibility for team performance, so all team members need to discourage unproductive behavior.

- Once members have learned to confront disruptive behaviors, they should try to use the same approach if these problems arise outside of meetings.

The power of the group solution is that it shines a spotlight on toxic behavior and gets everyone involved in controlling it. Sometimes the attention alone causes the toxic person to behave more appropriately. If not, then the situation must be addressed by the manager as a job-performance problem.

Individual Approach. The leader of the group has ultimate responsibility for dealing with the toxic person's behavior. Executives sometimes ignore a manager's performance problem because they are not comfortable discussing the issue. They may also believe that disciplinary procedures do not apply above a certain organizational level. This attitude is unfortunate, since poor performance by a higher-level manager can wreak much more havoc than the behavior of any lower-level employee. Having a toxic person on your management team represents a problem that probably extends beyond team issues: the odds are good that someone this destructive is also a poor manager.

The toxic person's disruptive behavior should be handled in the same manner as any other performance problem. The leader can use these steps to conduct a useful performance discussion with the difficult team member:

- Don't delude yourself into expecting a personality transformation. The structure of this person's character was formed long ago and is probably set for life. Your goal is not to change personality but to insist upon appropriate behavior so that your team is able to function.
- Target one or two particularly troublesome behaviors for the toxic manager to work on. Asking the person to eliminate all faults and irritating habits is unrealistic, so focus only on the areas that are causing you the greatest difficulty. Do not use this conversation as an opportunity to vent all your frustrations.
- Do not act like a parent or judge. Discuss the problem in an adult-to-adult fashion, clearly indicating that the toxic person is responsible for changing his own behavior. This is his problem to solve, not yours.
- Specifically describe the behavior that is a problem. Be sure to focus on behavior, not personality characteristics. Saying "I need for you to stop arguing with others in meetings" is more effective than saying "You need to develop a more positive attitude."
- Explain in detail the effect that the toxic person's behavior is having on others: team members, yourself, customers, upper management, and anyone else. Give specific examples. One vice president of finance had a terrible temper and would habitually scream, yell, and curse at employees. (Oddly enough, he was always able to control his anger when talking with his boss!) To help him

understand the effect of this behavior, the CEO explained that good employees were leaving for other jobs, employment applicants were rejecting offers based on rumors about his management style, employees were afraid to offer new ideas for fear of his reaction, and people in other departments were losing respect for him.

- Specifically describe the desired behavior. For example, you might say "I would like for you to find two good points about a new proposal before you talk about any problems with it" or "I would like for you to listen until others have finished speaking."
- Tell the toxic person that she must decide whether or not she can change this behavior. Again, stress that this is her problem, not yours. If she is able to change the problem behavior, then you expect her to do so. To stress the seriousness of the situation, you may wish to give her a day or two to think about this decision.
- Specify what happens if there is no change. Prior to the meeting, you should carefully think through what you will do if the toxic person continues to be a problem. The next step—whether a disciplinary warning, demotion, removal from important projects, or termination—should be clearly explained.
- If the behavior changes, thank the person for making this effort and continue to reinforce his improvement. If the behavior does not change, then you need to follow through with the steps that you previously warned him about. This is critical! Failure to take promised action sends the message that the problem isn't important and that you do not mean what you say.

Ultimately, a toxic person who does not change must be removed from the team and probably should not be allowed to manage others. Someone who can make a valuable contribution as an employee might be retained; otherwise, termination is the only alternative. Keeping a truly toxic person on the payroll is an abdication of your responsibilities as a manager.

Problem Two: Hostile Cliques

Many groups have informal cliques, but some develop entrenched factions that promote disharmony and dissension. This division among team members is a group-level problem that is most effectively addressed through group solutions.

Symptoms

Hostile cliques are usually easy to spot because team members always divide into the same groupings. The same people sit together in meetings, talk during breaks, have lunch together, and interact at social functions. They also support one another during discussions and take the same position on issues. Of course, we all tend to spend more time and agree more frequently with some people than with others, so some division among team members is to be expected. There are signs, however, that indicate cliques have become a problem:

- Certain people or groups never talk to one another and seem to avoid contact.
- Frequent comments are made emphasizing the differences between people or groups ("Those of us who have been here for a while . . . " or "If you really understood what it was like in the field . . .").
- People in one group often make negative remarks about those in the other.
- Members of one faction try to influence the leader's opinion against positions taken by the other side.
- People don't share helpful information with those in the other group.

Whenever these behaviors are present, the cliques are having a destructive effect on the team.

Suggestions for a Cure

Because this is a group-level problem, the solution needs to be focused on the group as a whole. Talking with team members individually and directing them to break up the cliques is not likely to have any effect, since a cure requires changing the group dynamics. The leader may choose to address the situation with a direct approach, an indirect approach, or both. In any case, the first step is to determine the cause of the division in the group.

Diagnosis. Most of the time, the reason for division within a team is fairly obvious. In one group, cliques formed based on length of service in the organization. When several people retired simultaneously, a group of new managers was brought in. They regarded their long-service coworkers as "old fogies" who were set in their ways, while the old-timers saw the newcomers as young whippersnappers who lacked experience. Another team divided along corporate and field lines; yet another formed subgroups based on a clear difference in management philosophy. Demographic factors (age, race, gender, nationality) can also generate cliques. If the basis for forming subgroups is not clear to you, ask some team members. You can simply say, "I've noticed that the same people always seem to hang out together. Why do you think that is?" Team members are usually able to tell you.

Direct Approach. Addressing the problem directly means discussing the situation as a group and exploring the underlying issues. This is best accomplished during a staff retreat, where people are more relaxed and can devote sufficient time to the discussion. (Staff retreats are covered in Chapter Seven.) If the group has entrenched cliques whose members have some animosity toward one another, using an experienced facilitator is recommended. Be sure that your facilitator specializes in working with difficult group issues and has dealt with similar situations in the past. Check references.

These general suggestions may be useful to the team leader, who should work closely with the facilitator to develop a specific plan for the retreat:

- Consider having team members provide an assessment of team functioning prior to the retreat. Their views are easily obtained by using a short survey. This strategy helps you develop an effective plan for the retreat and ensures that all opinions are expressed, not just those of the most talkative people. At the retreat, you can start the discussion of issues by sharing the group's own observations.
- During the retreat, describe the negative behavior you have observed and its effect on teamwork and accomplishment of results. If team members have provided an advance assessment, compare their observations with your own. Discuss the common goals that should be of concern to everyone on the team—or better yet, involve the group in identifying the goals.
- Allow the facilitator to guide the discussion of issues. At some point, the facilitator may wish to divide the managers into cliques to identify the views of the different groups. Teams sometimes resist this approach, saying that they want to discuss everything openly. The real reason for their reluctance, however, is usually that they fear what the discussion will reveal. Since small-group discussions are often the only way to have members express their true feelings, you should be supportive if your facilitator recommends this activity. A good facilitator is able to effectively manage the process.
- Be sure to end the retreat with an action plan detailing the specific steps members must take to improve relationships and function more effectively as a complete team. If the group only discusses issues without agreeing on new behaviors, nothing is likely to change.

With a good facilitator and team members who have positive intentions, the direct approach usually helps break down walls between cliques. If one or more team members want this process to fail, however, you may need to deal with them individually (see "Toxic Team Members" on page 221).

Indirect Approach. With the indirect approach, the team leader does not openly discuss the existence and cause of cliques. Instead, specific steps are taken to increase communication and interaction between the groups, with the goal of gradually altering group dynamics. Even if you use the direct approach to surface team issues, you may still wish to use some indirect methods to encourage and reinforce changes in behavior.

- Assign people from different cliques to work on projects. When trying to mend a divided group, make a special effort to create projects that members can complete together. One management team that had split into two distinct subgroups faced some serious ethical issues in the department. The leader told team members that she wanted to develop a seminar for employees on ethical decision making. She then assigned two people from each clique to work together on creating the workshop. Other approaches might have been used to address the ethical issues, but this solution provided an opportunity to start breaking down the cliques. Another divided management team that was going through a strategic planning process put members of different cliques on planning teams together. Although a single project is not likely to create instant harmony, over time this approach usually improves communication among team members.
- Send people from different cliques on trips together. If you have multistate or multinational operations, arrange for warring team members to visit them at the same time. If you need to send representatives to a conference or workshop, have people from different factions attend together. (This strategy often helps to develop relationships, but it can backfire if prolonged contact proves to be irritating.)
- Periodically have members change jobs to help break down barriers based on position. One company intentionally moved people between field and corporate jobs to promote understanding of these different aspects of their operations; thus field managers who had previously been part of the corporate staff became much more aware of the latter's point of view, and vice versa. This tactic may not be feasible, however, if your positions require specialized skills and experience.
- If switching jobs is unrealistic, require team members to learn more about one another's departments. Increased understanding sometimes helps reduce animosity.
- Break up seating patterns in meetings. Change the room arrangement. Use small group discussions and mix up clique members. Or simply say that you have observed that everyone tends to sit with the same people, so you are going to change their perspectives by having them switch seats.
- Assign seats at group lunches and social events to promote conversation among people who seldom interact. Few people ignore those around them throughout an entire meal.

The direct approach tries to change behavior by changing attitudes. The indirect approach, on the other hand, tries to change attitudes by changing behavior. A combination of the two is often the most effective solution.

Problem Three: Intense Rivalries

Rivalries are different from cliques. Cliques are subgroups that form around a shared characteristic. Rivalries develop when team members are competing for the same reward. The desired reward can take many forms: raises, bonuses, promotions, resources, special trips, important projects. Whatever the cause, the result is competition among people who need to work cooperatively. Rivalries are likely to be an organization-level problem to some degree, since reward systems are often outside the control of the group or its members.

Symptoms

A certain amount of competition is normal and even healthy among team members. Problems arise when competition becomes so intense that people no longer focus on common goals or engage in cooperative efforts. Signs that a rivalry has gotten out of hand include self-promoting statements or actions, subtle put-downs of other team members, comments or actions meant to minimize the contributions of others, and one-upmanship during team meetings. Rivals may attempt to undercut one another's efforts by withholding information, manipulating data, or refusing to share resources. They aim to polish their own reputations by spotlighting accomplishments, while damaging the credibility of competitors through gossip and insinuation. At worst, they engage in blatant attempts to sabotage the other person or group. One government manager used his political connections to have a rival audited and to have legislation introduced that would eliminate the rival's funding. The rival, meanwhile, attempted to wrest control of a joint project by excluding the other department from the planning process. Needless to say, this situation did nothing to improve the functioning of their management team or their organization.

Interestingly, rivals often appear to be perfectly friendly on the surface. Strangers observing their interactions would seldom suspect the intense negative feelings beneath the calm exterior. Many highly competitive people have learned to mask this aspect of their personalities, since organizations place a high value on amiability and strongly prohibit open expression of hostility. Violating these norms places one at a competitive disadvantage, so rivals tend to comply. Observation over time usually reveals the truth behind the façade, however, as the competitors try to outmaneuver one another. Another indication of their insincerity is that rivals are quite cordial in meetings but studiously avoid one another as soon as the required interaction is over.

Suggestions for a Cure

Rivalries usually escalate when competitive personalities are operating under a competitive reward system. Again, competition in itself is not bad; it is only a problem if you need cooperation to achieve the best results (as you do on a management team). To resolve this problem, you must first figure out what the rivals are competing for and then either change the reward system or refocus their attention on common goals and encourage cooperative behavior. These suggestions can be helpful:

- Identify the source of the competition. People most frequently compete for money, power, attention, or prestige, although these basic drivers take many forms.
- Evaluate how rewards, recognition, and resources are allocated in your organization. If these systems encourage harmful competition among individuals or groups, try to change the allocation system or develop some team-based rewards. One management group, for example, based a percentage of members' bonuses on the success of team projects. Reward and recognition systems send a powerful message about how people should behave.
- Be sure that the rivals clearly understand team goals and the need for cooperation in achieving them. Competitive people tend to focus on their own needs and interests; they require frequent reminders about common objectives.
- If the rivalry is getting out of hand, the team leader should meet with the parties, individually or together, to discuss their competitive behavior. Simply surfacing the issue may make them more cautious about their actions. Don't expect to change their feelings, but do insist on a change in behavior. Share your observations about the negative impact their rivalry is having on the team, and tell them specifically how you expect them to behave toward one another in the future.
- Assign the rivals to shared projects that can only succeed through collaboration. Putting them in a situation where competition makes them both look bad may help them develop new ways of communicating. The experience of shared success might also improve their relationship.
- If you are the team leader and the rivals are competing for a promotion that is within your control, stress that teamwork counts heavily in deciding who gets the position. In one company, for example, three candidates to succeed the president served on the executive team. The CEO told each of them that the position of president required extensive cooperation with business partners, customers, and members of the board; therefore, he intended to carefully assess their ability to cooperate with one another.
- If the desired promotion is not within your control, talk about the importance of teamwork in today's organizations. Stress that when you are asked for

an assessment of a team member's potential, the ability to work cooperatively with others is a major factor in your evaluation.

Rivalry is usually an organization-level problem because managers are competing for an organizational reward. The solution, therefore involves making them aware that the organization values cooperation and that intense competition is not the best path to their desired outcome. If the rivalry has been personalized to the point that the primary goal is not to gain a reward but to destroy the other person, then you are dealing with an individual performance problem and need to address it as such (see "Toxic Team Members" on page 221).

Problem Four: Autonomous Managers

With some management groups, the problem is that there essentially is no team. Group goal setting, problem solving, and decision making do not exist. A group of managers is present, but they are a team in name only. This problem is usually organizational in nature, because the organization is not requiring the group to function as a team.

Symptoms

Meetings of a "nonteam" serve primarily for information sharing (assuming that the group has meetings at all). Even if relationships are friendly and managers eat lunch together regularly, they seldom interact with one another in the course of their work. On a nonteam, most decisions are made by individual managers or bounced up to the next level for resolution. The leader meets with managers individually but rarely initiates group decision making. This tactic is sometimes a way for the leader to retain more control. The commissioner of one government agency had monthly informational meetings with the top thirty managers in his organization, but the six division directors—who would normally have constituted the top management team—never met as a group. All decisions were referred to the commissioner, who would mediate and resolve disagreements among the divisions. Not surprisingly, operations in this organization were quite fragmented, and all power resided with the commissioner.

Suggestions for a Cure

The solution to this problem is to create a structure and forum to encourage teamwork and then help members learn to act in a team-oriented fashion. If people are accustomed to working autonomously, they do not turn into a team overnight just because they have been told to do so. Developing the habits and skills needed for teamwork takes time, so expect managers to face a learning curve. (See Chapter Six for suggestions on changing behavior.) The team leader may find these suggestions helpful for turning a group into a team:

- You might kick off the change in team culture with an initial retreat where you announce your intention to create a true management team. Be specific with the managers about your new goals and expectations; otherwise, they may be confused, suspicious, and uncooperative. During the retreat, the group can engage in some of the activities described below. If a retreat is not possible, hold a meeting to announce the change.
- Involve the group in identifying common goals. If these managers have never engaged in strategic planning, participating in such a process helps both to focus their efforts appropriately and to develop teamwork. In the commissioner-dominated government agency, strategic planning was the initial tool used to help team members learn to function cooperatively.
- Ask the group to identify areas in which shared decision making would be beneficial, and give them some initial decisions to work on. Encourage managers to develop the habit of bringing important decisions to the team for discussion, especially those that affect other departments. If managers continue to bring issues to you for resolution, help them collaborate with others who are involved. Whenever appropriate, put issues on a staff meeting agenda for group discussion.
- Discuss the links between departments, and encourage team members to determine how they might assist one another. Have managers from each department identify specifically how the others can help simplify their work or improve their results.
- Identify synergies between departments. One company found that three divisions were serving the same customers. By sharing information and engaging in joint planning, their managers served the customers more effectively, increased sales, and eliminated duplication of effort.
- Hold regular management team meetings that emphasize problem solving and decision making, not just sharing information.

Turning a nonteam into a team is relatively simple if you follow these steps and if members' intentions are positive. Just remember that people don't abandon entrenched habits overnight, so expect team members to change their behavior gradually. If you continue to encourage cooperation and teamwork, they will eventually develop a new set of habits.

Problem Five: High Turnover

Rapid turnover is really a symptom rather than a problem in its own right. Teams with high turnover definitely have a serious problem, but the trick is to determine whether turnover is creating a sick team, or a sick team is creating turnover. In either case, continually losing members makes team development an impossible task.

Symptoms

The symptoms of high turnover are obvious: managers frequently leave the team within a year or two after they arrive. In some instances, recruiting replacements is also difficult.

Suggestions for a Cure

To cure high turnover, you must first diagnosis the cause and then fix the problem.

Diagnosis. Identifying the true cause of turnover requires gathering data to pinpoint the source of the problem. Too often, managers in this situation make the wrong assumptions about why people are leaving and then proceed with a useless solution. These managers either do not want to take the time to gather data or do not want to face the possibility that they themselves may be the problem. One CEO kept tinkering with the compensation plan to encourage managers to stay with the company, not realizing that they were leaving because he was so difficult to work with. To pinpoint the cause of management turnover, these data-gathering approaches are useful:

- Compare your management compensation plan with those of similar organizations. People often give higher pay as the explanation for taking a new job when they are actually leaving for other reasons. If pay really is the problem, however, you can easily identify and remedy it.
- Hold exit interviews with people who are leaving. To encourage honest dialogue, the team leader should not conduct these interviews personally. Having someone from human resources perform this task provides better information, although many managers are still reluctant to complain to anyone inside the organization for fear of burning bridges. To further remove the company from the situation, you might consider hiring an external consultant to conduct the interviews.

- Conduct a companywide opinion survey; include questions that can help illuminate the reasons for management turnover. (Be sure to separate management and employee responses to the survey.)
- Hire an organizational development consultant to do a management study. By interviewing your current managers, a consultant usually learns why people have left and can then make suggestions for correcting the problem.
- If you use a search firm, ask their recruiters about the reputation of your organization. Recruiters usually hear through the applicant grapevine about problems that cause people to steer clear of particular companies. One CEO learned from a recruiter that his company had a terrible reputation among engineers because of the president's demands for frequent design changes and excessive overtime work. "You're known as an engineering sweatshop," said the recruiter. The revelation helped explain why engineering managers kept leaving for opportunities elsewhere.

Fixing the Problem. Some problems that create turnover are simple to fix; most are not. Pay is one of the simplest. If high turnover among your managers is the result of an uncompetitive compensation plan, change it. Replacing managers is a costly proposition in many ways, so you save money by paying them competitively to begin with. Use your human resource department or a compensation consultant to develop an appropriate pay program.

If turnover is caused by the behavior of a particular executive, steps must be taken to change the situation. (See the discussion of performance problems under "Toxic Team Members" for some suggestions.) If the executive cannot learn to function effectively as a manager of people, then find a replacement. Executives who cause high turnover among managers are of no benefit to your organization, no matter what other strengths they possess.

As the team leader, what happens if you find that you yourself are contributing to the turnover problem? You can do one of two things: deny the truth of the feedback and miss an opportunity to become a more effective person, or take steps to change your own behavior. Most managers opt for denial. But if you are the rare exception, consider the suggestions for behavioral change outlined below under "Ineffective Team Leadership."

Problem Six: Problems with Upper Management

Top managers have a great impact on everyone below them. An incompetent, ineffective, or toxic person in a high-level position may cause an otherwise effective team to become dysfunctional. Specific top management problems vary widely, but the effect is the same: diverting the team's energy and attention from producing results to coping with the difficult executive.

Symptoms

If top management is a problem, you probably don't need to look for symptoms among team members. The difficulty is usually obvious. One exception occurs when a manager joins a company but has only met executives during the interview process. In this situation, new team leaders can learn a lot from their team members. One newly arrived vice president was shocked by his managers' remarks about the CEO during a staff meeting. Unfortunately, the reason for their comments became apparent as soon as he began to work for his new boss. If team members frequently complain about top management, have well-established jokes about top management problems, and spend considerable time developing strategies to overcome obstacles presented by top management, then the odds are good that some real difficulties exist. (If it looks like a duck and quacks like a duck . . . well, you know the rest.)

Suggestions for a Cure

Serious difficulties with top management usually require mediation by the team leader. Addressing this situation means reviewing the problem with your boss, your team, your peers, or yourself—or possibly all four. In some cases, you may find a solution, while in others you simply need to learn to cope with the situation.

Talking with Your Boss. If your immediate manager is not the source of the problem—that is, the difficult executive is at a higher level—you may find it helpful to ask your boss for advice on how to overcome the obstacles you are facing. Describe the specific problems you are having and the assistance you need. Ask your boss to suggest strategies for dealing more effectively with upper management. In some situations, you might have your boss arrange a meeting in which both of you can talk with the higher-level manager about the situation. In other circumstances, however, this direct approach does more harm than good.

If your boss is the problem, the conversation gets a little trickier. Complaining about your manager's work style, behaviors, or personality characteristics is not likely to yield positive results. Few people like to hear criticism, and executives are more averse to it than most. After all, their style and personality got them where they are today, so why should they change? A more effective approach is to outline the problems you are having with your work (without citing your manager as the cause) and request specific assistance from your boss. Offer solutions that involve your taking responsibility and doing any extra work that is required.

One woman worked for a CEO who took forever to sign off on policies and approve expenditures. She would send documents to his office for approval and wait weeks for their return. The delays were causing problems both for her and for the managers on her team, but frequent verbal and written reminders had no effect. Finally, she met with the CEO and said, "I'm trying to improve efficiency in my department, so I need to be able to move policies and purchases along more quickly. I know that you are extremely busy and have to deal with a constant flood of paperwork, so I thought we might agree on a time when I could bring the documents that need your approval and have you sign off on them all at once. I'll be glad to prepare a summary sheet that describes each one so that you can review them. Is there a time when it would be easier for you to meet with me?" The CEO suggested that they meet twice a month at 7:30 A.M., when he was not likely to be interrupted by people or phone calls. The manager was more than happy to come in early in order to solve her problem.

Talking with Your Team. If the executive is not likely to change, you need to help your team cope with the situation. Just telling them to stop complaining is a mistake, since team members may then become reluctant to share negative information with you. Instead, acknowledge the difficulties that you are all facing and try to focus the group on developing strategies to manage the situation. Conduct a problem-solving session in which you and the team specifically outline the challenges being created by the top manager's behavior, and brainstorm strategies for coping with them. (Be sure not to publicize this event, though, or you may soon have an even bigger problem.)

In one situation, the management team of a large business unit had a CEO with no sense of time and little consideration for others. He would schedule a meeting and then keep people waiting for hours. Despite repeated feedback about the problem, he showed no interest in changing his behavior. On one occasion, the management team spent an entire day in the corporate lobby waiting for a business review to begin. They decided that in the future they would leave after thirty minutes and have the CEO's secretary call when he was ready.

Another problem created by his behavior was that applicants for top-level jobs would be scheduled for interviews and then kept waiting for considerable periods of time. This treatment created quite a poor impression of the company and its management. To address this problem, the human resource department decided to schedule interview appointments with a series of other managers and work the CEO into the schedule whenever he was ready. They could then say to the applicant, "We had planned for you to see our CEO later, but he would like to talk with you now. We'll reschedule your other interviews for a later time." This approach made applicants feel that the CEO was anxious to meet them instead of giving the impression that he was too busy to see them on time.

Talking with Peers. Having a problem-solving session with your peers may also help you develop new approaches to coping with upper management challenges. If some people in your organization seem to be particularly effective in working with the difficult executive, you should find out what strategies help them get results. Making an effort to modify your own style is probably more realistic than expecting the executive to change. Any solutions that seem useful can be shared with your team members.

Talking with Yourself. If the situation becomes too stressful, you may need to have a good talk with yourself. When problems with top management start to harm your health, family relationships, or self-image, it may be time to leave. Remember that you always have a choice about whether to leave or stay in your job. If you are receiving certain benefits in terms of pay or status that are hard to give up, then you may not feel as though you have a choice, but in reality you have simply decided that the benefits of staying outweigh the costs of leaving.

Problem Seven: Ineffective Team Leadership

Teams sometimes become sick because they have poor leadership. If you yourself are the poor leader, you are not likely to recognize the problem. If the poor team leader reports to you, then you are in a better position to resolve the issue.

Symptoms

Any one of these symptoms may be a sign of poor team leadership:

- The team lacks direction and clear goals.
- The team fails to achieve results.
- Relationships on the team have deteriorated.
- No coordination exists among different functions on the team.

If you spot any of these problems, then evaluating the quality of leadership is a wise move.

Suggestions for a Cure

The steps listed below (which are directed to the weak leader's boss) provide suggestions for diagnosing and correcting a team leadership problem. As the manager of an ineffective team leader, you need to discuss your observations of the group's performance and your reasons for taking action. Team leaders who have become aware of difficulties with their own leadership style may decide to take some of these steps themselves. If you are a member of a team with a weak leader, you might suggest some of the strategies in Chapters Two through Six in order to help make the group as a whole more effective.

- If you are the weak leader's boss, then you need to decide how much time and money you are willing to invest in developmental activities. Managers who have never had good role models, management training, or effective coaching may have potential for great improvement. On the other hand, some people are not likely to change, and some situations are too critical to allow time for a manager to develop new skills and habits.
- If you decide that developmental activities will be beneficial, set clear performance expectations for the leader and the team. Clearly describe the results that you expect the team to produce. Have the leader put these in writing to show that you were understood correctly.
- Get feedback on the leader's behavior from employees, coworkers, and internal customers. Since people may not give honest information to you directly, use a human resource representative or outside consultant to develop a feedback process. If a survey instrument is used to collect this information, the process is referred to as 360 degree feedback, or multirater assessment. (This technique is also discussed in Chapter Four, under group interaction problem four, "The Team Leader Manages Conflicts Poorly.") The feedback process is usually quite effective, since the manager receives observations about behavior from a variety of people in his or her work environment. In fact, many executives have found this to be a powerful developmental experience for all their managers. The surveys in this book can also obtain members' perceptions of management team effectiveness. If you prefer not to use a survey, then interviews can be conducted (although the manager may be less likely to accept the validity of information acquired in that way).
- Based on the feedback received, create a development plan to help the ineffective leader improve critical skills and abilities. Helpful activities include training, coaching sessions, reading assignments, working with a mentor, visiting other organizations, and many other possibilities. Be sure to follow up to find out what the leader learns through these experiences.

- Hold regular meetings with the team leader to discuss job performance. Review the five success factors and help the leader implement them with the management team.
- Consider hiring a professional executive coach to work with the manager. An experienced coach is familiar with strategies that can help change behavior. Being able to talk with someone from outside the company also helps the manager develop a more objective view of strengths and weaknesses.
- If the leader's behavior doesn't change or if the situation is so critical that there is no time to wait for change, then remove the manager. Management work is not for everyone. If you are assessing your own leadership abilities and feel that they fall short, consider the possibility that you may simply be in the wrong job. The head of one customer support department found that he really hated dealing with constant decisions and employee problems. When he voluntarily stepped back into a customer training position, he was much happier. Many poor managers are much more effective in a role of individual contributor.

Without an effective leader, teams cannot achieve their full potential. Strong leaders help facilitate positive interaction and accomplishment of results, while ineffective leaders become an obstacle to team performance. If the head of a management team has poor leadership ability, the entire organization suffers.

Being part of a sick team is a frustrating and discouraging experience for both members and leaders. Fixing such a sick team is a difficult task, requiring the leader's attention for an extended period of time. Team leaders who are tearing their hair out with frustration may find that working with an outside consultant helps them develop a plan of action and preserves their sanity.

When all else fails, the ultimate solution for a sick team is to reorganize in such a way that the team is disbanded. If the team's problem reflects troubles in the larger organizational culture, however, even this solution will not be successful.

True Story: Warfare on the Board

Part Two: The Solution

Not all problems can be solved. Despite several attempts to improve their performance and their working relationships, members of the warring board are just too angry with one another to function effectively. Unfortunately, this group of nonprofit directors is causing significant damage to the organization.

Because they put most of their energy into group battles, the board neglects many of its responsibilities in running the agency. When one irate member leaks some information about poor management practices to the press, several articles appear in the local paper criticizing the organization for possible misuse of government funds. The agency's reputation is severely damaged, which makes it more difficult to convince potential donors to make contributions.

The executive director is fired, but not everyone agrees with the decision. This creates further division among members, causing several of them to stop speaking to one another. Potential applicants for the executive director position are turned off by the bad publicity and the obvious negative feelings among board members. Whenever a promising candidate emerges, the rift on the board makes it impossible to reach agreement on filling the job. If a candidate is supported by one faction, others are automatically opposed.

All this turmoil causes several bright and competent staff members to leave for other jobs, which prevents the agency from meeting its annual goals. Without an executive director, recruiting replacements is difficult, so the remaining staff members become increasingly overworked, tired, stressed, and frustrated.

Finally, this particular leadership group begins to disband. The chairperson does not run for another term, nor do any of the other officers elect to continue in their roles. Several members resign from the board and are replaced by newcomers, who have no involvement with the previous conflicts. Unfortunately, they are quickly recruited by the warring factions. The new occupants of leadership positions vow to avoid the mistakes of their predecessors but quickly find themselves in disagreement about meeting times and locations. Whether the new board will become any better than the old one is still an open question.

CONCLUSION

TWELVE GUIDING PRINCIPLES FOR HIGH PERFORMANCE

Previous chapters have presented many strategies for improving management team performance. Underlying these specific suggestions are some broad, general principles that increase the effectiveness of individuals or groups in almost any work situation—and in many personal circumstances as well. For each of the twelve guiding principles described below, key questions are provided to focus management team discussions appropriately. To illustrate the principles, let's consider one last true story. Because this example involves a family business, it illustrates how the principles relate to both work and personal issues.

Principle One: Determine Your Purpose

Before you make a decision, undertake a project, or start a new venture, you need to clearly understand why you are doing so; thoroughly explore your own motivations and the expectations of others.

Key questions:
Why are we doing this?
What is our ultimate or long-range goal?

The Family Business

Our final true story is about a family business that is experiencing a drop in sales because of disagreements in the marketing department. Many years ago, Mom and Dad started the business, which now also employs Older Son, Younger Son, Daughter, and Son-in-Law. After several attempts to resolve the marketing problems on their own, Mom and Dad decide to bring in a consultant, who conducts in-depth interviews with the key family members and everyone in marketing. This assessment reveals that the entire business is in turmoil thanks to family conflicts. Because Mom and Dad are getting on in years and starting to consider retirement, the family hostilities are particularly troubling to them. They want to turn the business over to the children but know that doing so under current circumstances is likely to harm family relationships beyond repair. Although initially they focused on the marketing department as the problem, Mom and Dad now realize that the real need is to determine the future of the business: Can they keep it in the family, or will they have to sell it?

Principle Two: Define Desired Outcomes

Once you are clear about your purpose, decide exactly what you want to accomplish and how you define success.

Key questions:
What are the results that we want?
How will we know if we have succeeded?

The Family Business

Now that they realize their primary purpose is to determine the future of the business, Mom and Dad identify two desired outcomes related to work and family. The work-related goal is to develop a plan for retirement from the business, while the family goal is to repair relationships and keep the family together. If achieving the latter goal means they have to sell the business, then so be it.

Principle Three: Base Decisions on Complete Information

Although a decision may be influenced by a hunch or gut feeling, intuition should be informed by data. Making data-based decisions means gathering all relevant information, from both subjective and objective sources—including the feelings and reactions of important people as well as appropriate facts and figures.

Key questions:

What information must we have to make a good decision?

Have we considered both objective and subjective information?

The Family Business

Mom and Dad see that to make an informed decision about the future of the business, they not only need financial data and market projections but also have to find out how their children feel about running the business and working together. They have never asked such questions because they aren't really sure they want to hear the answers. If the children wish to keep the business in the family, then Mom and Dad also need an assessment of the abilities and talents of each one. This evaluation can help family members match their skills with necessary business functions and determine where they need outside expertise.

Principle Four: Learn from Others

A key component of effective decision making is to learn from those who have gone before you. All too often, we waste time reinventing the wheel even though there is a wagon maker just down the road.

Key questions:

Who else has experience or expertise in this area?

How can we learn from them?

The Family Business

Having recognized the importance of planning for retirement, Mom and Dad begin reading about transition in family businesses and talking with others who have been through the experience. Gathering this knowledge helps them identify strategies to consider and pitfalls to avoid.

Principle Five: Value Different Viewpoints

We often tend to discount views different from our own instead of exploring and learning from them. Making good decisions means taking off our blinders and trying to see through the eyes of others.

Key questions:

What are some other ways of looking at this issue?

What does the situation look like from the viewpoint of the other people involved?

The Family Business

Conflicts in the business seem to center on one child, Younger Son. He has been identified by the others as The Problem. According to Mom, Dad, and everyone else in the family, Younger Son is highly critical and frequently likes to tell everyone else what they're doing wrong. He doesn't do it in a very nice way, so his criticism touches off arguments, which often escalate into verbal battles.

From Younger Son's viewpoint, however, the situation looks different. Younger Son was given additional responsibilities, but no one has allowed him to make changes to accommodate the heavier workload. He says he can see many ways their growing business can be improved, but whenever he suggests a new idea or approach, he is turned down or brushed off. As business increased, He is becoming increasingly frustrated and chronically irritable. When a work style analysis reveals that Younger Son is the only family member with an innovative, big-picture approach to situations, the group begins to realize why he keeps saying "I'm so misunderstood!" and why they persist in ignoring his suggestions. Learning to value his style and use his strengths is important for the health of both the business and the family.

Principle Six: Involve Everyone Affected

Each person or group who is affected by a decision needs to be included in the planning or communication of the decision.

Key questions:

Who is affected by our actions?

How shall we involve them?

The Family Business

All the family members have to be included in determining the future of the business, regardless of their level of involvement with the company. Son-in-Law, for example, only works there a few hours each week; still, he has a right to participate in discussion of the family's future (even though he may be less involved in the final decision). Spouses who do not work in the business should also be part of the conversation, since the final decision affects their lives. Once the family is in accord about the future, employees can be informed and involved in those aspects of the transition that affect them.

Principle Seven: Explore Resistance

When someone objects to an idea or change that you are proposing, the natural tendency is to fight that resistance, giving all the reasons why your views are correct. This approach usually just locks other people into their own perspective as they try to counteract your arguments with their own. A more effective strategy is to ask questions, listen, and learn their view of the situation. Establishing real two-way communication often gives you valuable information.

> **Key questions:**
> What are your concerns?
> Why do you not like this idea?

The Family Business

While exploring the option of continuing the family business, the children discuss how they might take over the duties currently performed by Mom and Dad. But whenever they mention reassigning responsibilities, one of the parents raises an objection. After Mom and Daughter get into a heated discussion about how purchasing might be handled in the future, Older Son says, "Mom, every time we talk about taking over your responsibilities, you and Dad find some reason why it won't work. What are you concerned about?"

"I'm afraid you'll screw it up," replies Mom. "You kids have never done a lot of these things."

"So you're afraid we'll make mistakes?"

"Yes," Mom says. "I get really nervous when I think about it."

"Well, I guess we might make some mistakes since we'll be learning a lot of new things. Why would that be so awful?"

Dad joins in. "Most of our retirement income has to come from this business. If the business fails . . . well, I don't know what we'll do. Move in with you, I guess."

"So it's money you're worried about?" asks Daughter.

"Sure," says Dad, "But I guess it also feels kind of funny after thirty years to be just shoved aside. I know that it's time to retire, but I'm not exactly sure what Mom and I are going to do all day."

Having identified the source of Mom and Dad's concern, the family calmly discusses how the parents' involvement in the business can gradually be reduced, providing them with an easier transition into retirement and giving the children a chance to learn from Mom and Dad's experience.

Principle Eight: Turn Conflict into Problem Solving

When disagreements arise, try to avoid a "tennis match" conversation in which everyone repeats his or her own point of view more and more emphatically. Instead, attempt to identify the underlying problem that needs to be solved. Find goals the parties can agree on, and explore their different perspectives on how to solve the problem.

Key questions:

What is the problem that we need to solve?

What are our common goals?

The Family Business

The family has asked the consultant to facilitate a discussion of people's present and future roles in the business.

"You're just lazy," says Daughter to Older Son. "You don't really want to do any work around here."

"Hold on," says the consultant. "Attacking people's personalities probably isn't going to be very helpful. What's bothering you about Older Son's role in the business?"

"He doesn't pull his weight, but he pulls a pretty good paycheck," says Daughter. "I don't think it's fair."

The consultant turns to Mom and Dad. "How do you make decisions about what to pay people?"

Mom and Dad look at each other. "Well, I guess we just try to give everybody in the family what they need. Other people, we just pay them more than they made at the last place they worked."

"So one problem is that you have no compensation plan, no systematic way to set salaries, right?" asks the consultant. Everyone nods. "And do you all agree that it would be a good idea to have procedures in place to relate people's pay to their job duties?"

"We sure need that before the kids take over the business!" exclaims Dad. "Otherwise they'll kill each other." The rest of the family agrees.

"Then let's list a compensation study as one of our action items," says the consultant.

Principle Nine: Express Appreciation

We find it so easy to see problems and so hard to see blessings. Our health, for example, becomes quite precious when we're sick, but the rest of the time we don't think much about it. The same is true of our reactions to the people with whom we live and work: we notice what we don't like and take the good things for granted. Developing the habit of expressing genuine appreciation to people not only makes you more effective in your work but also makes you a happier person. (Be sure to try this one at home.)

Key questions:

What do other people or departments do that makes our life easier or helps us succeed?

How can we express our appreciation to them?

The Family Business

"In this family," Older Son says, "we spend too much time thinking and talking about each other's weaknesses and irritating habits. We don't even see our strengths and positive traits."

"I agree," Daughter says.

"You know," the facilitator offers, "if you're trying to define everybody's role, maybe you should start by listing the talents and abilities that each of you brings to the business."

"Well," Younger Son immediately responds, "I'd sure like to be seen as something besides 'The Problem' around here."

"You're right," Son-in-Law concedes. "I for one have always thought that you do a great job in developing our advertising materials."

"And you've made some really good suggestions about how to improve our work processes," Daughter offers, as the mood of the discussion shifts noticeably. "Even though the rest of us seem to have a 'talent' for criticizing all your new ideas!"

Principle Ten: Follow Through

Finish what you start—as long as what you start is worthwhile. If you have a good idea, implement it. If you see a problem, solve it. If you start a valuable project, complete it. Intentions are worthless without action.

Key questions:

What is the first step we need to take?

And the next step?

And the next?

The Family Business

The family members unanimously agree to keep the business in the family and pass it on to the next generation.

To solve their work-related problems, however, they must do more than just define their new roles in the business. "We have to stick to our plan for the division of labor," Older Son says.

"Yes," Daughter agrees. "If I'm going to be put in charge of sales, then Dad is going to have to stop trying to manage the sales function for me.

"That's right, Dad," says Older Son. "You'll have your hands full reorganizing the customer service department."

Any family business has to face the challenge of separating work and personal issues. When family difficulties begin to infect the working environment, then family members must take steps to improve their personal relationships.

Daughter and Son-in-Law have some marital problems that often spill over into the workplace, so they agree to see a marriage counselor for help in resolving the issues. Since the transition plan calls for Son-in-Law's role in the business to increase greatly, this step is particularly important. In both work and family areas, everyone needs to follow through with their part of the plan if the transition is to succeed.

Principle Eleven: Evaluate Results

When you do anything of importance, find out whether you accomplish what you intend. Too often, we go from one activity to the next without assessing the results of our previous actions.

Key questions:

How well have we succeeded in accomplishing our goals?

What went well and what went poorly?

The Family Business

As the family implements their transition plan, they need to stop at certain points and determine whether it is meeting the needs of both the business and the individual family members. How well is everyone performing in his or her new role? How do they feel about their new responsibilities? How is the business doing financially? Are Mom and Dad gradually letting go? Are the children learning how to run the business successfully? How well is everyone getting along? In short, they need to determine whether they are achieving their desired goals of implementing a successful transition plan while maintaining positive family relationships.

Principle Twelve: Learn Life's Lessons

If you fail to learn the lessons that life presents, you will fall into destructive patterns and continue to experience the same problems repeatedly. To become more effective, every person, management team, and organization must take responsibility, determine how they have contributed to their own problems and successes, and change their behavior based on the feedback they receive.

Key questions:

What did we do that created successful results?

How did we contribute to the problems we experienced?

What will we do differently next time?

The Family Business

As the children take the business into the next generation, life will offer them lessons about work and family, and how to combine the two. If they develop the habit of learning from these experiences, then they are quite likely to succeed.

Conclusion

Management teams have more power than they realize. As managers sit around a conference table discussing their problems and concerns, they seldom feel terribly powerful. Usually, they are much more aware of factors over which they have little or no control: the behavior of customers, the maneuvers of competitors, the decisions of political bodies, the actions of upper management. But in fact the decisions made by a management team determine the fate of its organization or department and shape the future of everyone working there. The ripple effect from their actions touches the lives of customers, taxpayers, suppliers, competitors, and many others whom they will never meet.

As a leader or member of a management team, you too have more power than you know. By asking key questions and encouraging effective habits of thinking and acting, you can stimulate your group members to become superior problem solvers and decision makers. If you help your management team implement the five success factors discussed in earlier chapters and follow the twelve guiding principles in this one, you will make a valuable contribution to your organization.

REFERENCES

Argyris, C. *People: Managing Your Most Important Asset.* Boston: Harvard Business Review, 1987.

Belbin, R. M. *Management Teams: Why They Succeed or Fail.* New York: Wiley, 1981.

Bruner, J. *A Study of Thinking.* New York: Wiley, 1956.

Byrum-Robinson, B., and Womeldorff, J. D. "Networking Skills Inventory." In *The 1990 Annual Developing Human Resources.* San Diego: University Associates, 1990.

Clark, S. A. "Entice Investors with Profit, Not Potential." *Atlanta Business Chronicle,* Oct. 1993, p. 42A.

Cota, A., and others. "The Structure of Group Cohesion." *Personality and Social Psychology Bulletin,* 1994, *3,* 572–580.

De Bono, E. *Six Thinking Hats.* New York: Little, Brown, 1985.

Hackman, J. *Groups That Work (and Those That Don't).* San Francisco: Jossey-Bass, 1990.

Harrison, A., and Bramson, R. *Styles of Thinking.* New York: Anchor Press, 1982.

Kanter, R. M. "The New Managerial Work." *Harvard Business Review,* 1989, *67,* 85–92.

Katz, D., and Kahn, R. L. *The Social Psychology of Organizations.* New York: Wiley, 1978.

Katzenbach, J. K., and Smith, D. K. *The Wisdom of Teams.* Boston: Harvard Business School Press, 1993.

Larson, C., and LaFasto, F. *Teamwork.* Thousand Oaks, Calif.: Sage Publications, 1989.

Larson, J. R., Foster-Fishman, P., and Keys, C. "Discussion of Shared and Unshared Information in Decision-Making Groups." *Journal of Personality and Social Psychology,* 1994, *3,* 446–461.

Leavitt, H., and Lipman-Blumen, J. "Hot Groups." *Harvard Business Review,* 1995, *73*(4), 109–116.

McGrath, M. E. *Setting the Pace in Product Development.* Boston: Butterworth-Heinemann, 1996.

McKenney, J. L., and Kern, P.G.W. "How Managers' Minds Work." In *Harvard Business Review: On Human Relations.* New York: HarperCollins, 1979.

Mintzberg, H. *The Nature of Managerial Work*. New York: HarperCollins, 1973.

Morgan, G. *Images of Organization*. Thousand Oaks, Calif.: Sage Publications, 1986.

Myers, I., and McCaulley, M. *A Guide to the Development and Use of the Myers-Briggs Type Indicator*. Palo Alto, Calif.: Consulting Psychologists Press, 1985.

Osborne, D., and Gaebler, T. *Reinventing Government*. Reading, Mass.: Addison-Wesley, 1992.

Pugh, D., and Hickson, D. *Writers on Organizations*. Thousand Oaks, Calif.: Sage Publications, 1989.

Schein, E. H. "What You Need to Know about Organization Culture." *Training and Development Journal*, 1986, *40*, 30.

Scott, K., and Townsend, A. "Teams: Why Some Succeed and Others Fail." *HRMagazine*, 1994, *23*, 62–67.

Senge, P. *The Fifth Discipline*. New York: Doubleday, 1990.

Sessa, V. I. "Can Conflict Improve Team Effectiveness?" *Center for Creative Leadership* (newsletter), 1994, *14*, 1–5.

Simon, H. A. *Administrative Behavior*. Old Tappan, N.J.: Macmillan, 1947.

Simon, H. A. *The New Science of Management Decision Making*. New York: HarperCollins, 1960.

Simon, H. A. "The Strategic Decision Process: A Behavioral View." In J. Higgins (ed.), *Organizational Policy and Strategic Management: Text and Cases*. Orlando: Dryden Press, 1983.

Tjosvold, D. "Achieving Productive Synergy: Integrating Departments into a Company." *Journal of Business and Psychology*, 1988, *3*, 42–53.

VanGundy, A. B. *Managing Group Creativity*. New York: AMACOM, 1984.

Watson, W., Michaelsen, L. K., and Sharp, W. (1991). "Member Competence, Group Interaction, and Group Decision Making." *Journal of Applied Psychology*, 1991, *76*, 803–809.

Zander, A. *Making Groups Effective*. San Francisco: Jossey-Bass, 1994.

INDEX